AN ECONOMIC HISTORY OF MEXICO

After a turbulent modern history of conquest and colonialism, Mexico has developed as an economy that may be emerging but still displays significant levels of poverty, particularly in relation to its neighbor to the north, the United States.

Drawing on archival data, decades of new Mexican historiography, and considering issues of political economy, this book explores how Mexico ended up in the relative economic position that it did. Beginning with Hernán Cortés and the invention of the Conquest of New Spain, it explores the economic history of Mexico through the lens of political economy, incorporating environment and demography, politics and power, and industrialization and inequality. The aftermath of the Conquest brought about a complete restructuring of the economy as a result of death from disease, the introduction of European-style agriculture, and a more intensive exploitation of the peasantry. The eighteenth and nineteenth centuries saw "reform" followed by a series of crises and rebellions under which sustained economic growth was impossible. Globalization and the expansion of agricultural exports provided some opportunities in the late nineteenth and twentieth centuries, but they failed to provide the booming rural population with a sustainable means of supporting domestic demand. The so-called Mexican Miracle—the period of rapid growth in the 1950s, 1960s, and early 1970s—disguised a failure to address the economic inequality embedded since the colonial period. As this book clearly demonstrates, this inequality was sometimes challenged in Mexican history but never decisively addressed, let alone reversed.

This accessible and engaging book is vital reading for students and scholars of the history of Mexico and Latin America and those interested in economic development in historical perspective.

Richard J Salvucci was a tenured associate professor (Mexican history) at the University of California, Berkeley, and a professor of economics at Trinity University. He has authored two books—*Textiles and Capitalism: An Economic History of the Obrajes, 1539–1840* and *Politics, Markets and Mexico's "London Debt" 1823–1887*—and has been elected a corresponding member of the Academia Mexicana de la Historia in Mexico City.

AN ECONOMIC HISTORY OF MEXICO

Contested Conquest, Ambiguous Development: 1519-2000

Richard J Salvucci

Routledge
Taylor & Francis Group
LONDON AND NEW YORK

Designed cover image: Amelia Fuentes Marin

First published 2025
by Routledge
4 Park Square, Milton Park, Abingdon, Oxon OX14 4RN

and by Routledge
605 Third Avenue, New York, NY 10158

Routledge is an imprint of the Taylor & Francis Group, an informa business

British Library Cataloguing-in-Publication Data
A catalogue record for this book is available from the British Library

ISBN: 978-1-032-87420-3 (hbk)
ISBN: 978-1-032-87419-7 (pbk)
ISBN: 978-1-003-53258-3 (ebk)

DOI: 10.4324/9781003532583

Typeset in Times New Roman
by Apex CoVantage, LLC

CONTENTS

Acknowledgments		*vi*
List of Figures		*vii*
List of Tables		*viii*
	Introduction	1
1	"New" World, New Rulers, New Rules	6
2	A Century of Shocks	43
3	A Century of Revolutions and "Miracles"	91
Epilogue		*127*
Data Appendix		*131*
Index		*136*

ACKNOWLEDGMENTS

I wish to acknowledge the assistance of some people and institutions that helped me find my way through this manuscript. My friend and colleague Bernardo García Martínez probably had more influence on me than any other scholar. He has been absent now for some time, but I found myself often wondering what Bernardo would say or think about something. Since I could only guess at the answer, his loss has been sorely felt, both personally and professionally. Other generous colleagues have read or discussed some of the ideas here (or facilitated their production), which, of course, does not implicate them in any way. They include Moramay López Alonso, Alma Parra, Josefina Vázquez, Amílcar Challú, Aurora Gómez Galvarriato, Arturo Grunstein, Ivan Escamilla, Diana Montaño, Manuel Bautista, Sergio Cañedo, Ricardo Fagoaga, and Juan Carlos Moreno Brid. Jeffrey Williamson subjected himself to early drafts of various parts of the manuscript. His criticisms and encouragement were invaluable. William Taylor, who has been saving me from myself since our time together in the Mexican archives in 1976, remains my model of a senior colleague. Seminars and the like at El Colegio de México, Universidad Nacional Autónoma de México, and the Instituto Nacional de Antropología e Historia gave me some sense of what would fly and what would not. And, as usual, Linda Kerrigan Salvucci knew when I needed a push or a few days off. My especial thanks to David Andrew at Autumn Lane Investments in Houston, Texas. David knows that money is time, and vice versa. And, not least, Andy Humphries, my Editor at Routledge, continues to value books in economic history. Thank you.

FIGURES

1.1 Maize-Deflated Real Wages 8
1.2 IEEAS and Ten-Year Moving Average, 1519–1599 10
1.3 PDSI 1500–1599 Centered on Amealco with Ten-Year Smoothing 10
1.4 Indigenous Population of Central Mexico versus Cattle, Sheep, and Goats, 1550–1610 15
1.5 IEEAS and Ten-Year Moving Average, 1600–1699 18
1.6 Index of Real Wages for New Spain, 1540–1660 19
1.7 PDSI 1600–1699 Centered on Amealco with 10-Year Smoothing 20
1.8 Alcabala (Value-Added Tax) Collected in Guanajuato versus Querétaro 23
1.9 PDSI 1700–1799 Centered on Amealco with Ten-Year Smoothing 29
1.10 IEEAS 1700–1799 and Ten-Year Moving Average 30
2.1 Wage-Rent Ratio for Querétaro, 1818–1845 44
2.2 Average Property Instrument (Hipoteca) in Querétaro versus Coinage at Guanajuato, 1818–1845 (in Current Pesos) 45
2.3 PSDI 1750–1850 Centered on Amealco with Ten-Year Smoothing 48
2.4 Implicit Index of Tariff Protection, 1821–1845 50
2.5 Age Structure of Querétaro Population, 1844 52
2.6 Crude Birth and Death Rates, Querétaro 52
2.7 Mexico Population Pyramid, 1895 69
2.8 Wage-Rent Ratio in Porfirian Mexico 75
3.1 Secular Trend versus Realized Output 104
3.2 Trend Growth in Manufacturing, 1900–1948 105
3.3 N-Gram Using "Import Substitution" as a Search Term 114
Figure Epilogue 1 Rate of Economic Growth in Mexico, 1960–2021 (the left axis represents the percentage and the heavy line denotes Mexico) 128

TABLES

1.1 Wage-Rent Ratio in the Valley of Mexico, 1509–1606 12
2.1 Railroad Mileage versus Share of Nontraditional Exports 72
3.1 Total Factor Productivity Change in Agriculture, 1940–2019 98
3.2 Annualized Growth Rate of GDP, 1966–1982 111

Base 802540 (R01257) 3-97

MAP 0.1 Map of Mexico

Used by permission of the University of Texas Libraries, The University of Texas at Austin

INTRODUCTION

History is written with a purpose. Economic history in particular has one. The great British economist Lionel Robbins famously observed that people would like to have everything if they could. But they cannot. Hence the need to ration scarce resources to accommodate virtually unlimited wants.[1] So, then, economic history is a way of examining how that process takes place over time, or how changing material constraints will produce different outcomes under different circumstances. It is about scarcity, and it is about change over time. Or it is neither history nor economics.

The purpose of this book is not to test a particular class of models or to validate a particular economic ideology or brand of theory. It is instead an account of how Mexico, the geographical focus, got to be where it is (or was) in terms of income, population, wealth distribution, and other economic variables: why Mexico is where it is and what it is. Or, as Robbins might have it, Mexico in terms of the logic of scarcity. Robbins was, moreover, particularly convinced that one started from facts and proceeded empirically. Of course, facts do not select, much less speak, for themselves. The historian—or the economic historian—makes those choices. They do not proceed uncritically, unthinkingly, or in a vacuum. An analysis of scarcity—what economists term "factor endowments"—may point in one direction or another as far as explanation is concerned. But observation and theory condition each other or should. Neither simply leads while the other follows, blinkered.

This book is somewhat different from other economic histories of Mexico, not for the sake of difference but because its purposes are different. I try not to simply repeat what others have written, both where I think they have gotten it right and where I think they have not. I do try to draw upon and synthesize a generation's worth of Mexican scholarship, much of which has escaped significant notice outside the country. The Mexican work is data-driven, archival-based, and directed

DOI: 10.4324/9781003532583-1

at answering large and important economic questions first posed in the 1960s and 1970s but left unresolved because of changes in historians' interests, especially in the English-speaking world. An older generation of historians—Silvio Zavala, Pierre Chaunu, Francoise Chevalier, Charles Gibson, Woodrow Borah, and David Brading, among others, left a legacy of scholarship whose relevance remains, mostly taken up by historians in Mexico. I have tried to follow their lead as best I could, although my efforts or those of any single scholar will be incomplete. Work coming out of the Instituto Mora, the Instituto de Investigaciones Históricas (UNAM), the Instituto Nacional de Antropología e Historia (INAH), the Centro de Investigaciones y Estudios Superiores en Antropología Social (CIESAS), and the Colegio de México (COLMEX), to mention only a few, provide the foundations of this study, as its scholarly apparatus shows. That makes this history different, more responsive to debates abroad than at home. It is useful to pay more attention to what scholars in Mexico are doing. Our major concerns in the United States—race, class, and gender—are important, but they are hardly the only ones that matter. People not only shape but are shaped by their material circumstances as well. I take that as a given. As Karl Marx wrote, "Men make their own history, but they do not do it as they please."

Although primarily a synthesis, the book contains a significant amount of new research in primary sources, archival and otherwise. This is particularly true of the section on the nineteenth century. There is a growing and important secondary literature on the period, but scholars have barely scratched the surface, particularly in light of advances in archival organization and documentation in Mexico since 1980. The military archives of the Secretaría de Defensa Nacional (SEDENA) have been a particularly important source of socioeconomic data, as have various ecclesiastical records and the archives of the state of Querétaro. The COVID outbreak has, unfortunately, made it much more difficult to undertake research than it might have otherwise been in some other archives, but that has been a problem for everyone, and not just for me.

I was once asked, in good faith by a colleague, "Does anyone agree with you?" Really, I hope not. We learn more from our considered differences than our ritual acknowledgments of mutual wisdom. That path too often leads to sterility. While I have no interest in sectarian warfare, what I have written is somewhat different because I think differently. This is probably because I have spent so much time working in a discipline, economics, other than what I might properly call my own, Latin American history. For example, few if any continue to subscribe to the "men from Mars" version of the Conquest of New Spain, but, frankly, more advanced thinkers anticipated much of what is now consensus 40 years ago, especially about conquest as a kind of civil war among different indigenous ethnic groups ("tribes"). Moreover, one sees precious little consideration of differing conceptions of property rights, European versus Amerindian, in the existing literature. From a development standpoint, nothing could matter more, and yet the questions apparently raise little interest. That is an error, and a serious one. What we call these differences, "capitalism," "mode of production" and the rest is of less interest, at least to economic historians concerned with substantive mechanisms of accumulation, impoverishment, growth, and change. A historian like Enrique Semo may have called his seminal work a history of capitalism in Mexico, but he was more concerned to show how political power and colonialism rather than relative productivity shaped what were clearly commercial outcomes, at least at the level that counted. That is really the only sense in which such discussions are of much interest.

This book is composed of three chapters, organized around the question of factor endowments, scarcity, and their determinants, natural or otherwise, and following chronological limits (colonial, long "nineteenth," and perhaps "shortened" twentieth centuries) simply because they are familiar, and not because they are necessarily unquestionable or somehow canonical. For sure, historians like Robert Brenner reminded us 30 years ago that supply and demand mattered, but they are not all that matter: power does as well. This is particularly true in Mexico, which is what Semo emphasized in his *Historia del Capitalismo*. Semo and Brenner, as well as Tony Judt, have influenced me; so, if there is a historical context in which to situate this book, they are the historians who mostly provide it.[2]

But sound economic analysis matters as well, and that does not necessarily mean fancy econometrics or even elaborate formal models. The colonial section of this book, and much of the first half of the nineteenth-century section, was read and critiqued—vigorously—by Jeffrey Williamson, to whom I am much indebted. Williamson's work is a model for all of us, not least because it understands that markets are powerful but that their power can cut more than one way—for or against people. It is a mistake to dismiss neoclassical economics, or what one thinks neoclassical analysis ("anathema," a reviewer once told me) is, simply out of an understandable dislike for its misapplication or oversimplification. Economics is a tool like any other. It can be used or abused, but arguably, it should never be ignored.

This project has had a lengthy history. It began as an encyclopedia entry, "Mexico" (https://eh.net/encyclopedia/the-economic-history-of-mexico/) for the EH.Net Encyclopedia of Economic History (https://eh.net/encyclopedia-2/advisory-board-members-and-consulting-editors/) and was originally commissioned by Robert Whaples. It took far longer to write that entry than I had ever intended, because trying to take a comprehensive view of Mexico's economic history was a daunting task. The results proved satisfactory, and save for an occasional updating, I intended to let matters rest there. Nevertheless, my friend, colleague, and teacher, Stanley J. Stein, insisted that I should consider expanding the original essay, and particularly, to push well beyond my field of expertise, colonial and neocolonial New Spain and Mexico. I suspect he had a short interpretive volume in mind, and that was what I have tried to do, although he did not live to see the results, about which I am certain he would have had much to say. I wish it would have been otherwise.

Briefly, the three chapters of this book are as follows.

The first chapter is devoted to the colonial period, beginning with the consequences of the European incursion. It emphasizes environmental factors, demographic change, and the way in which changing factor scarcities altered the institutional landscape of New Spain. We explicitly construct an index of environmental stress in an attempt to verify its relevance for an analysis of the entire colonial period. There is an intentional reinterpretation of the so-called Depression of the Seventeenth Century, and then a more general account of the ways in which fiscal, political, environmental, and demographic factors interacted to produce the dramatic changes that characterized the eighteenth century. If one were so inclined, it might be possible to see two very long cycles in the colonial period, one in which the sixteenth and eighteenth centuries move in opposite directions, with the point of inflection coming around the middle of the seventeenth century. The ratio of labor to land and the consequent rent-wage ratios are of great importance, fairly sketching out a kind of stylized history of accumulation, distribution, and its reversal under three hundred years of colonial rule. There is also an extended consideration of the Conquest, not only as a demographic event but as the one in which the regime of property rights decisively changes. While we end with the outbreak of the Insurgency, we clarify the material framework of that rebellion, which grew out of a complex of changes, some intentional, others not, that cannot be reduced simply to one variable or another.

The second chapter deals with the nineteenth century from the Insurgency (1810–1823) to the Revolution (1910–1940). While we take up the same issues for the colonial period, we focus especially on the demographic costs of political instability. The point is not why Mexico did not grow but why any reasonable expectation should exist that it would. Conventional wisdom about the absence of costs of political instability is not convincing, especially when potential output (i.e., what would have been produced in its absence) is considered. There is novel demographic data for the entire century and an explicit calculation of the costs of peasant expropriation during the Porfiriato, not to mention the long-run effects of events such as the War with the United States (1846–1848), the War of the Reforma (1858–1860), and the French Intervention (1862–1867). We present a lagged model connecting railroad building to agricultural output and the diversification of the export basket. Again, there is an emphasis on factor endowments, scarcity, and the changes that resulted from exogenous political events such as wars and insurrections.

Finally, in Chapter 3, we take up the relation between the Revolution, agrarian reform, industrialization, and the so-called Mexican Miracle (roughly 1954–1982). To repeat, this is not a political history but an economic one, with much more emphasis on agriculture than customary. It is also impossible to understand the end of the "Miracle" without reference to the end of the Bretton Woods era (1944–1971), which makes Mexico much less unique in terms of some of the problems it faced in the 1970s and afterwards. Similarly, we consider Mexico's problems in the

1980s to be a not particularly remarkable variant of the problems faced by all the oil-producing countries of OPEC, even if Mexico remained outside. It simply will not do to hold Mexico's import substitution industrialization responsible for difficulties that were caused by its drinking from the poisoned chalice of oil. There were poor decisions, but there was also very bad luck involved in what was to transpire. Many factors, and not simply one or two, lead to that conclusion.

I argue that the agrarian reform, while well intentioned and even politically astute, was poorly designed economically. It did little or nothing to support domestic demand. This is why economists have always seen agriculture as the basis of development. In effect, Mexico inadvertently reproduced an impoverished peasantry that could purchase little of what "industrial" Mexico wanted to produce. For this reason, the industry did not benefit from ordinary economies of scale and required substantial tariff protection. But this is important—Aurora Gómez Galvarriato has documented the beginnings of the process with the Revolution and the failure to modernize textile technology. It was scarcely just the failure of the so-called Mexican Miracle. Frankly, one could really go back to the mid-nineteenth century as well and discern the origins of inefficient import substitution. As Stephen Haber has correctly argued, "It did not begin with ["Raúl]Prebisch."

As many historians have concluded, including one no less distinguished than Eric Hobsbawm, it is very difficult to write the history of events in which one is intimately involved. In my case, this begins in the 1970s and continues through 2000. The sharp discontinuities and multiple crises which characterize this period are not easily summarized in simple terms, but it is clear that Mexico changed dramatically thereafter. While I end, for that reason, with the epochal election of 2000, I go no further other than to reflect on what historians now say about the "dilemma" of Mexican development.

The future lies beyond the historian's remit. Economists have a mediocre record of prediction. And economic historians, frankly, none at all. We may not be able to penetrate, as the Roman historian Livy put it, "the mists of antiquity," but for us, it is the future, not the past, that is truly the unknown country.

Notes

1 Lionel Robbins, *An Essay on the Nature and Significance of Economic Science* (London, UK: Macmillan & CO, Limited, 1932).

2 T.H. Aston and C.H.E. Philpin, *The Brenner Debate: Agrarian Class Structure and Economic Development in Pre-industrial Europe (Past and Present Publications)* (New York, NY: Cambridge University Press, 1987). Tony Judt, "A Clown in Regal Purple: Social History and the Historians," *History Workshop Journal* 7 (1979): 66–94, https://doi.org/10.1093/hwj/7.1.66. Enrique Semo, *Historia del capitalismo en México* (Mexico City Ediciones Era, 1973).

1

"NEW" WORLD, NEW RULERS, NEW RULES

Factor Endowments, Conquest, and Power

In recent years, it has become fashionable, not to say conventional, that the "Spanish Conquest" of Mexico would ultimately leave more intact of indigenous society, culture, and institutions than it destroyed. There were, to be sure, battles, the overthrow of dynasties, internecine conflict, and all the trappings of a civil war. Yet it is also true that the consequences of the European incursion completely altered the resource endowments of the indigenous peoples, if only by accident. Labor (population), which in the preconquest world, had been abundant, was now decimated by a series of epidemics and armed conflicts. The land, which remained, had been previously scarce but was now relatively abundant. And it was to this remarkable shift that the newly implanted colonial institutions and the surviving indigenous population must adapt. The essence of economic history is to recognize the logic of scarcity. And that is what we undertake here.

As Alfred Crosby demonstrated more than 30 years ago, the ecological and biological implications of the European incursion were profound. New pathogens and biota were introduced that altered the ways in which Mesoamericans interacted with their world—indeed, in the very ways in which they *could* interact with their world. More, Eleanor Melville memorably put it, not the least of it was a "plague of sheep" that multiplied as rapidly as the indigenous people died. Within these radically changed parameters of their material existence, the indigenous peoples had to cope. And cope they did, sometimes in unexpected ways.

The stories of these interactions are, for the most part, known, but some of their subtler implications have gone unappreciated, not to say ignored.[1] Intense, but ultimately fruitless and irrelevant debate over what one observer called "numbers from nowhere," the speculative reconstruction and debate over the size of the pre-contact

DOI: 10.4324/9781003532583-2

populations, obscured what truly matters, which was the change in relative factor endowments, the ratio of productive labor to useable land.[2]

The Europeans initially behaved as if they were surrounded by a virtually innumerable and inexhaustible population—a perfectly elastic labor supply. To their chagrin and to the natives' sorrow, time proved otherwise. From an economic standpoint, the Conquest was of fundamental significance, whatever its cultural, social, or even political implications were. To argue otherwise is plainly absurd.[3]

New Spain, as the colony was to be called, was an agrarian society with a high-pressure demographic regime (i.e., characterized by both high fertility and mortality). This regime, in turn, was shaped not only by actions of conquerors, military, administrative, judicial, and otherwise but also by both demographic and climatological conditions. While many basic economic conditions, such as the influence of time preference (i.e., consumption or production now versus consumption or production in the future) on the decisions of conqueror and conquered alike is mostly evident from broad ex post changes in behavior. But the historical study of climatic, epidemiological, and demographic conditions has made dramatic progress of late. It was formerly difficult to make much more than anecdotal reference to climate, rainfall, hunger, and disease. An ample body of archival evidence has now been examined systematically by Virginia García de Acosta, Juan Manuel Pérez Zevallos, and América Molina del Villar.[4] There is now systematic research into dendrochronology, that is, the historical relation between soil moisture, environmental stress, and the configuration of tree rings. Paleoclimatology has made substantial advances—to the point where it is now apparent that the European invasion occurred during a period of drought (1521–1524) comparable to the infamous "year of hunger" (1785–1786) in the late colonial period. Such considerations must now be integrated into a modern understanding of the Conquest and its sixteenth-century aftermath.[5]

In many ways, a natural point of departure and comparison is with the literature on the demographic and economic effects of the European Black Death in the fourteenth century. With some modification, that model will inform the remainder of this chapter, beginning with the catastrophic demographic collapse of the native population in late sixteenth-century New Spain. We conclude with the subsequent demographic reversals of the eighteenth century. The economic logic we pursue is as follows.

With the irruption of the Black Death in Western Europe in the fourteenth century, approximately 25 percent of the existing population perished. Land and physical capital (productive assets) were not affected by disease, but the population declined. Assuming diminishing returns to labor, a reduction in population raises real wages and drives down residual rents and the returns to physical capital. Therefore, the relative price of labor-intensive goods will rise and that of land-intensive goods will fall. Since per capita real income (the actual purchasing power over goods) and wealth rises, there is a boom in the market for luxury goods while the relative prices of necessities tend to fall. Thus, the simple predictions of neoclassical economics.[6]

According to the Berkeley School (in this context, Woodrow Borah, Sherburne Cook, and Leslie Simpson), labor scarcity took root in the outbreak of the catastrophic *cocoliztli* epidemic of 1545 that resulted in 12 to 15 million deaths, perhaps 45 percent of the native population of Central Mexico. The disease is now thought to be enteric fever causing salmonella that struck again in 1576. Only Yucatán, for whatever the reason, appears to have been spared.[7] Using real wage data of unskilled native labor assembled by Woodrow Borah and Sherburne Cook that appear in Figure 1.1 (expressed in terms of purchasing power over fanega of corn scaled to 100), it is apparent that real wages remained essentially unchanged from the 1530s through the 1550s. Then the regime changed dramatically: two factors produced the change.

One, of course, was labor scarcity. The second was the subsequent emergence of a labor market in New Spain in the 1550s. No such market existed in Mesoamerica, let alone under the Aztecs, prior to the arrival of the Europeans. The emergence of a labor market was the result of the New Laws of the 1540s which regulated the existence and duration of the encomienda, or distribution of native labor to the Europeans, and in a supplementary clause of 1549, mandated the payment of wages and the definitive suspension of the native people to provide personal services to the conquerors. In a market, prices (maize wages) and quantities (population) are inversely related, just as they are here.[8]

Critics of the encomienda and of other similar institutions, such as the friar Jerónimo de Mendieta or the jurist Alonso de Zurita, concluded that the post-conquest labor regime, in conjunction with environmental factors and newly

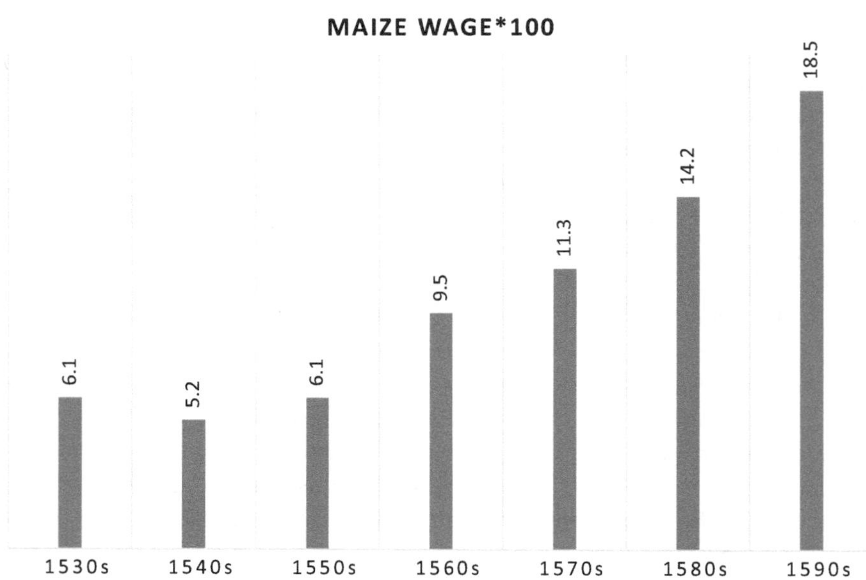

FIGURE 1.1 Maize-Deflated Real Wages

introduced pathogens, was killing off the native population. The wasteful employment of native labor at a zero price gave way to a belated recognition to rationing at a nonzero price was the only alternative, even if the colonists themselves often looked for ways to circumvent the laws. The Europeans—and by the 1550s and the reign of King Philip II, there is no great anachronism involved in calling them "Spaniards"—may have come to Mexico with the ambition of living like feudal lords, but the disappearance of the native population ultimately imposed the constraints of markets and commercial society upon them, even if only in an uneven and tentative way. History has a way of defying ideological categorization: an evolving reality is far messier. Alonso de Zorita's residence in Mexico coincided with the outbreaks of *cocoliztli* in 1559 and 1566. His account of natives falling dead by the roadside distinctly recalls accounts of the Black Death in Europe. Zorita understood that the pre-1550 labor regime was no longer viable. He pointedly observed that the colonists could have forced labor or native survival. Do you want them to make woolens in the manufactories (*obrajes*) under compulsion and perish, or do you want them to survive?[9]

Underlying the rise of real wages, the evolution of royal law, and the demographic collapse of the native population was a complex of meteorological, epidemiological, and zootic factors that can now be quantified. Population collapse led to a rise in real wages; the rise in real wages was embedded in evolving law and property rights. These had an irreducible climatological component that conditioned and complicated all such responses. It was generally impossible to account for these in much more than an anecdotal way in the past. But recent comprehensive samplings of archival data involving its features can be linked into systematic research into dendrochronology—the historical relation between soil moisture, environmental stress, and the configuration of tree rings.

Thus, real wages rose in the latter part of the sixteenth century and the relative prices of labor-intensive goods rose as well in response to climatological and environmental changes mediated through population movements, which, in turn, reflected prevalence of diseases due to climate-related malnutrition. Let us explore how.

We begin by examining Figures 1.2 and 1.3. Figure 1.2 charts an index of environmental, epidemiological, and agricultural stress (IEEAS) across sixteenth-century Mexico after the Conquest. Figure 1.3 shows a plot of the Palmer Drought Severity Index (PDSI) centered on Amealco in the Eastern Bajio region of Central Mexico. The technical details and method of computation (for the IEEAS) and some discussion of the PDSI both appear in the Data Appendix. The analysis presented is made in light of the considerations outlined there, all of which are relevant. An interested reader should consult that Appendix for qualifications, cautions, and relevant limitations. Here it is enough to add that both figures present smoothed data for intelligibility and to reveal the underlying trends.

Figure 1.2 shows considerable chatter, so it is more helpful to look at the ten-year moving average. This index of stress climbs into the mid-1540s. It then falls away

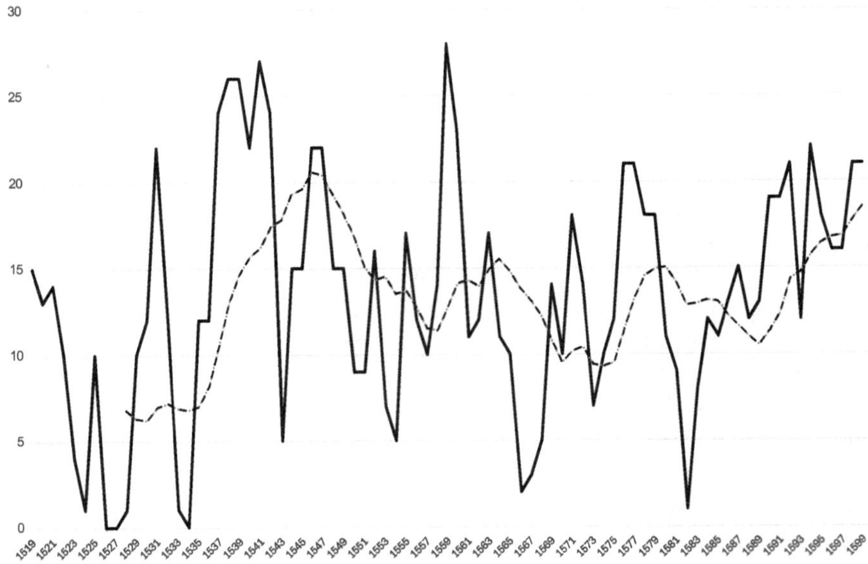

FIGURE 1.2 IEEAS and Ten-Year Moving Average, 1519–1599

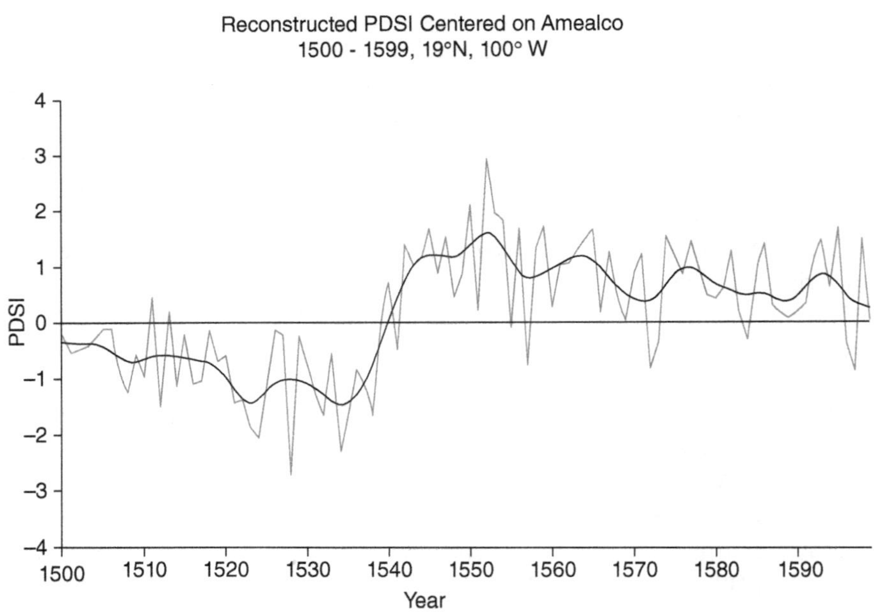

FIGURE 1.3 PDSI 1500–1599 Centered on Amealco with Ten-Year Smoothing

to a perceptibly lower level, until it begins to increase again in the late sixteenth century. If we look at Figure 1.3, which is the reconstructed PDSI centered on Amealco, (in the Bajío), it too strongly suggests that there are two distinct parts to the sixteenth century, where one is based on climatic considerations alone. Again, the break (or inflection) comes in the 1540s, which may be interpreted as a transition from a drier to a wetter period in Central Mexico.

If we mentally combine the two graphs, something like the following picture emerges. Both changes in the legal regime—which is to say legislation associated with the New Laws—and in coinciding climatic factors seem to have taken over after the very turbulent period of the Conquest. In part, of course, the coincidence was fortuitous. Legal and institutional change does not "cause" climate change in any sense. But the two may reinforce each other, of course. A legal regime that is gradually moving toward a more rational private allocation of labor can relieve the pressure that an exploitative "seigneurial" or feudal mode of production that requires personal service to an almost unlimited extent entails. At the same time, more abundant rainfall—assuming it is not catastrophically overabundant—can certainly enhance agricultural productivity. It will moderate agricultural price increases being driven by labor scarcity as well. In this very specific way, the Conquest mattered, and mattered a great deal, because nothing remotely approximating a labor market existed before it.

Historians have long known this, but perhaps need to be reminded. As Charles Gibson correctly and eloquently concluded from "traditional" historical methods more than a half century ago, "Officials in New Spain took the royal orders seriously, although they never fully eradicated unrecompensed labor. . . . They implied that coercion was unnecessary, and that Indians would work voluntarily if a sufficient wage were provided. . . . The uneconomical labor institutions of the first colonial years would no longer suffice." Where Gibson erred was in observing that "in Mexican history significant changes have rarely occurred as a consequence of law." This was one of those rare instances. Even the natives on the property of the Cortés family in the Marquesado were included. No one was exempt.[10]

Drawing on the agricultural and labor history of the sixteenth century as an example, what, precisely, were the conquerors about? Unfortunately, the answer seems all too obvious: scarcity and markets worked against them. If anything, their open rent-seeking, i.e., rearranging the boundaries of who got what out of existing production, rather than "capitalism" (or the accumulation of new productive assets) per se worked to impoverish the native peoples. As Gibson noted, Juan Suárez de Peralta in his *Noticias Históricas de la Nueva España* (published in 1878) observed, "the moment these rules took effect everything had to be bought . . . and people found themselves in need."[11] Which people exactly? As Evsey Domar observed, whom scarcity tends to impoverish or enrich is a matter of relative factor scarcity, not ideology. Of course, Robert Brenner concluded that there is nothing mechanical about the response to scarcity. Class power and institutions matter. But people respond to material forces, not disembodied abstractions of mode of production or even to capitalist stage theories of development.[12]

Another way of understanding the matter is by observing precisely why the European settlers resisted the implications of scarce labor in the Valley of Mexico, which at an early moment was largely, if not exactly, coterminous with what was called New Spain anyway. In Table 1.1, we show that from 1570–1575 through

TABLE 1.1 Wage-Rent Ratio in the Valley of Mexico, 1509–1606

Years	*Land Index(A)*	*Labor Index(B)*	*(Land/Labor)*
1570–1575	100	100	100
1576–1590	50	143	286
1591–1606	33	286	867

Sources: Calculated from Rebecca Horn, *Postconquest Coyoacán: Nahua-Spanish Relations in Central Mexico (1519–1650)*, p. 208; and José Ignacio Urquiola Permisán, "Salarios y precios en la industria manufacturera textil de la lana en la Nueva España: 1570–1635" in Virginia García Acosta, *Los Precios de Alimentos y Manufacturas Novohispanas* (Mexico City: CIESAS, 1995), pp. 195–229.

1591–1606, the price of unskilled labor in the Valley of Mexico nearly tripled while the price of land in the south-central Valley fell by nearly two thirds.

In other words, the price of labor relative to land increased by nearly 800 percent. The evolution of relative prices (on balance) would have inevitably worked against the employers of labor and in favor of its suppliers as real wages rose. This was not exactly what Cortés and his soldiers had in mind: struggling landlords and a wealthy peasantry.

To repeat, the emergence of a labor market was associated with both institutional and demographic changes. And both were related to the Spanish Conquest. A clear example was the appearance of the *sonsaque* (no poaching labor) laws regarding the *obrajes* of Tepeaca, Puebla and Tlaxcala, beginning in the 1580s, coming hard on the heels of the terrible *cocoliztli* epidemic of the mid-1570s, and continuing into the 1590s, as real wages skyrocketed. The sharpening competition for labor was documented in a series of laws and ordinances that prohibited the owners of textile manufactories from raiding each other's work forces. If competition for labor (or forbidding as much) is not evidence of pressures of an emerging labor market, then what was? The fact market relations were far from universal or complete is hardly a surprise and not an argument against economic analysis. In early sixteenth-century England, perhaps no more than 20 to 35 percent of agricultural labor was wage labor. Yet few hesitate to identify the emergence of a market economy there.[13]

While institutional history has fallen out of favor with historians of Latin America, quite the opposite has occurred among economic historians, largely thanks to the work of Douglass North. To an economic historian, neglect of "institutional" history makes little sense, because it is tantamount to forgetting the bases on which incentives are created in an exchange economy, however inchoate. Put more simply, one inevitably asks why agents exchange property rights as they do?[14]

The issue of property rights—the right of exclusion—under an early modern European versus an Amerindian regime is a crucial reason for reconsidering the Conquest. It is not clear that the Nahua and the Spaniards regarded property rights in the same way, even if they constitute the very basis for exchange. It seems hard to believe, but the difference was amply recognized by Andrés Molina Enríquez in *Los Grandes Problemas Nacionales* in which he termed the Papal Bull *Noverint Universi* "the origins of property in our country."[15]

The matter of property rights is a crucial reason for reconsidering the Conquest since the Nahua and the Spaniards did not regard property rights in precisely the same way. Yet these rights constitute the basis of exchange. Crossed signals (or more formally, elevated transaction costs) would result in fewer exchanges, because they lead to increased uncertainty. Less exchange ultimately produces less economic growth and development.

But did the Conquest and its transition lead to higher transactions costs? Clearly, the fraught contest over the policy of *congregación* (village reorganization) in the Valley of Mexico in the sixteenth and seventeenth centuries was whether the native village (*altepl*, or pl. *altipemi*) should be organized along ethnic or territorial lines, or some combination of both, or neither.[16] The indigenous *altepetl* was only secondarily spatial or territorial, whereas the *pueblo de indios* represented a territorial projection of what may have been a scattered settlement. The *altepetl* and the reconstructed "Indian" village under the Spaniards had only a tenuous connection. The laws whereby property rights of the villages were defined were essentially Castilian and mostly came after 1570. To the Spaniards, the *village* was nothing other than property fixed in space. The native *altepetl* was a symbolic representation of the cosmos whose basis was as much ethnic as anything else. About this, the Spaniards could have cared less; the *congregación* of the late sixteenth and early seventeenth centuries made few distinctions between the native peoples they included. Ultimately, the differences persisted far beyond the colonial period in the specification of land titles, rights to collecting wood, and even privileges of water usage.[17] A specific study of the Chalco region in Central Mexico emphasizes that the basis of the altepetl was nonterritorial. It often had multiple access to resources disconnected from the altepetl itself. The reality changed only gradually from the 1560s to the 1640s with the depopulation of indigenous lands and their distribution in land grants or *mercedes* to the colonizers mostly, peaking around1600. This was a private property, familiar to the Spaniards, whatever the communal status of the previously indigenous property was. The process contributed to the development of an active land market. It did not happen overnight, but it would not have happened at all if the Conquest had not intervened.[18]

Very few historians have dealt explicitly with the question. One was James Lockhart in *The Nahuas After the Conquest.* The other is Rebecca Horn in *Postconquest Coyoacán.* Lockhart is forthright. For example, he concludes, unobjectionably: "It is a fair statement that there was movement in the direction of a more individualized concept of landholding in the European style in which the landholder stood in contrast to larger entitles rather than forming part of them."[19] This is a middle ground statement. Previous authors such as Pedro Carrasco discounted the existence of private property in Mesoamerica, but Lockhart takes a more measured and less doctrinaire position.[20] His student, Horn, concludes "Nahua land tenure was extremely complex. Although residual rights to land rested with the corporate body, Nahua lands were not worked in common."[21] As for the Maya prior to the Conquest, Robert Patch observes, "Maya land tenure principles, in sum, were quite complex and still somewhat mysterious."[22]

So, for the Maya, the matter is open. But it is not correct to conclude that the Nahua had no notion of private property even if, by and large, their use of property was mediated territorially by the *calpolli*, itself a clan-based entity. Yet theirs was far from any generalized notion of land as a commodity that could be bought or sold at will (if legally unencumbered) that is closer to the European notion that gradually took hold in Mexico. As a result, in the interim between the Conquest and the end of the sixteenth century, huge tracts of land made vacant by massive depopulation passed into Spanish control, formally and otherwise.[23] What, in an agrarian society, could have been more conducive to the formation of a broadly unequal distribution of wealth, even as the very notion of property was in flux? Not to speak of differing notions of the distribution of and claims on output—for example, of distribution by average versus marginal product—about which we essentially know nothing? Could these changes, if indeed they were changes, insofar as they were associated with the Conquest, have been trivial? Again, markets depend on clear property rights, and these rights came after the Conquest and with the Spaniards.

As real wages rose and land values fell, there were numerous changes in agricultural technology which reflected just such alterations. These transformations—from labor- to land-intensive techniques and products, or away from *chinampas* (artificial islands, thus all essentially 100 percent labor) and toward haciendas (which are *relatively* less labor intensive than chinampas—labor costs were 60–70 percent of producing corn and wheat on haciendas in Central Mexico) and from the digging stick to the introduction of draft animals and the European plow were a direct consequence of changes in relative factor scarcities.[24]

As Teresa Rojas Rabiela has argued, intensive agriculture and garden plots that depended on irrigation works, levelling and terracing—all labor intensive—were transformed. Growing European plants unleased effects "that ranged from complementation to displacement and substitution (cotton for sugar cane). "Diverse results included complex agricultural calendars, with new crop rotations and associated labor . . . and an increase in production from new species resistant to lower temperatures." Agriculture underwent "a profound transformation."[25]

As a simple model based on factor endowments would hold, the relative prices of land-intensive goods should have fallen. Anything requiring large inputs of land, such as wool and meat (ranching in general) were land intensive. An example of the expansion of land-intensive products was provided by Charles Gibson over half a century ago. The expansion of the population of cattle, sheep, and goats was dramatic in the face of population decline. In a memorable graph following Gibson, the staggering increase in the livestock population, generally taken as exogenous, is displayed in Figure 1.4.

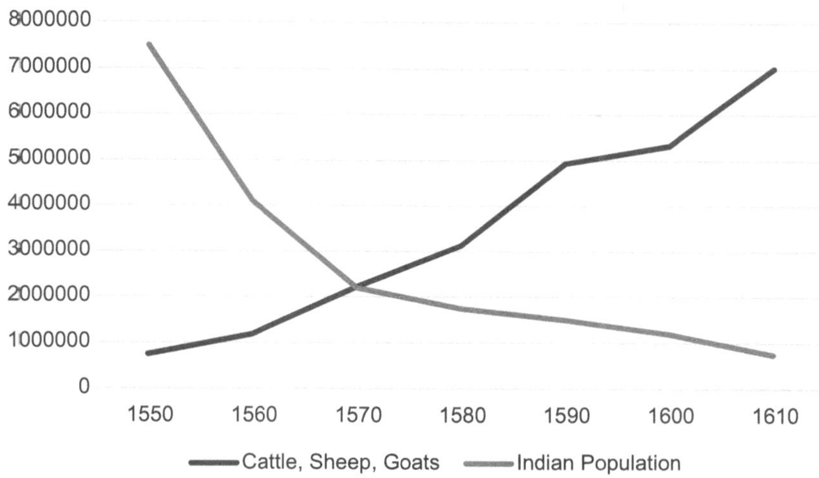

FIGURE 1.4 Indigenous Population of Central Mexico versus Cattle, Sheep, and Goats, 1550–1610

Even in Yucatán, so often very different from Central Mexico, the initial decline of the native population produced a similar result: "The Maya population decline had resulted in a surplus of land, which the Spaniards began to put to use for stock raising."[26] Nor was central Veracruz much different. The Native American population was wiped out by disease, and essentially replaced by sheep and cattle. It was, in the words of Antonio García de Leon, "the absolute failure (*hundimiento*) of the indigenous world."[27]

While the increase in livestock is a characteristic of the rise of the hacienda in Central Mexico, the pattern was in place by the 1550s.[28]

Nor was the example of ranching unique. In the sixteenth century, maize continued to be produced under labor-intensive indigenous techniques, and its price consequently rose sharply. Maize, a bulky commodity was produced mostly for regional markets. There is no reason to assume price convergence, much less the law of one price across New Spain (i.e., the same good traded within a given market should, exclusive of transportation and transaction costs, trade at the same price). Maize prices in the bishopric of Puebla derived from tithing data show a 50 percent increase between 1559 and 1583. If anything, Richard Garner's "maize" price series shows an even greater increase between 1557 and 1595, with an index basically doubling over the period. Here was an example of incomplete (technological) specialization, for maize production on chinampas never completely disappeared even as it shifted mainly to haciendas.[29]

If anything could provide a unified explanation for economic trends in the sixteenth century, it would be the consequences of a massive population decline, itself the result of a deadly colonial labor regime played out against a persistent, cyclical background of disease, dearth, and drought. These ultimately required a substantial reorientation of "modes of production," technology, and an accompanying change in the distribution of wealth and its principal forms of accumulation—as land rather than as tributary labor, with a new element of price rationing not always to the liking of the Spaniards. The result was extensive rent-seeking behavior to modify market outcomes and the persistence of both free and forced labor, depending heavily on regional circumstances and the political influence of the users of labor.[30] We tend to call this "capitalism" for want of a better term, but over the years, debates about the word have been both sterile and inconclusive. The "Conquest," like other historical events, was an invention, but an invention with dramatic economic consequences, particularly when Conquest is considered in environmental and demographic terms. Cultural and linguistic analyses are a necessary part of the discussion, not sufficient in themselves to appreciate the magnitude and nature of the changes underway. As Robert Brenner astutely observed, *both* power and scarcity were at issue.

Depression, Recovery, or Both?

Historians have written about the "General Crisis" of the seventeenth century for more than 50 years. In the words of Peter Clark, the discussion had two interconnected themes. The first was to explain an outbreak of political instability in Europe in the mid-century. The second examined whether the period marked a turning point from feudalism to capitalism. More recently, Geoffrey Parker has recast the debate in terms of climate change, specifically, global cooling with its agricultural and demographic implications. The debate will no doubt continue.[31]

The first indication that events in New Spain were linked to a "general crisis" came in 1976 with the publication of a paper by J. I. Israel.[32] Looking back at Figure 1.2, we note that Mexico participated in the "crisis of the 1590s," at least to judge from the sharp upturn in the moving average of the IEEAS then. But what about the seventeenth century? Parker is ambivalent, discussing "American exceptionalism."[33] There is a case to be made for New Spain, but as much as a spillover or echo of events in Spain than as an endogenous development in Mexico. As Parker explains in detail, European events came to a head in 1647 and 1648, somewhat later than the peak of the IEEAS for Mexico around 1640, when anti-Portuguese and anti-Semitic hysteria broke out in Mexico as Olivares faced the Revolt in Portugal in 1640.[34]

The relevant point is that Mexico in the seventeenth century cannot be considered independent (in economic terms) of Mexico in the sixteenth century. The adjustments demanded by indigenous population decline were simply too large as a fall in total production occurred. Because of population decline, land and physical capital went uncultivated or underemployed. But they did not disappear. If diminishing returns to labor held-and why would they not-a reduction in population was accompanied by a rise in marginal product and in real wages, precisely as we have seen.

Yet this, in turn, implied a change in the distribution of wealth. Those private parties, especially the newly emerging class of large landowners or owners of haciendas, the new "lords of the land," were driven to compete for fewer laborers. The "labor share" of income rose, just as the "property share" composed of rents and profits declined. The Spaniards themselves understood that prices and wages would rise and said so. They called the seventeenth century, as Claude Morin notes, "the century of the scarce Indian," a scarcity exacerbated by vast drainage and flood control projects in the Valley of Mexico that continued to rely on forced labor that competed with the private sector. The implications were profound. "The moment you take away the Indians, people will lose whatever wealth or profit they have."[35]

While Morin spoke of scarce Indians, he could have as easily spoke of abundant land. The classic institutional adaptation to the fall of relative price of land was, as we previously noted, the hacienda. By the beginning of the seventeenth century, the institution, rooted in the later sixteenth century, made a more general appearance and slowly supplanted indigenous agriculture as a source of Spanish (and principally urban) supply. According to Gisela von Wobeser, the first use of the term "hacienda" in the sense of an agricultural unit dates to 1579, in the zone of Zacatula, Guerrero, where there was a reference to the "casa and hacienda of Villegas." While the system first appeared in Central Mexico, it spread slowly from there, especially to what would become the Northern mining districts. In the beginning, the term was mostly associated with cereal agriculture while cattle ranching, as Chevalier observed, gravitated to the North. While hacienda had a specific meaning, there was considerable variation in the production of maize, maguey (agave), and cotton.[36]

Spaniards acquired land by a variety of devices and under vastly different circumstances. Land could simply be appropriated, especially if vacated by the native people after one of the periodic outbreaks of epidemic disease. Or it could be had by royal grant or outright purchase, or by exchange. Agricultural land commanded no value—it was essentially a free good—without a source of indigenous labor. That typically meant that early settlements existed cheek by jowl with native communities. The villages may have been existing or reconstituted once the twin processes of "composition" (regularization of title) and "congregation" (relocation of scattered settlements) had been undertaken.[37]

Both were important steps in the creation of a colonial agricultural regime in which the now scarce indigenous population (labor) was applied to abundant land. As Gibson pointed out, the initial attempt by Spaniards to employ a rotating draft of village labor, the *repartimiento*, but by 1632–1633, it had been judged unsatisfactory and abolished.[38]

As Woodrow Borah realized many years ago, a reduction in creole wealth (by the loss of indigenous labor: the additional accumulation of additional vacant land was of little value at the margin) may have been a depression for the landed class, but not necessarily for the indigenous population. There is no question that the abolition of such devices as the *repartimiento* reduced agricultural output (total product)

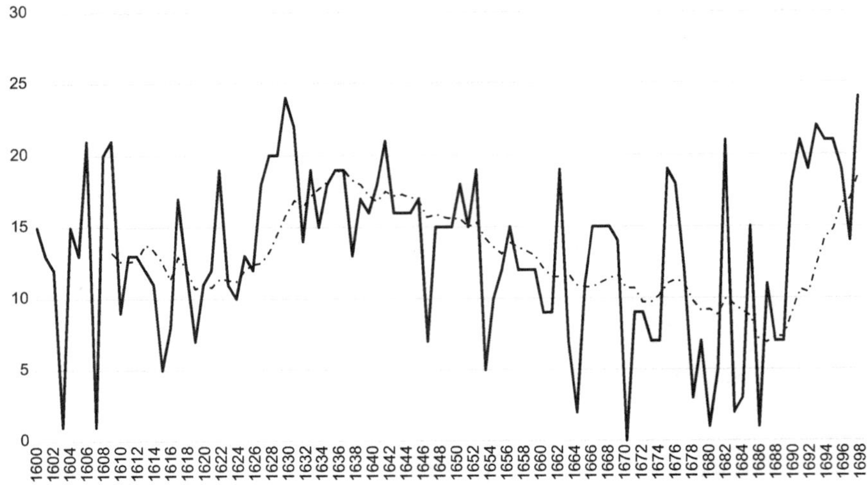

FIGURE 1.5 IEEAS and Ten-Year Moving Average, 1600–1699

against which the creoles (Spaniards) could make claims. A canon of the ecclesiastical cabildo of Tlaxcala observed that the decline in the tithe (an indirect and very loose measure of agricultural output) in Atrisco (in Puebla) of wheat consequent to the abolition of the *repartimiento* in 1632 was 7.5 percent, a very substantial amount. There was no longer enough labor to sustain planting and harvesting.[39]

In short, as the native population fell and the ability of the Spaniards to coerce them into working fell as well, agricultural output fell and so did the Spanish share of a shrinking pie, even as the natives were now remunerated at higher rates. This was the "depression" of the seventeenth century in New Spain. Whether it constituted a crisis really comes down to "crisis for whom?" The IEEAS shown in Figure 1.5 falls almost continually for half a century in Mexico after the 1630s. By this standard, at least, ecological and environmental pressure on the colonial population was diminished, and the basis for a recovery of sorts was established.

The work of Leticia Arroyo and her collaborators supports this conclusion. In Figure 1.6, I draw on Arroyo's findings. Like Borah, Arroyo finds real wages beginning to rise in the late sixteenth century. Her wage series continues to increase into the 1660s (actually, into the 1670s in her original work), after which it begins a measured decline (and the rate of increase declines after 1630). Indicators of substitutes for free labor—slave sales—appear to have peaked in Puebla in 1630 or so and then to have fallen sharply thereafter. Or to put it differently, the relative price of free versus slave labor peaks around 1630, even if real wages increased for some time thereafter.[40]

With some important regional differences, the long-run recovery of population in Central Mexico got underway between 1640 and 1670. Toluca, for example, stabilized around 1640 through 1690, after which growth resumed. There was a strong

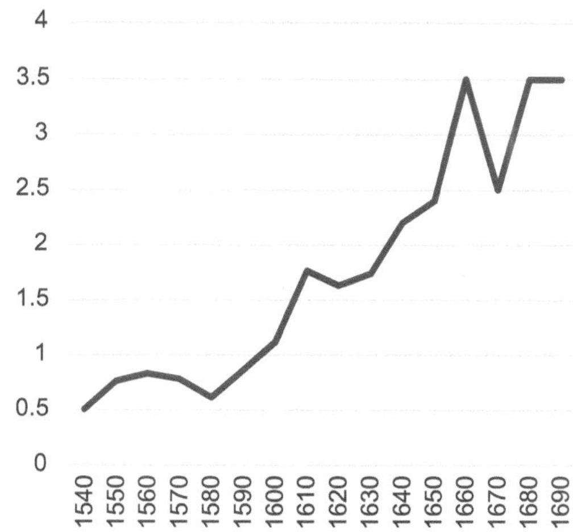

FIGURE 1.6 Index of Real Wages for New Spain, 1540–1660

Note: The basis of Calculation here differs from that shown in Figure 1.1.

increase in population in Tlaxcala (Santa Inés Zacatelco) after 1647. In Querétaro, the number of tributaries increased between 1644 and 1688. A similar impression emerged for Veracruz between 1640 and 1670.[41]

In the Mixteca Alta, which embraces parts of Oaxaca, Puebla, and Guerrero, the Spaniards did not set out immediately to exert control. They never evidenced much interest in holding indigenous lands, leaving stock raising to the Indians until well into the seventeenth century. Nevertheless, they had managed to make their presence felt by the later sixteenth century. It was then that the monetization of the indigenous economy and the penetration of Spanish goods intro tribute was underway. From the mid-sixteenth through the first quarter of the seventeenth century, Spanish commercial activity in the Mixteca increased, the decline of the native population notwithstanding. The pattern changed after 1625 with some evidence of stagnation and decline through 1660. The principal source of change were the *alcaldes mayores*, who shifted from ordinary merchants to a kind of cartel of lenders seeking commercial control. The South thus did not share in the larger economic currents of central and northern New Spain (silver mining was marginally present) and was less open to the market forces that seemingly worked in favor of the native peoples of Central Mexico. It was simply a matter of the intensity of Spanish occupation and native land retention in the South, altogether different from patterns in Central Mexico.[42]

In a Malthusian model of preindustrial society, population decline is linked to rising real wages and to a rise in fertility, the number of children that a woman will bear. Thus a consequence of rising real wages in the long run is population growth, precisely what one finds occurring in late seventeenth-century New Spain, albeit

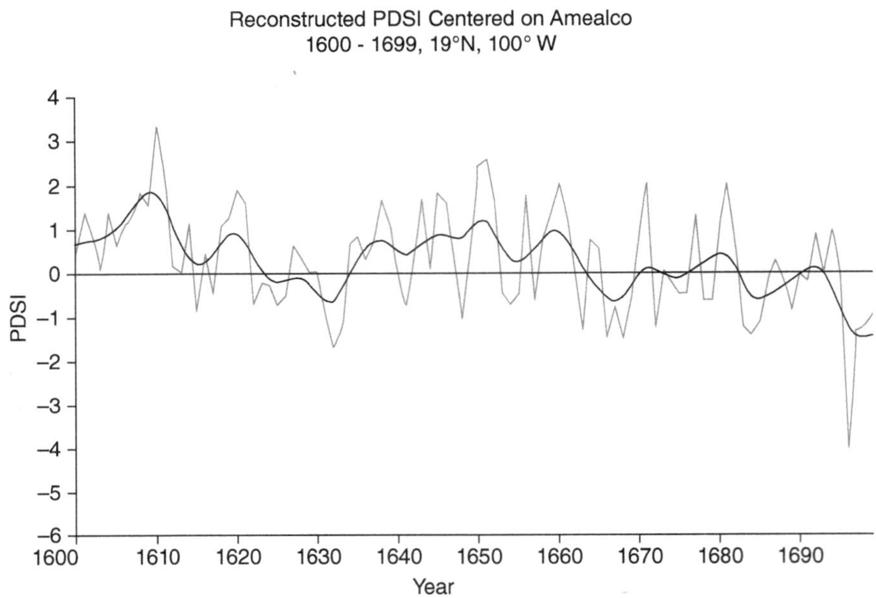

FIGURE 1.7 PDSI 1600–1699 Centered on Amealco with 10-Year Smoothing

with strong regional and, indeed, local variations. Yet there was clearly something else at work as well. As Figure 1.5 shows the IEEAS for 1600–1699, climatic and epidemiological conditions entered a relatively benign phase in the mid-1630s and continued so into the 1680s. These reinforced the long-run recovery of the population which finally got underway between 1640 and 1670. Again, Figure 1.7, which carries forward the PDSI from 1600 to 1699, shows roughly, but not exactly, the same pattern. The dry period in the seventeenth century was from the 1620s through the 1640s. So climate itself, especially from the 1640s through the 1660s, would have reinforced the population recovery, probably through rising agricultural productivity. The overall picture is consistent. Even if the seventeenth century was a "depression" for the creole population of Mexico, it was not for the indigenous people. As far as "crisis" is concerned, it reflected fiscal pressures under Olivares (The King's chief minister) in Spain. In New Spain, it figured in the property seizures of the Inquisition, but not as an economic variable per se. There was no General Crisis of the Seventeenth Century in Mexico, not in any European sense.[43]

Money, Silver, and Silver Mining

We have left money, silver and silver mining to now, not in strictly chronological order. Of course, all three embraced the entire colonial period and beyond. All three are complex. They are in no sense identical. And, to a greater (money) or lesser (mining) extent, all are imperfectly understood. There are, of course, plenty of numbers: about coinage, mints, and silver shipments. But numbers alone are not enough.

There is, for one thing, a difficult historical question. The Nahua existed within an exchange economy, at least as far as commodities other than labor was concerned. The famous account of Bernal Díaz del Castillo of the market at Tlatelolco, which Díaz del Castillo favorably compared to the commercial fair of Medina del Campo in Spain, requires no retelling.[44] Yet the thorny issue of what was used as a medium of exchange or of prices is unclear. Indeed, in European records, prices are ubiquitous. Kenneth Hirth has provided an exemplary introduction to the Aztec economy, one that had markets but was not a market economy.[45] This is almost certainly correct, although Hirth leaves open how commodity exchange functioned. In any commercial economy, a medium of exchange is a necessity, for it represents social claims on output. Yet we have only the dimmest of notion of what money was in the Aztec economy, much less how it supported markets of the kind of sophistication and density that the Spaniards observed. Lockhart points out two of the original borrowings into Nahuatl were "peso" and "tomín," monetary units.[46] But if the thing exists, why is there no native word for it? In this case, the absence of evidence does indeed appear to be evidence of absence. The Spaniards clearly brought money in a European sense to Mexico. What existed prior to the Conquest is anyone's guess. There are examples of payment in cacao beans to indigenous workers, but the documented examples are all, unfortunately, postconquest.

Aside from the existence of money, how to measure it and its effects? While by law, silver mined and refined was to be brought to a royal mint for registration and the payment of the King's seignorage fee (*quinto*), in practice, much silver circulated illegally, in the form of ingots. How much is simply unknown. How much silver was diverted to sumptuary as opposed to monetary uses? Again, unknown. New Spain was not a closed economy; silver was its major export. There was a balance between mining, mintage, nonmonetary uses, and exports. What was it? No one knows.[47]

As if these uncertainties were not enough, if merchants functioned as bankers in New Spain, essentially by taking deposits and issuing bills of exchange (*libranzas*), even if only to finance trade, they were creating circulating debt, and therefore, money. Silver was high powered money, in modern jargon (the raw material from which liquid purchasing power was created), but the size of a putative money multiplier is unknown. It matters. And whether money should be treated as a stock or as a flow variable matters too. Unfortunately, the answer to virtually every significant monetary question is an unknown.[48]

In a closed economy, the price level should be directly proportional to the stock of money (M), $MV=PQ$, where V is the velocity and Q is the "real" income or quantum (nominal income is PQ; velocity is determined, among other factors, by technology; it is typically assumed to be constant in the short run. There can—and in the case of New Spain should—be an adjustment (k) for what proportion of the economy passes through the market, but that can be left aside). This is the well-known Equation of Exchange. Yet we could also regard the price level as an outcome of the supply and demand for money. In some sense, Q is also a function of population, because one assumes more people will require more money to finance transactions. In other words, if population and the money supply grow at the same rate, other things remaining the same, the price level should be stable.

But suppose population is falling, as it was in sixteenth-century Mexico. Then the injection of more money, which would have paralleled the expansion of silver output in the second part of the century, should have resulted in a higher price level. Since real wages are money wages deflated by the price level, by implication, they must have been rising rapidly enough as the population declines to push up real wages. In Figure 1.6, a measure of real wages basically doubles (from 0.5 to 1.0) in the sixteenth century, which is consistent with population decline and an increase in silver output. The relative jump is even larger (from about 1 to 3.5) in the seventeenth century, peaking around 1680, after which the entire pattern reverses. Since we know silver output in Mexico began to rise enough in Mexico after 1645 for the colony to outstrip Peru as the principal source of silver in the Spanish Empire, the corresponding fall in real wages after 1680 must have been due in part to the incipient recovery of population in the period from 1640 to 1670. Falling money wages were abetted by an increase in the demand for money—among other things—that population growth supported. This is admittedly speculative, but not wildly so.[49]

Once the ore was extracted (labor cost), it could be regarded as a sunk (irrecoverable) cost. The relevant question was then the most profitable way to extract the silver. In most cases, the ore's middling quality justified the use of the amalgamation process, where raw materials alone, such as maize, mules, straw, and the rest were 50 percent of costs. These were mostly of local provenance.

Silver also had important fiscal dimensions. Inputs to mining represented a large share of domestic spending, perhaps 7 to 10 percent of gross output at the end of the colonial period. Agriculture alone represented a larger share, but a part of the agricultural output (such as maize) was taken up by mining in refining (as fodder for mules). As one observer noted, "The landscapes of states like San Luis, Zacatecas and Guanajuato were forever changed by the frenzied exploitation of their woodlands. Silver mines needed wooden ladders and pit props. The smelting of silver ore required vast quantities of firewood."[50]

[51]For a mining town like Zacatecas, Peter Bakewell argued, "The development of the Bajío can therefore be seen as a direct consequence of the prosperity of mining."[52] While the labor force of the mines may have been drawn from all over New Spain, assuring an adequate supply of labor for the mines was inevitably a primary goal of every viceroy from Antonio de Mendoza (the first Viceroy) forward. Supplying the mines created aggregate demand. It was the Mexican version of Say's Law.

Indirect evidence for the fiscal importance of silver mining is shown in Figure 1.8, a comparison of the sales tax or *alcabala* revenues collected in two different jurisdictions, Guanajuato and Querétaro, both in the Bajío. Guanajuato was the principal mining center of New Spain when these data were collected. Querétaro, in turn, had become the center of woolen manufacture and of its *obrajes*. It was also the distribution center for merchandise sent into the interior and the

FIGURE 1.8 Alcabala (Value-Added Tax) Collected in Guanajuato versus Querétaro

Far North, *tierradentro.* Both were extremely important. From 1785 through 1810 (some data are missing), tax collections in Guanajuato almost inevitably exceeded those of Querétaro. In other words, the tax on inputs of silver mining, though there were exemptions made to encourage mining, not to mention retained consumption goods, far exceeded a comparable charge on those in Querétaro, a more populous city, where raw wool, dyestuffs, and other inputs on woolen manufacture were in plentiful demand, not to say the same kinds of consumer goods sold in Guanajuato. Since the *alcabala* was a tax on value added, value added in mining exceeded that of manufacturing by an order of magnitude. This is the fiscal effect of mining: its linkages and the derived demand for inputs.

As for effects on the price level or monetary effects, these are difficult to determine. While the production of silver was not completely endogenous (determined by economic factors), there was no intrinsic reason while the output of the mines and that of the real economy (agriculture and industry) should vary in the same way. There was, in fact, no reason why the two sectors should have balanced at all other than ex post—after the fact. The quantity of money—however measured—and its relation to real production were ex ante independent because there was a large element of simple chance on the side of mining. You either struck it rich or you did not.

Therefore, the influence of money on prices was there, but unpredictable. As one observer put it in 1574:

> Everything [in Mexico] . . . comes only from that. If [silver mining] should stop, the tributary maize, manta and other goods would be of no value, and would

> revert to their former prices, which among the Spaniards was so low as to hardly sustain His Majesty's courts and officials. . . . So supporting silver and the mines raises the value of everything.[53]

The author of this statement, Pedro Moya de Contreras, the Archbishop of Mexico, himself a graduate of the University of Salamanca, was aware of the teachings of Martín Azpilcueta Navarro, a pioneer monetary theorist of the "School of Salamanca" in which the quantity theory of money figured so prominently.[54]

For the seventeenth century, this is about as far as the data can lead us. If we follow the work of Richard Garner, John TePaske, and Engel Sluiter, all available on Garner's previously cited web site, we could very crudely calculate that the amount of silver retained in New Spain between the 1560s and the 1640s may well have doubled, but this is simply a guess. What is not at issue is whether the seventeenth century was one of General Crisis or Depression. It was not. It would make more sense to characterize it as a period of adjustment to the enormous demographic, fiscal, environmental, monetary, and institutional changes that were occurring, during which the decline of population came to a halt and then reversed. Real wages appear to have risen and the monetization of the economy, which remained quite fragmented as a series of regional entities, probably increased. If the situation in Central Mexico resembled anything, it may have been that of Spanish Central America, where the pressure on the native population had been somewhat reduced, although, we are told, forced labor and land seizures continued almost unabated, even in the emergence of debt peonage.[55]

How to Lose a Colony in a Century

"Death to the Viceroy and his defenders. . . . Death to the Spaniards and the *gachupines* who consume our maize. . . . Is this not our land? What then do the Spaniards want with it?"[56]

As the seventeenth century concluded, environmental pressures increased exponentially (see Figure 1.5). A bloody food riot took place, perhaps the worst disaster the city had witnessed since the Great Flood of 1629—it was now nearly 70 years later, 1692. The "long" eighteenth century started inauspiciously. Pressures would increase, but it took a century and a change of political dynasty—from the Hapsburgs to the Bourbons—for the results to become manifest. The recovery of population that had begun in the seventeenth century reversed the evolution of the wage-rent ratio: real wages declined and property income rose. Metropolitan fiscal and commercial policies complicated the results of demographic changes. Output increased but was subject to the increasing fiscal demands of the Spanish Crown.

Population growth that resumed in the mid- to late seventeenth century continued into the eighteenth. Regional and urban-rural disparities were marked, but overall rates of 1 to 2 percent were common. Places like Michoacán and Guanajuato almost certainly support estimates closer to 2 percent, which was sustained over the century.[57] There were ethnic differences, but their economic significance is debatable. Overall, aggregate population estimates suggest a doubling or tripling of souls.

Direct measures of output, other than mining, are unavailable. Historians typically rely on the tithes as a crude measure of agricultural production, but the difficulties in interpreting them are well known: they are incomplete, subject to administrative changes and time lags, and directly available only at nominal levels. Coverage is highly variable across regions, so comparisons are hazardous. Only long-run trends can be of much value. Even these are of doubtful reliability. Nevertheless, some rough patterns across New Spain do appear: the tithe increased in the South, in the Mixteca, and in the Bajío. In Oaxaca, collections increased at less than 1 percent a year. In the Bajío, at San Luis de la Paz, midway between San Luis Potosí and Querétaro, a series deflated by local prices doubled between 1680 and 1750, a growth rate of 1 percent per year. In Michoacán, Morin concluded that the tithe quadrupled over the eighteenth century. Agricultural production certainly increased, but more slowly in the South than in the Bajío, and even there growth was uneven.[58]

Growth was one thing, distribution quite another. Changing relative factor supplies again told the tale. A rise in the population relative to land produced a clear reversal of the wage-rent ratio that was previously obtained. Employing data from the Bajío collected by Brading, we might estimate that the wage-rent ratio fell by nearly 70 percent between 1700 and 1810. This is, of course, a substantial decline, even if it was less than the corresponding rise in the sixteenth century. Brading concluded:

> All our evidence points in the same direction. In the years before 1810, the laboring classes experienced a decline in their standard of living. . . . That it was the surplus of manpower which was largely responsible for the fundamental change in the relation of labor and capital can be demonstrated in the parallel trends in mining and agriculture, with labor no longer scarce, rents were raised. In mining [similar reductions in real earnings occurred]. There can be little doubt that it was the play of the market which determined the distribution of income between labor and capital.[59]

While population increase may explain a fall (or stagnation) in money wages, the source of rising land prices is less obvious. In León, the eighteenth century witnessed a pattern of estate consolidation at the expense of smallholders and indigenous villages. The effect was dramatic. Brading identified a class of "cottage farmers," impoverished smallholders who emerged in two ways. There was a subdivision of landed property that occurred naturally as population increased in a regime of partible inheritance. It was also a consequence of the silver mining boom, which Brading estimated (in terms of improved haciendas) as a tripling of values.[60] Only those with ample fortunes could participate in a rising market. The incentive for many smallholders to sell out was nearly irresistible. Brading also emphasized that the changes in the Bourbon commercial regime (*libre comercio*, or the abolition of the flota or convoy system of Atlantic trade which took full effect after 1789) encouraged a withdrawal of mining and mercantile capital from commerce into land in the latter part of the eighteenth century.[61] Brading's focus was the Bajio, but others have emphasized similar forces at work in Jalisco as well.[62]

The significance of this process for a country whose colonial history ended in violent agrarian rebellion in the 1810s is obvious. Yet the exact mechanism by which a society response to scarcity, or increasing land scarcity, is perhaps more contingent than one usually supposes.

In his study of the Dutch rural economy in the golden age, Jan de Vries notices that there are at least two possible responses to demographic pressure in agricultural societies. One, which he calls the "peasant model" is essentially Malthusian. The other, which he terms the "specialization model" owes its origins to Ester Boserup (and Adam Smith). Her model is based on the importance of exchange (trade) and the development of a commercial society in rural areas that acts in symbiosis with an urban system. Peasants do not simply remain landless in the countryside. They most assuredly do not become passive holders of miniscule plots of land. They migrate to cities and into growing urban industries—perhaps even labor-intensive export industries—whose existence is underwritten by rising agricultural productivity. This is simply a comparative advantage: economies develop naturally as specialization and division of labor occur. Accumulation is facilitated by exchange, and whether it is called capitalism or commercial society is mostly of ideological or taxonomic interest. The point is how growth occurs. To make things worse (or better), it occurs almost effortlessly as well. There is no "underdevelopment" with which to cope.

Then there is the "peasant" model. Here a process of subdivision of land occurs but the peasantry remains attached to it. At the same time, they adopt practices such as artisan weaving that enable them to supplement a subsistence income. This inevitably reduces the demand for industrial goods produced in the urban industry and depresses agricultural productivity as well. Inequality widens as land ends up in the hands of wealthy merchants or miners. As DeVries put it, "moneyed men are encouraged to buy land and to organize production in order to profit from the strong demand for grain" [which DeVries explains as a consequence of population increase and the relative inefficiency of agriculture].[63]

In fact, the similarity of the "peasant model" to the Mexican Bajío is so close that one might be forgiven for thinking that deVries was writing about New Spain. All of it—rising land prices, rising relative grain prices, the diffusion of rural industry (variously described as *telares sueltos* or putting out around Puebla, in the Bajío, and really, almost universally throughout Central Mexico in the 1780s and 1790s), and the slow decline of the urban *obrajes* (woolen textile manufactories established in the sixteenth and seventeenth centuries when pastoral land was abundant) fits

New Spain very closely.[64] It is not "capitalism" or "the market" that is the villain here: quite the opposite. As DeVries puts it, the peasantry strives to avoid market dependence. In the same way that users of labor in other parts of the economy circumvented the market, particularly in the sixteenth and early seventeenth centuries because "the market" favored labor, so too did rural agriculture. Enrique Florescano's predatory haciendas could well be described by De Vries' analysis, along with some element of price setting in maize that the passage of land into extended kin groups facilitated in Chalco, Michoacán, and Puebla.[65] Thus, maize prices (and hacienda rents and profits) tended to rise (and real wages to fall) at least in part, because of the changing structure of production and land ownership. Perfect competition in agriculture was never a possibility, and not simply because of Mexican geography. There were missing markets. Peasants could not borrow to buy land based on future profitability, even into the twentieth century.[66] There were few market opportunities for them from which to profit. The result was rural impoverishment and the persistence of a deeply retrograde and conservative society in the countryside. It is not capitalism at work, to put it bluntly, but rent seeking by a politically powerful landed and mercantile class that maintained social order more interested in the conservation of privilege and maximizing its own wealth than anything else.[67]

Policy moves, the "Bourbon Reforms," were an exogenous source of change and heightened social and economic tensions. Whether the *flota* system was a contrived Iberian monopoly on the American colonial trade or a response to economic uncertainty, its demise had consequences.[68] After 1700, the *flota* system never worked as intended, and all sorts of exceptions were made to its operation.[69] After 1765, the extension of "free trade" to Cuba indirectly provisioned Veracruz with foreign goods to the tune of 3 million pesos per year, and the British South Sea Company's activity in Portobello (Panama) and Veracruz may have accounted for as much as 6 percent of all British exports at the beginning of the nineteenth century.[70] Combined with the extension of the reforms, it thus accelerated the change in relative prices already underway. After the extension of free trade to Mexico after 1789, the volume of trade simply grew. Mexico's traditional big merchants then complained of too much abundance and saturated markets.[71] Prices and quantities are, inevitably, inversely related. The Bourbon Reforms improved Mexico's terms of trade: the prices of imports—mostly manufactures such as textiles—fell relative to agricultural goods or even silver.[72] The reforms thus accelerated the change in relative prices already underway. At some point, the Mexican peso—its "real" exchange rate—became overvalued, which made it even more difficult for things like textiles produced in Mexico to compete. The computations are crude, but nevertheless suggestive.[73]

The fall in price of such goods as imported British cottons drove Mexico's *obrajes* out of business and caused unemployment, other than during periods of international warfare, when transatlantic trade routes were blocked. This may not have been classic deindustrialization as Jeffrey Williamson describes, but that was because the fall in real wages only encouraged the expansion in putting out (the *telares sueltos*) that the "peasant model" had presupposed. This is what happened in the Puebla-Tlaxcala basin and the South, and to a lesser extent, in the Bajío as well.[74] The rising relative price of agricultural goods simply accelerated the consolidation of the hacienda system. The increased purchasing power of silver over such goods as cloth was because wages and labor costs in mines such as Real del Monte in Guanajuato simply fed large mining fortunes and accelerated the growth of inequality.[75] How unequal? According to well-known data collected from Manuel Abad y Queipo, the Bishop-elect of Michoacán, at the end of the colonial period, the top 10 percent of New Spain's population could have accounted for 60 percent of the colony's income. If this is what Humboldt meant when he called Mexico "the land of inequality," he was not exaggerating.[76]

Viewed as a fiscal program, the intent of the Bourbon Reforms was to increase the economic yield of the colonies to the metropolis. With the replacement of the Hapsburgs in 1713, Spain became increasingly linked to France, not only in its program of administrative change but also in its foreign policy.[77] Increasingly entangled in the complex wars for trade and empire that marked the eighteenth century, Spain's fiscal needs grew apace. By circumstance, it was to New Spain to which the Bourbons would increasingly turn to revenue.[78] The evolution of increasing fiscal pressure in New Spain took time, but over the course of the century, the share of Mexican output taken as taxes by the peninsula increased by 167 percent. Richard Garner concludes that the impact of the royal fisc "could have reached a substantial if not destructive scale by the end of the colonial period, and nominal treasury receipts grew at a pace of four to five percent per year."[79]

Taxes, of course, reduce spending, demand, and with it, economic growth. So, whatever the rate of growth in New Spain, the Bourbon Reforms could have only reduced it. That much is clear, because some portions of the colony—for instance, the Puebla-Tlaxcala basin—may have been affected more than others given the way imperial revenue transfers were structured.[80] Yet the reforms were not limited to increasing taxes. The Crown also provided incentives to silver mining by reducing the prices of reagents used in mining and refining, mercury and gunpowder (for blasting). However one views silver production, these subsidies helped mining grow at about 1.4 percent per year.[81] Royal policies thus had countervailing effects: one promoting, one reducing growth. What was the result?

According to Humboldt, the Bourbons could raise about 20 million pesos in taxes per year. Using Rosenzweig's revised output figure of 190 million per year, that would suggest taxes took around 10.6 percent of output per year. Silver accounted for about 9.4 percent of output; a generous allowance for mining subsidies would be 50 percent of value added. So the Crown created 4.7 percent of output and taxed away 10 percent, which leaves a negative balance of 5.3 percent—John Coatsworth estimated a 4 percent "fiscal burden" 40 years ago.[82] The balance against Mexico was then 4 to 5 percent per year at the end of the colonial period. That was hardly trivial, and for now, that is where the matter rests. Changing shares of labor (falling) and (rising) capital income took place within the context of what was probably a modest growth in output that had been reduced by Bourbon policies. Mexico was poorer, and the laboring classes perhaps significantly poorer than they otherwise have been. And social conflict sharpened too. Exogenous factors such as climate change played a part in this process as well. In Figure 1.9, we observe the pattern of rainfall in the eighteenth century, especially after 1740. Conspicuously, there are two distinct phases: one, from about 1740 through 1780, is typically wet. The other, from 1780 through 1810, is much drier. Historians like Florescano have amply demonstrated the sharp—and largely irreversible—rise in maize prices after 1790 that corresponded to dry weather (and to increasing concentration in ownership (diminished competition) of the grain producing hacienda). Moreover, the ten-year moving average for the eighteenth-century IEEAS (Figure 1.10) shows a reasonably consistent increase after 1760 through 1800, which suggests that climate stresses translated into dearth and epidemiological expressions as well. The second half of the eighteenth century, was, in retrospect, a "perfect" storm" of climatic, demographic fiscal, and institutional changes. The trigger—as historians of revolution would have it—was political and came with the collapse of the *ancien regime* in 1808 and the abdication of the Bourbon monarchy. Regime change, planned or otherwise, has bedeviled all empires since Rome.

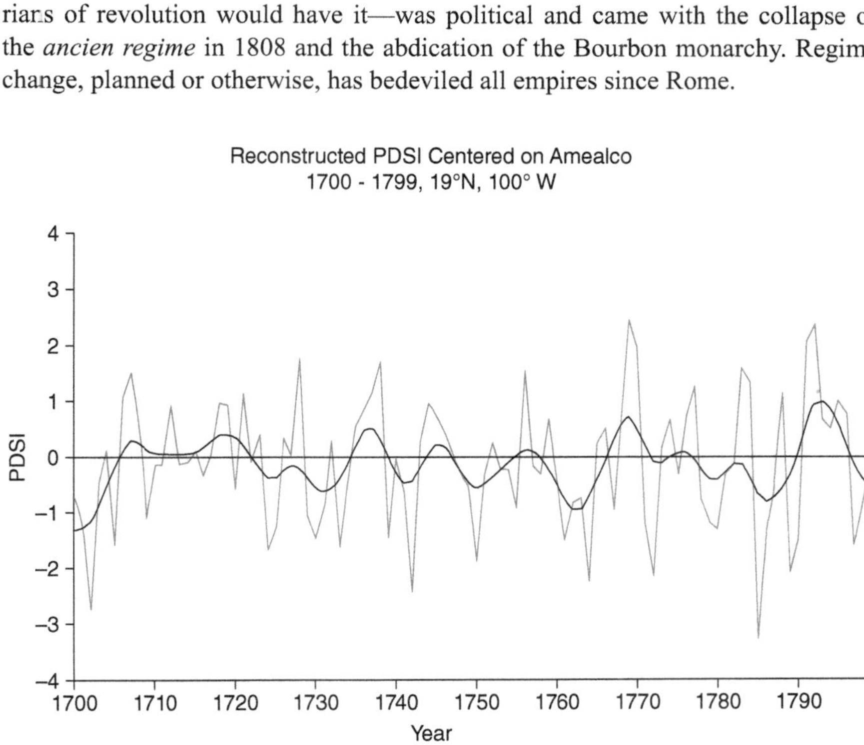

FIGURE 1.9 PDSI 1700–1799 Centered on Amealco with Ten-Year Smoothing

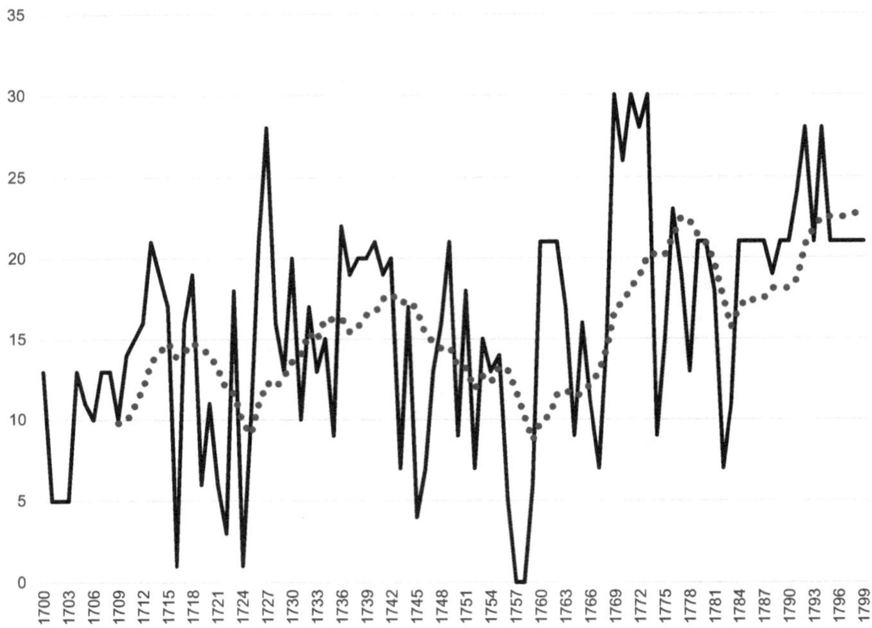

FIGURE 1.10 IEEAS 1700–1799 and Ten-Year Moving Average

Final Thoughts

Thus, our argument on a stylized economic account of New Spain can be summarized as follows. Factors endowments matter. Scarcity matters. Relative prices matter. From the sixteenth through the eighteenth centuries, the evolution of population relative to land was critical. In the sixteenth century, a dense (perhaps 25 million in Central Mexico according to the Berkeley School) indigenous population made labor the abundant factor of production. Social and technological arrangements reflected this abundance, in labor-intensive chinampa agriculture, and in tribute, the extraction of a small surplus from large numbers of subject peoples organized as *altepetl*.

The arrival of the Europeans was a shock. Novel pathogens that jumped to humans from large animals played havoc with indigenous populations that had no immunity against them. So too did those spread directly by human contact. A dramatic reduction in indigenous population took place, perhaps the most sweeping collapse in recorded history, something on the order of 90 percent by the beginning of the seventeenth century. Labor, previously the abundant factor, was replaced by land. The shift was reflected in the end of labor-intensive practices such as the *encomienda* and *repartimiento*; in the introduction, however unevenly, of wage labor and the rise of pastoralism and extensive agriculture, the characteristic haciendas, ranchos, and associated pueblos were based in land rather than in shared ethnicity or descent. By the end of the sixteenth century, these transformations were well underway.

The seventeenth century saw a rise in real wages and a fall in rents—a "depression" from the perspective of the colonizers, yet anything but for the subject peoples. The rise in real wages stabilized population decline and slowly reversed it. This occurred within a far reduced indigenous access to land, of course. It was not necessary for pre-contact population to be reattained (it was not) for real wages to fall. And so, by the end of the seventeenth century, the initial reversal of relative scarcities was once more moving in the opposite direction, as was the wage-rent ratio. Dearth and disease were the context in which falling real wages occurred and land rents rose once more, and sharply so after 1769. The outbreak of epidemics and massive hunger are two characteristics of the later eighteenth century, with the outbreak of *matlazahuatl* in 1736–1739 and the early frost and subsequent maize crop failure in 1785–1786, "starvation time.'[83] Current thinking in economic history sees all preindustrial growth as consumed by population growth one way or another. Mexico is no exception. There are numerous variations in the so-called Malthusian models, but their basic finding—that population change works against secular increases in income, is well established,[84] although in Mexico, the twist may well have been that the land was *owned* rather than *completely used*.

Moreover, it is all too clear that the elements of a market economy—and particularly of a labor market—that evolved alongside colonial institutions created a justifiable ambivalence in the colonial elite. It is not hard to understand why. Markets reward scarcity. As indigenous labor became scarcer, mobilizing it under highly unfavorable conditions drove the Spaniards to circumvent markets whenever they could. The archival record that documents the all too ordinary attempts of colonial masters to employ coercion speaks directly to scarcity: it benefitted the wrong party in the colonial arrangement, especially in the sixteenth and seventeenth centuries. So there was a tension between laws enacted that sought to ensure native welfare (not to say, survival) and the ordinary ways of running any sort of profitable business. Here, perhaps, was one of the key "noneconomic" obstacles to economic growth in New Spain: a system that relied less on relative productivity than on political power and influence to mobilize labor and other resources. That such arrangements produced chronic misallocation of resources is hardly surprising. Knowing the viceroy and knowing how to operate an *obraje* were hardly the same thing. The longer such arrangements endured, the higher their cumulative cost—a deadweight loss—would have been. Economic historians trained in economics opposed finding a "colonial heritage" in Mexico, but one is hard pressed to think of a better name.

Finally, we come to a troubling conceptual question. When we speak of a colonial Mexican economy, does it make any sense at all? We know transportation costs were high and that information could move no more rapidly than people. Consider, for example, the distribution and ratio of maize prices in Celaya to Mexico in 1721–1784. The shape of the distributions was very different, so much so that it is impossible to think whatever mechanism producing them was the same. While the prices do rise and fall together, the correlation between the series is 0.08—basically nonexistent.[85] As the crow flies, the two cities are 260 kilometers apart. They might as well be in different worlds. Examining the trends in the ratio of Celaya to Mexico maize prices shows no trend. They neither diverge nor converge. The law of one price may well have held for silver, or even for beef between Valladolid and Mexico City between 1700 and 1780 when the source was cattle on the hoof for which the marginal cost of transportation was essentially zero, but there were *telares sueltos* and looms to produce cottons all over New Spain. Cloth and maize were two of the staple items of popular consumption; if they faced no "national" market, there may as well have been no national market at all.[86] The implications of this simple fact had to do with comparative advantage, specialization, and exchange. Ever since Adam Smith, specialization and division of labor have been recognized as the basis for creating wealth. Hence Smith's famous observation in *The Wealth of Nations* that peace, low taxes, and a tolerable administration of justice would lead to economic growth. But only in the presence of markets, the extent of which famously limited the degree of specialization. In Mexico, transportation costs were so high that it was impossible to ship grain from Puebla to Cuba more cheaply than it was to supply Cuba from Pennsylvania.[87] So Mexico's comparative advantage, both internal and external, could not be realized, much less exploited to any great extent, until those costs were reduced. The potential for arbitrage was considerable because factor endowments and comparative advantage differed substantially between regions, as we shall see in the next chapter of this history on Mexico's "long nineteenth century."

Notes

1 Alfred Crosby, *Ecological Imperialism: The Biological Expansion of Europe, 900–1900*, 2nd ed. (New York, NY: Cambridge University Press, 2004). Eleanor Melville, *A Plague of Sheep: Environmental Consequences of the Conquest of Mexico* (New York, NY: Cambridge University Press, 1994).

2 David Henige, *Numbers From Nowhere. The American Indian Contact Population Debate* (Norman, OK: University of Oklahoma Press, 1998). More temperate and reasonable accounts, although hardly uncritical, may be found in Lourdes Márquez Morfín and Rebecca Storey, "Population History in Precolumbian and Colonial Times," in *Oxford Handbook of the Aztecs*, eds. Deborah Nichols and Enrique Rodríguez-Alegría (New York, NY: Oxford University Press), 189–200. Robert McCaa, "The Peopling of Mexico From Origins to Revolution," in *A Population History of North America*, eds. Michael R. Haines and Richard H. Steckel (New York, NY: Cambridge University Press, 2000), 241–304.

3 Bradley Benton, *The Lords of Tetzcoco: The Transformation of Indigenous Rule in Postconquest Central Mexico* (New York, NY: Cambridge University Press, 2017) argues that local nobles made a place for themselves in the Spanish structure, their reduction to colonial status notwithstanding. The book captures much of the flavor of revisionist research.

4 Virginia García Acosta, Juan Manuel Pérez Zevallos, and América Molina del Villar. *Desastres Agrícolas en México. Catalogo Histórico*, 2 vols (Mexico City: Fondo de

Cultura Económica, 2003). Also Gustavo G. Garza Merodio, *Variabilidad climática en México a través de fuentes documentales (siglos XVI al XIX)* (Mexico City: Instituto de Geografía, Universidad Nacional Autónoma de México, 2017).

5 David W. Stahle, Edward R. Cook, Dorian J. Burnette, José Villanueva, Julián Cerano, Jordan N. Burns, Daniel Griffin, Benjamin I. Cook, Rodolfo Acuña, Max C.A. Torbenson, Pasul Szejner, and Ian M. Howard, "The Mexican Drought Atlas: Tree-Ring Reconstruction of the Soil Moisture Balance During the Late Pre-Hispanic, Colonial and Modern Eras," *Quaternary Sciences Reviews* 149 (2016): 41.

6 A good summary is Ronald Findlay and Kevin O'Rourke, *Power and Plenty. Trade, War and the World Economy in the Second Millennium* (Princeton, NJ: Princeton University Press, 2007), 111–24.

7 Angus Chen, "One of History's Worst Epidemics May Have Been Caused by a Common Microbe," *Science* (January 16, 2018), https://doi/org.10.1126/science.aat0253. Robert W. Patch, *Maya and Spaniard in Yucatán, 1648–1812* (Stanford, CA: Stanford University Press, 1993), 41.

8 Kenneth G. Hirth, *The Aztec Economic World. Merchants and Markets in Ancient Mesoamerica* (New York, NY: Cambridge University Press, 2016). Silvio Zavala, *Estudios Acerca de la Historia del Trabajo en México. Homenaje del Centro de Estudios Históricos a Silvio Zavala*, ed. Elías Trabulse (Mexico City: Colegio de México, 1988), 204.

9 Benjamin Keen, *Life and Labor in Ancient Mexico: The Brief and Summary Relations of the Lords of New Spain*, trans. and ed. Benjamin Keen (Norman, OK: University of Oklahoma Press, 1963). Rodolfo Acuña-Soto, Leticia Calderón Romero, and James H. Maguire, "Large Epidemics of Hemorrhagic Fever in Mexico, 1545–1815," *American Journal of Tropical Medicine and Hygiene* 62 (2000): 733–39.

10 Charles Gibson, *The Aztecs Under Spanish Rule. A History of the Indians of the Valley of Mexico, 1519–1810* (Stanford: Stanford University Press, 1964), 223, 224, 225. But *servicio personal* and "unwaged" labor did not simply disappear at the stroke of a quill. The practices continued and even blurred with the beginning of the "coerced but paid" *repartimiento* system. See Silvio Zavala, *El servicio personal de los indios en la Nueva España, 1550–1575* (Mexico City: El Colegio de México, 1985), 79–112, 377.

11 Gibson, *Aztecs*, 223.

12 Evsey Domar, "The Causes of Slavery or Serfdom: A Hypothesis," *Journal of Economic History* 30 (1970): 8–32. Robert Brenner, "Agrarian Class Structure and Economic Development in Pre-Industrial Europe," *Past & Present* 70 (1976): 30–75.

13 Bas Van Bavel, *The Invisible Hand. How Market Economies Have Emerged and Declined Since AD 500* (Oxford, UK: Oxford University Press, 2016), 211. Zavala, *Servicio personal, 1550–1575*, 445–47. Also see Carlos Sempat Assadourian, "La despoblación indígena en Perú y Nueva España durante el siglo XVI y la formación economía colonial," *Historia Mexicana* 38 (1989): 419–53. By contrast, Andrés Reséndez, *The Other Slavery. The Uncovered Story of Indian Enslavement in America* (New York, NY: Houghton, Mifflin Harcourt, 2016), 68, which seems quite misleading.

14 Douglass North, "Institutions," *Journal of Economic Perspectives* 5 (1991): 97–112.

15 Andrés Molina Enríquez, *Los grandes problemas nacionales*, repr. ed. (1909; Mexico City: Ediciones Era, 1978), 94–95. Also see Jarquín O. María Teresa, *Formación Y Desarrollo De Un Pueblo Novohispano: Metepec en el Valle de Toluca* (Toluca, México: El Colegio Mexiquense, 1990), 143–48.

16 Omar Olivares Sandoval, *Atlas Histórico del Estado de México* (Toluca, México: Fondo Editorial Estado de México, 2013), 65–66, 161–67.

17 Federico Fernández Christlieb and Ángel Julián García Zambrano, *Territorialidad y Paisaje en el Altepetl del Siglo XVI* (Mexico City: Fondo de Cultura Económica, 2006), 96, 144, 148, 204. Also see Ernesto de la Torre Villar, *Las congregaciones de los pueblos de indios: Fase terminal: aprobaciones y rectificaciones* (1995; Mexico City: Instituto de Investigaciones Históricas, 2018), accessed May 8, 2024, https://historicas.unam.

mx/publicaciones/publicadigital/libros/313/congregaciones_indios.html. Brian Hamnett, *Reform, Rebellion, and Party in Mexico, 1836–1861* (Cardiff, Wales: University of Wales Press, 2022), 102.

18 Tomas Jalpa Flores, *Chalco: Tierra y Sociedad* (Mexico City: Instituto Nacional de Antropología e Historia, 2008).

19 James Lockhart, *The Nahuas After the Conquest: A Social and Cultural History of the Indians of Central Mexico, Sixteenth Through Eighteenth Centuries* (Stanford, CA: Stanford University Press, 1992), 175.

20 Pedro Carrasco and Guillermo Céspedes, *América Indígena: La conquista* (Madrid: Alianza Editorial, 1985).

21 Rebecca Horn, *Postconquest Coyoacán. Nahua-Spanish Relations in Central Mexico, 1519–1650* (Stanford, CA: Stanford University Press, 1997), 111–12.

22 Patch, *Maya and Spaniard in Yucatán,* 73.

23 Sandoval, *Atlas Histórico del Estado de México,* 167–289, examining the increasing scarcity of vacant land as time went by makes the point clearly, if anecdotally. Also see Flores, *Tierra y sociedad,* 138–52.

24 Alejandro Tortolero, *De la Coa a la Maquina de Vapor. Actividad agrícola e innovación tecnológica en las haciendas mexicanas: 1880–1914* (Mexico City: Siglo Veintiuno Editores, 1995). A calculation certainly subject to great uncertainty, being based on the production of one hacienda (Del Moral) in Chalco in 1881, considering only corn and wheat, 229–31.

25 Teresa Rojas Rabiela, "Agriculture," in *The Oxford Encyclopedia of Mesoamerican Cultures. The Civilization of Mexico and Central America*, 3 vols, ed. David Carrasco (New York, NY: Oxford University Press, 2001), 1: 3–8.

26 Patch, *Maya and Spaniard in Yucatán,* 35.

27 Antonio García de León, *Tierra adentro, mar en fuera. El puerto de Veracruz y su litoral a Sotavento, 1519–1821* (México City: Fondo de Cultura Económica, 2011), 263 et ff.

28 Chevalier's classic account of the rise of the hacienda is a case of factor endowments as well. The fall in relative land prices encouraged land-intensive methods of production. See Francois Chevalier, *Land and Society in Colonial Mexico: The Great Hacienda* (Berkeley, CA: University of California Press, 1963).

29 Aristides Medina Rubio, *La iglesia y la producción agrícola en Puebla, 1540–1795* (Mexico City: El Colegio de México, 1983), 129; Richard Garner, "Inside My Desk. History Data Desk," accessed May 10, 2024, www.insidemydesk.com/hdd.html (mexicoprices.xls). The economics of chinampas is treated in detail in Teresa Rojas Rabiela, ed., *La Agricultura Chinampera. Compilación Histórica* (Mexico City: Trajín, 2022).

30 Ethelia Ruiz Medrano, *Gobierno y Sociedad en Nueva España: Segunda Audiencia y Antonio de Mendoza* (Zamora, MICH: Colegio de Michoacán, 1991), esp.343–47.

31 Peter Clark, ed., "Introduction," in *The European Crisis of the 1590s* (London, UK: Allen & Unwin, 1985), 3, 8, 11 which Clark summarizes as "high mortality, extensive social stress, popular disorder and severe strains on government" whose "most obvious source" was bad weather. Geoffrey Parker, *Global Crisis. War, Climate Change and Catastrophe in the Seventeenth Century*, abrid. and rev. ed. (New Haven, CT: Yale University Press, 2017).

32 Jonathan Israel, "Mexico and the 'General Crisis' of the Seventeenth Century," *Past and Present* 68 (1974): 33–57.

33 Parker, *Global Crisis*, 3, 43, 341–42–44–45.

34 Graphically illustrated by prosecution of Inquisition cases in Solange Alberro, *La Actividad del Santo Oficio de la Inquisición en Nueva España, 1571–1700* (Mexico City: Instituto Nacional de Antropología e Historia, 1981), 147. For a discussion of the peninsular political context, see Solange Alberro, *Inquisición y Sociedad en México, 1571–1700*, kind. ed. (1988; Mexico City: Fondo de Cultura Económica, 2015), Part 7, which also explains the complex relation between fiscal, political, and religious events in Mexico.

35 Parecer of Andrés de Tapia, México, March 11, 1550 in Silvio Zavala, *El servicio personal de los indios en la Nueva España, 1521–1550* (Mexico City: El Colegio de México, 1984), 47, 73; Claude Morin, *Michoacán en la Nueva España del Siglo xviii. Crecimiento y desigualdad en una economía colonial* (Mexico City Fondo de Cultura Económica, 1979), 33. Vera S. Candiani, *Dreaming of Dry Land. Environmental Transformation in Colonial Mexico City* (Stanford, CA: Stanford University Press, 2014), 58–9.

36 Gisela von Wobeser, *La formación de la hacienda en la época colonial: El uso de la tierra y el agua*, 2nd ed. (Mexico City: Universidad Nacional Autónoma de México, 1989), 50.

37 Bernardo García Martínez, *Los pueblos de la Sierra. El poder y espacio entre los indios del Norte de Puebla hasta 1700* (Mexico City: El Colegio de México, 1987).

38 Gibson, *Aztecs*, 235.

39 Woodrow Borah, *New Spain's Century of Depression* (Berkeley, CA: University of California Press, 1951); Zavala, *Servicio personal, 1636–1699,* 23.

40 Letica Arroyo, Elwyn Davies, and Jan Luiten van Zanden, "Between Conquest and Independence: Real Wages and Demographic Change in Spanish America, 1530–1820," *Explorations in Economic History* 49 (2012): 149–66; Pablo Miguel Sierra Silva, *Urban Slavery in Colonial México. Puebla de los Ángeles, 1531–1706* (New York, NY: Cambridge University Press, 2018), 128.

41 Nadine Béligrand, *Entre lagunas y volcanes. Una historia del Valle de Toluca (finales del siglo XV-siglo XVIII)*, 2 vols (Zamora, MICH: El Colegio de Michoacán, 2017), 1: 292, Gráfica B. Claude Morin, *Santa Inés Zacatelco (1646–1812), Contribución a la demografía histórica del México colonial* (Mexico City: Instituto Nacional de Antropología e Historia, 1973). María García Eugenia Ugarte, *Breve Historia de Querétaro* (Mexico City: Fondo de Cultura Económica, 1999), 83. de León, *Tierra adentro, mar en fuera*, 435–37.

42 María de los Ángeles Romero Frizzi, *Economía y vida de los españoles en la Mixteca Alta, 1519–1720* (Mexico City: Instituto Nacional de Antropología e Historia, 1990), 64, 83, 133, 149, 173–77, 196–97, 249–52. Carlos Sempat Assadourian, *Zacatecas. Conquista y transformación de la frontera en el siglo xvi. Minas de plata y evangelización* (Mexico City: El Colegio de México, 2008), 83. William B. Taylor, "Landed Society in New Spain: A View From the South," *Hispanic American Historical Review* 54 (1974): 387–413.

43 See Solange Alberro, *Inquisición y Sociedad en México, 1571–1700* (Mexico City Fondo de Cultura Económica, 1988), Gráfica VI and compare to Parker, *Global Crisis*, esp.215, which show the close correspondence to trials for heresy by the Inquisition in Mexico around 1640, which resulted in property seizures from crypto-Jews, with the revolt of the Portuguese and the Catalans in Spain, the fiscal problem of Olivares, and more loosely, ecological and climatic instability in the long run. What was in the minds of crypto-Jews in New Spain regarding liberation from Castilian oppression, the ostensible reason for heightened inquisitorial activity, is not recorded here, although that motivation clearly existed. Also see John Lynch, *The Hispanic World in Crisis and Change, 1598–1700* (Oxford, UK: Basil Blackwell, 1994), esp. 155. For a recent treatment of the so-called General Crisis in Latin America, see Herbert S. Klein, "Current Debates About the Colonial Economy and Government From the Spanish Royal Treasury Records," *Hispanic American Historical Review* 104 (2024): 213–42, esp. 216.

44 *Historia de la Conquista de Nueva España (1632)*, 10th ed., Chap. XCII (92) (Mexico City: Editorial Porrua, 1974), 171–172.

45 Hirth, *The Aztec Economic World*.

46 Lockhart, *The Nahuas*, 178–80.

47 A starting point: Fausto de Elhuyar, *Indagaciones sobre la Amonedación en Nueva España* (Madrid, Mexico City: Imprenta de la Calle de la Greda, 1818).

48 Pedro Pérez Herrero, *Plata y Libranzas. La articulación del México Borbónico* (Mexico City: El Colegio de México, 1988) is a basic study. Silver reached 17 to 22 million pesos

by the end of the eighteenth century. The standard estimate of total output for the era first produced by José María Quirós was 250 million pesos. The computational issue of double-counting in Quirós was taken up by Francisco Rosenzweig, who came to a figure closer to 190 million pesos. If Rosenzweig were correct, there was virtually no growth in per capita income in nominal terms through about 1840, as we will see. Francisco Rosenzweig, "La economía Novohispana al comenzar el siglo xix," in *El Desarollo Económico de México, 1800–1910* (Mexico City: El Colegio Mexiquense, 1989), 81. For definitions of money, see Karl Brunner, "High-Powered Money and the Monetary Base," in *Money. The New Palgrave*, eds. John Eatwell, Murray Milgate, and Peter Newman (New York: WW Norton, 1987), 175–78.

49 David A. Brading and Harry C. Cross, "Colonial Silver Mining: Mexico and Peru," *Hispanic American Historical Review* 52 (1972). A long debate over the causes of an ostensible decline (labor shortages versus the diversion of mercury supply for refining ore) in Mexican silver production in the seventeenth century has never been satisfactorily resolved, assuming production actually fell. See Michel Morineau, *Incroyable Gazettes et Fabuleux Métaux* (New York, NY: Cambridge University Press, 1985), 42–119, whose salient point was that European receipts of American silver typically exceeded accounts of American production in the seventeenth century.

50 "Geo-Mexico, the geography and dynamics of modern Mexico," accessed May 14, 2024, https://geo-mexico.com/?p=9664.

51 David Brading, *Miners and Merchants in Bourbon Mexico, 1763–1810* (Cambridge, UK: Cambridge University Press, 1971), 153–55.

52 Peter Bakewell, *Silver Mining and Society in Colonial Mexico. Zacatecas, 1546–1700* (Cambridge, UK: Cambridge University Press, 1971), 61, 237.

53 Sempat Assadourian, *Zacatecas*, 109–10.

54 Marjorie Grice-Hutchinson, *The School of Salamanca. Readings in Spanish Monetary Theory, 1544–1605* (Oxford, UK: Clarendon Press, 1952), 51–56.

55 Murdo J. McLeod, *Spanish Central America: A Socioeconomic History, 1520–1720* (Berkeley, CA: University of California Press, 1973), 224–25.

56 Carlos de Siguenza y Góngora, "El Motín de 1692," in *Lecturas Históricas Mexicanas*, 2nd ed., 5 vols, ed. Ernesto de la Torre Villar (Mexico City: Universidad Nacional Autonoma de Mexico, 1998), 1: 580–87.

57 Manuel Miño Grijalva, "Las Ciudades Novohispanas y Su Función Económica: Siglo XVI-XVIII," in *Historia Económica General de México*, ed. Sandra Kuntz Ficker (Mexico City: El Colegio de México, 2010), 149. Morin, *Michoacán*, 39–83.

58 Cecilia Rabell, *Los Diezmos de San Luis de la Paz. Economía en una Región del Bajío en el Siglo XVIII* (Mexico City: Universidad Nacional Autónoma de Mexico, 1986), 54. Morin, *Michoacán,* 102–26. Elías Trabulse, ed., *Fluctuaciones económicas durante el siglo xviii* (Mexico City: El Colegio de Mexico, 1979).

59 David Brading, *Haciendas and Ranchos in the Mexican Bajío. León, 1709–1860* (New York, NY: Cambridge University Press, 1979), 82, 196, 199–200.

60 Brading, *Haciendas and Ranchos*, 122, 134–36. Morin, *Michoacán*, 212–13.

61 Brading, *Miners and Merchants,* 115–16.

62 Eric Van Young, *Hacienda and Market in Eighteenth-Century Mexico: The Rural Economy of the Guadalajara Region, 1675–1820* (Berkeley, CA: University of California Press, 1981).

63 Jan de Vries, *The Dutch Rural Economy in the Golden Age, 1500–1700* (New Haven, CT: Yale University Press, 1978), 5–6.

64 Richard Salvucci, *Textiles and Capitalism in Mexico: An Economic History of the Obrajes, 1539–1840* (Princeton, NJ: Princeton University Press, 1987), 22–23, Map 1.1 and Map 2.2.

65 Enrique Florescano, *Precios del maíz y crisis agrícolas en México (1708–1810)* (Mexico City: El Colegio de Mexico, 1969), 26, 27, 101, 107, 117, 187–88. Brading, *Haciendas*

and Ranchos, 65, 70, 180–82; Morin, *Michoacán*, 280–83. D.J. Weiland, III, "The Economics of Agriculture; Markets, Production and Finances in the Bishopric of Puebla, 1532–1809 (PhD diss., University of Cambridge, 1995), 187.

66 Roger L. Ransom and Kerry Ann Odell, "Land and Credit: Some Historical Parallels Between Mexico and the American South," *Agricultural History* 60 (1986): 4–31.

67 A different view, Jeffrey Williamson, *Trade and Poverty. When the Third World Fell Behind* (Cambridge, MA: MIT Press, 2011), 154–56.

68 Jeremy Baskes, *Staying Afloat. Risk and Uncertainty in the Spanish Atlantic World Trade, 1760–1820* (Stanford, CA: Stanford University Press, 2013). Ivan Escamilla, *El Consulado de Comerciantes de México y la Monarquía Española, 1700–1739* (Mexico City: Universidad Nacional Autónoma de México, 2011). A recent treatment is Allan J. Kuethe and Kenneth J. Andrien, *The Spanish Atlantic World in the Eighteenth Century. War and the Bourbon Reforms, 1713–1796* (New York: Cambridge University Press, 2014).

69 Xabier Lamikiz, *Trade and Trust in the Eighteenth-Century Atlantic World: Spanish Merchants and Their Overseas Networks* (Woodbridge, UK: The Boydell Press for The Royal Historical Society, 2010).

70 Adrian Pearce, *British Trade with Spanish America, 1763–1808* (Liverpool, UK: Liverpool University Press, 2007), 20–21. Stanley J. Stein and Barbara H. Stein, *Apogee of Empire: Spain and New Spain in the Age of Charles III, 1759–1789* (Baltimore, MD: Johns Hopkins University Press, 2003), 174.

71 Brading, *Miners and Merchants*, 126.

72 For an exploration of the subject, Richard Salvucci, Linda Salvucci, and Aslán Cohen, "The Politics of Protection: Interpreting Commercial Policy in Late Bourbon and Early National Mexico," in *The Political Economy of Spanish America in the Age of Revolution, 1750–1850*, eds. Kenneth J. Andrien and Lyman L. Johnson (Albuquerque, NM: University of New Mexico Press, 1994), esp. 98–100.

73 R.J. Salvucci, "The Real Exchange Rate of the Mexican Peso, 1762–1812: A Research Note and Estimates," *Journal of European Economic History* 23 (1994): 131.

74 Williamson, *Trade and Poverty*, 119–44. Salvucci, *Textiles and Capitalism*, 22–23. Guy Thomson, *Puebla de los Angeles: Industry and Society in a Mexican City* (Boulder, CO: Westview Publishers, 1989).

75 Instituto Nacional de Estudios Históricos de la Revolución Mexicana, *Conflicto de Trabajo con los Mineros de Real del Monte (Año de 1766)* (Mexico City: INEHRM, 1960).

76 Data at http://gpih.ucdavis.edu and go to Mexico (accessed May 16, 2024). The calculation is mine, and only illustrative. A contrasting study is Diego Castañeda, "Moderate Opulence: the Evolution of Wealth Inequality in Its First Century of Independence," *Explorations in Economic History* 92 (2024).

77 Kuethe and Andrien, *Spanish Atlantic World*, 40–67.

78 David Ringrose, *Spain, Europe and the 'Spanish Miracle' 1700–1900* (Cambridge, UK: Cambridge University Press, 1996), 106–34.

79 Richard Garner (with Spiro B. Stefanou), *Economic Growth and Change in Bourbon Mexico* (Gainesville, FL: University Press of Florida, 1993), 35–36, 255.

80 Yovana Celaya Nández, *Alcabala y situados. Puebla en el sistema fiscal imperial, 1638–1742* (Mexico City: El Colegio de México, 2010), 117–23.

81 Garner, *Bourbon Mexico*, 112.

82 John H. Coatsworth, "Obstacles to Economic Growth in Nineteenth Century Mexico," *American Historical Review* 83 (1978): 80–100.

83 América Molina del Villar, *La Nueva España y el matlazahuatl, 1736–1739* (México: CIESAS, 2001).

84 Robert Lucas, *Lectures on Economic Growth* (Cambridge, MA: Harvard University Press, 2002), 109–88.

85 My calculations from mexmaizeprcesex.xls in www.insidemydesk.com/hdd.html (accessed May 18, 2024).

86 See the graph in Fernando Soria, "Dos mercados de Carne en el Siglo XVIII: Santiago de Querétaro y Valladolid," in *Integración y Desintegración del Espacio Económico Mexicano. Mercado interior y abastecimientos de las carnes desde la colonia al siglo XX*, coord. Michoacán in Enriqueta Quiroz (Mexico City: Instituto Mora, 2017), 125.
87 Salvucci, Salvucci, and Cohen, "Politics of Protection," 105–6.

Bibliography

Alberro, Solange. *La Actividad del Santo Oficio de la Inquisición en Nueva España, 1571–1700*. Mexico City: Instituto Nacional de Antropología e Historia, 1981.
Alberro, Solange. *Inquisición y Sociedad en México, 1571–1700*. Kind. ed. Mexico City: Fondo de Cultura Económica, 2015. First published 1988.
Arroyo, Leticia, Elwyn Davies, and Jan Luiten van Zanden. "Between Conquest and Independence: Real Wages and Demographic Change in Spanish America, 1530–1820." *Explorations in Economic History*, no. 49 (2012): 149–66.
Bakewell, Peter. *Silver Mining and Society in Colonial Mexico. Zacatecas, 1546–1700*. Cambridge, UK: Cambridge University Press, 1971.
Baskes, Jeremy. *Staying Afloat. Risk and Uncertainty in the Spanish Atlantic World Trade, 1760–1820*. Stanford, CA: Stanford University Press, 2013.
Béligrand, Nadine. *Entre lagunas y volcanes. Una historia del Valle de Toluca (finales del siglo XV-siglo XVIII)*. 2 vols. Zamora, MICH: El Colegio de Michoacán, 2017.
Benton, Bradley. *The Lords of Tetzcoco: The Transformation of Indigenous Rule in Postconquest Central Mexico*. New York, NY: Cambridge University Press, 2017.
Borah, Woodrow. *New Spain's Century of Depression*. Berkeley, CA: University of California Press, 1951.
Brading, David. *Miners and Merchants in Bourbon Mexico, 1763–1810*. Cambridge, UK: Cambridge University Press, 1971.
Brading, David. *Haciendas and Ranchos in the Mexican Bajío. León, 1709–1860*. New York, NY: Cambridge University Press, 1994.
Brading, David A., and Harry C. Cross. "Colonial Silver Mining: Mexico and Peru." *Hispanic American Historical Review*, no. 52 (1972): 545–79.
Brenner, Robert. "Agrarian Class Structure and Economic Development in Pre-Industrial Europe." *Past & Present*, no.70 (1976): 30–75.
Candiani, Vera S. *Dreaming of Dry Land. Environmental Transformation in Colonial Mexico City*. Stanford, CA: Stanford University Press, 2014.
Carrasco, Pedro, and Guillermo Céspedes. *América Indígena: La conquista*. Madrid: Alianza Editorial, 1985.
Celaya Nández, Yovana. *Alcabala y situados. Puebla en el sistema fiscal imperial, 1638–1742*. Mexico City: El Colegio de México, 2010.
Chevalier, Francois. *Land and Society in Colonial Mexico: The Great Hacienda*. Edited by Leslie Byrd Simpson. Translated by Alvin Eustis. Berkeley, CA: University of California Press, 1963.
Coatsworth, John H. "Obstacles to Economic Growth in Nineteenth Century Mexico." *American Historical Review*, no. 83 (1978): 80–100.
Crosby, Alfred. *Ecological Imperialism: The Biological Expansion of Europe, 900–1900*. 2nd ed. New York, NY: Cambridge University Press, 2004.
de la Torre Villar, Ernesto. *Las congregaciones de los pueblos de indios: Fase terminal: aprobaciones y rectificaciones*. Mexico City: Instituto de Investigaciones Históricas, 2018. Accessed May 8, 2024. https://historicas.unam.mx/publicaciones/publicadigital/libros/313/congregaciones_indios.html.
de Vries, Jan. *The Dutch Rural Economy in the Golden Age, 1500–1700*. New Haven, CT: Yale University Press, 1978.
Díaz del Castillo, Bernal. *Historia Verdadera de la Conquista de la Nueva España*. Mexico City: Editorial Porrúa, 1974. First ed. "Sepan Cuantos," 1964.

Domar, Evsey. "The Causes of Slavery or Serfdom: A Hypothesis." *Journal of Economic History*, no. 30 (1970): 8–32.
Elhuyar, Fausto de. *Indagaciones sobre la Amonedación en Nueva España.* Madrid: Imprenta de la Calle de la Greda, 1818.
Escamilla, Iván. *El Consulado de Comerciantes de México y la Monarquía Española, 1700–1739.* Mexico City: Universidad Nacional Autónoma de México, 2011.
Fernández Christlieb, Federico, and Ángel Julián García Zambrano. *Territorialidad y Paisaje en el Altepetl del Siglo XVI.* Mexico City: Fondo de Cultura Económica, 2006.
Findlay, Ronald, and Kevin O'Rourke. *Power and Plenty. Trade, War and the World Economy in the Second Millennium.* Princeton, NJ: Princeton University Press, 2007.
Florescano, Enrique. *Precios del maíz y crisis agrícolas en México (1708–1810).* Mexico City: El Colegio de México, 1969.
García Acosta, Virginia, Juan Manuel Pérez Zevallos, and América Molina del Villar. *Desastres Agrícolas en México. Catálogo Histórico.* 2 vols. Mexico City: Fondo de Cultura Económica, 2004.
García de León, Antonio. *Tierra adentro, mar en fuera. El puerto de Veracruz y su litoral a Sotavento, 1519–1821.* Mexico City: Fondo de Cultura Económica, 2011.
García Martínez, Bernardo. *Los pueblos de la Sierra. El poder y espacio entre los indios del Norte de Puebla hasta 1700.* Mexico City: El Colegio de México, 1987.
Garner, Richard (with Spiro B. Stefanou). *Economic Growth and Change in Bourbon Mexico.* Gainesville, FL: University Press of Florida, 1993.
Garner, Richard. "Inside My Desk. History Data Desk." Accessed May 18, 2024. www.insidemydesk.com/hdd.html, mexmaizeprcesex.xls.
Garza Merodio, Gustavo G. *Variabilidad climática en México a través de fuentes documentales (siglos XVI al XIX).* Mexico City: Instituto de Geografía, Universidad Nacional Autónoma de México, 2017.
Gibson, Charles. *The Aztecs Under Spanish Rule. A History of the Indians of the Valley of Mexico, 1519–1810.* Stanford, CA: Stanford University Press, 1964.
Gibson, Charles. *Spain in America.* New York, NY: Harper Torchbooks, 1966.
Global Price and Income History Group. "Nueva España [sic] 1790 Income Distribution." Accessed July 5, 2024. https://gpih.ucdavis.edu/Datafilelist.htm.
Grice-Hutchinson, Marjorie. *The School of Salamanca. Readings in Spanish Monetary Theory, 1544–1605.* Oxford, UK: Clarendon Press, 1952.
Hamnett, Brian. *Reform, Rebellion, and Party in Mexico, 1836–1861.* Cardiff, Wales: University of Wales Press, 2022.
Henige, David. *Numbers From Nowhere. The American Indian Contact Population Debate.* Norman, OK: University of Oklahoma Press, 1998.
Hirth, Kenneth G. *The Aztec Economic World. Merchants and Markets in Ancient Mesoamerica.* New York, NY: Cambridge University Press, 2016.
Horn, Rebecca. *Postconquest Coyoacán: Nahua-Spanish Relations in Central Mexico (1519–1650).* Stanford, CA: Stanford University Press, 1997.
Israel, Jonathan. "Mexico and the 'General Crisis' of the Seventeenth Century." *Past and Present,* no. 68 (1974): 33–57.
Keen, Benjamin. *Life and Labor in Ancient Mexico: The Brief and Summary Relations of the Lords of New Spain.* Edited and translated by Benjamin Keen. Norman, OK: University of Oklahoma Press, 1963.
Klein, Herbert S. "Current Debates About the Colonial Economy and Government From the Spanish Royal Treasury Records." *Hispanic American Historical Review,* no. 104 (2024): 213–42.
Kuethe, Allan J., and Kenneth J. Andrien. *The Spanish Atlantic World in the Eighteenth Century. War and the Bourbon Reforms, 1713–1796.* New York: Cambridge University Press, 2014.
Lamikiz, Xabier. *Trade and Trust in the Eighteenth-Century Atlantic World: Spanish Merchants and Their Overseas Networks.* Woodbridge, UK: The Boydell Press for The Royal Historical Society, 2010.

Lockhart, James. *The Nahuas After the Conquest: A Social and Cultural History of the Indians of Central Mexico, Sixteenth Through Eighteenth Centuries*. Stanford, CA: Stanford University Press, 1992.
Lucas, Robert. *Lectures on Economic Growth.* Cambridge, MA: Harvard University Press, 2002.
Lynch, John. *The Hispanic World in Crisis and Change, 1598–1700.* Oxford, UK: Basil Blackwell, 1994.
Maguire, James H. "Large Epidemics of Hemorrhagic Fever in Mexico, 1545–1815." *American Journal of Tropical Medicine and Hygiene*, no. 62 (2000): 733–39.
María Teresa, Jarquín O. *Formación Y Desarrollo De Un Pueblo Novohispano: Metepec en el Valle de Toluca*. Toluca, MEX: El Colegio Mexiquense, 1990.
McCaa, Robert. "The Peopling of Mexico From Origins to Revolution." In *A Population History of North America,* edited by Michael R. Haines and Richard H. Steckel. New York, NY: Cambridge University Press, 2000.
McLeod, Murdo J. *Spanish Central America: A Socioeconomic History, 1520–1720.* Berkeley, CA: University of California Press, 1973.
Medina Rubio, Arístides. *La iglesia y la producción agrícola en Puebla, 1540–1795.* Mexico City: El Colegio de México, 1983.
Melville, Eleanor. *A Plague of Sheep: Environmental Consequences of the Conquest of Mexico.* New York, NY: Cambridge University Press, 1994.
Miño Grijalva, Manuel. "Las Ciudades Novohispanas y Su Función Económica: Siglo XVI-XVIII." In *Historia Económica General de México*, edited by Sandra Kuntz Ficker. Mexico City: El Colegio de México, 2010.
Molina del Villar, América. *La Nueva España y el matlazahuatl, 1736–1739.* Mexico City: CIESAS, 2001.
Molina Enríquez, Andrés. *Los grandes problemas nacionales*. Repr. ed. Mexico City: Ediciones Era, 1978. First published 1909.
Morin, Claude. *Santa Inés Zacatelco (1646–1812), Contribución a la demografía histórica del México colonial.* Mexico City: Instituto Nacional de Antropología e Historia, 1973.
Morin, Claude. *Michoacán en la Nueva España del Siglo xviii. Crecimiento y desigualdad en una economía colonial.* Mexico City: Fondo de Cultura Económica, 1979.
Morineau, Michel. *Incroyable Gazettes et Fabuleux Métaux.* New York, NY: Cambridge University Press, 1985.
North, Douglass. "Institutions." *Journal of Economic Perspectives*, no. 5 (1991): 97–112.
Olivares Sandoval, Omar. *Atlas Histórico del Estado de México.* Toluca, MEX: Fondo Editorial del Estado de México, 2013.
Parker, Geoffrey. *Global Crisis. War, Climate Change and Catastrophe in the Seventeenth Century.* Abrid. and rev. ed. New Haven, CT: Yale University Press, 2017.
Patch, Robert W. *Maya and Spaniard in Yucatán, 1648–1812.* Stanford, CA: Stanford University Press, 1993.
Pearce, Adrian. *British Trade with Spanish America, 1763–1808.* Liverpool, UK: Liverpool University Press, 2007.
Pérez Herrero, Pedro. *Plata y Libranzas. La articulación del México Borbónico.* Mexico City: El Colegio de México, 1988.
Rabell Romero, Cecilia. *Los Diezmos de San Luis de la Paz. Economía en una Región del Bajío en el Siglo XVIII.* Mexico City: Universidad Nacional Autónoma de México, 1986.
Ransom, Roger L., and Kerry Ann Odell, "Land and Credit: Some Historical Parallels Between Mexico and the American South." *Agricultural History,* no. 60 (1986): 4–31.
Reséndez, Andrés. *The Other Slavery. The Uncovered Story of Indian Enslavement in America.* New York, NY: Houghton, Mifflin Harcourt, 2016.
Ringrose, David. *Spain, Europe and the 'Spanish Miracle' 1700–1900.* Cambridge, UK: Cambridge University Press, 1996.
Rojas Rabiela, Teresa, ed. *La Agricultura Chinampera. Compilación Histórica.* Mexico City: Trajín, 2022.

Rojas Rabiela, Teresa. "Agriculture." In *The Oxford Encyclopedia of Mesoamerican Cultures*. 3 vols, edited by David Carrasco. New York, NY: Oxford University Press, 2001.
Romero Frizzi, María de los Ángeles. *Economía y vida de los españoles en la Mixteca Alta, 1519–1720.* Mexico City: Instituto Nacional de Antropología e Historia, 1990.
Rosenzweig, Francisco. *El Desarollo Económico de México, 1800–1910.* Mexico City: El Colegio Mexiquense, 1989.
Ruiz Medrano, Ethelia. *Gobierno y Sociedad en Nueva España: Segunda Audiencia y Antonio de Mendoza.* Zamora, MICH: Colegio de Michoacán, 1991.
Salvucci, Richard. *Textiles and Capitalism in Mexico: An Economic History of the Obrajes, 1539–1840.* Princeton, NJ: Princeton University Press, 1987.
Salvucci, Richard. "The Real Exchange Rate of the Mexican Peso, 1762–1812: A Research Note and Estimates." *Journal of European Economic History,* no. 23 (1994): 131–41.
Salvucci, Richard, Linda Salvucci, and Aslán Cohen. "The Politics of Protection: Interpreting Commercial Policy in Late Bourbon and Early National Mexico." In *The Political Economy of Spanish America in the Age of Revolution, 1750–1850,* edited by Kenneth J. Andrien and Lyman L. Johnson. Albuquerque, NM: University of New Mexico Press, 1994.
Sempat Assadourian, Carlos. "La despoblación indígena en Perú y Nueva España durante el siglo XVI y la formación de la economía colonial." *Historia Mexicana,* no. 38 (1989): 419–53.
Sempat Assadourian, Carlos. *Zacatecas. Conquista y transformación de la frontera en el siglo xvi. Minas de plata y evangelización.* Mexico City: El Colegio de México, 2008.
Sierra Silva, Pablo Miguel. *Urban Slavery in Colonial Mexico. Puebla de los Ángeles, 1531–1706.* New York, NY: Cambridge University Press, 2018.
Siguenza y Góngora, Carlos de. "El Motín de 1692." In *Lecturas Históricas Mexicanas.* 2nd ed., 5 vols, edited by Ernesto de la Torre Villar, 1, 580–87. Mexico City: Universidad Nacional Autonoma de Mexico, 1998.
Stahle, David W. et al. "The Mexican Drought Atlas: Tree-Ring Reconstruction of the Soil Moisture Balance During the Late Pre-Hispanic, Colonial and Modern Eras." *Quaternary Sciences Reviews,* 149 (2016): 34–60.
Stein, Stanley J., and Barbara H. Stein. *Apogee of Empire: Spain and New Spain in the Age of Charles III, 1759–1789.* Baltimore, MD: Johns Hopkins University Press, 2003.
Taylor, William B. "Landed Society in New Spain: A View From the South." *Hispanic American Historical Review,* no. 54 (1974): 387–413.
Thomson, Guy. *Puebla de los Angeles: Industry and Society in a Mexican City.* Boulder, CO: Westview Publishers, 1989.
Tortolero, Alejandro. *De la Coa a la Máquina de Vapor. Actividad agrícola e innovación tecnológica en las haciendas mexicanas: 1880–1914.* Mexico City: Siglo Veintiuno Editores, 1995.
Trabulse, Elías, ed. *Fluctuaciones económicas durante el siglo xviii.* Mexico City: El Colegio de México, 1979.
Urquiola Permisán, José Ignacio. "Salarios y precios en la industria manufacturera textil de la lana en la Nueva España: 1570–1635." In *Los Precios de Alimentos y Manufacturas Novohispanas,* edited by Virginia García Acosta. Mexico City: CIESAS, 1995.
Van Bavel, Bas. *The Invisible Hand. How Market Economies Have Emerged and Declined Since AD 500.* Oxford, UK: Oxford University Press, 2016.
Van Young, Eric. *Hacienda and Market in Eighteenth-Century Mexico: The Rural Economy of the Guadalajara Region, 1675–1820.* Berkeley, CA: University of California Press, 1981.
von Wobeser Gisela. *La formación de la hacienda en la época colonial: El uso de la tierra y el agua.* 2nd ed. Mexico City: Universidad Nacional Autónoma de México, 1989.
Weiland, III, D.J. "The Economics of Agriculture; Markets, Production and Finances in the Bishopric of Puebla, 1532–1809." PhD diss., University of Cambridge, 1995.
Williamson, Jeffrey. *Trade and Poverty. When the Third World Fell Behind.* Cambridge, MA: MIT Press, 2011.

Zavala, Silvio. *El servicio personal de los indios en la Nueva España, 1521–1550*. Mexico City: El Colegio de México, 1984.
Zavala, Silvio. *El servicio personal de los indios en la Nueva España, 1550–1575*. Mexico City: El Colegio de México, 1985.
Zavala, Silvio. *Estudios Acerca de la Historia del Trabajo en México. Homenaje del Centro de Estudios Históricos a Silvio Zavala*. Edited by Elías Trabulse. Mexico City: Colegio de México, 1988.

2

A CENTURY OF SHOCKS

No Such Thing as a Free Insurgency

Three hundred years of colonialism in Mexico came to a catastrophic end with the Insurgency or rebellion against the Bourbon rule that began in 1810. Historians now downplay the significance of the date as a "break point" in much the same way they downplay the significance of the Conquest. From a socioeconomic perspective, this is incorrect. It is incorrect because the demographic effect of the Insurgency reversed the wage-rent trends of the late eighteenth century. As much as anything else, the reversal explains the features of Mexican economic history between the Insurgency and the outbreak of the War with the United States. There were, of course, confounding environmental, technological, and political changes that occurred. Yet fundamentally—like the colonial story—this one is rooted in the economic consequences of demographic and environmental changes as well.

The violent insurgency that overthrew the Bourbon regime came at a significant physical and human cost. These costs, understood as such, allow us to view the 1810–1840 period or so as a single unit of analysis. Population fell because of the direct and indirect effects of warfare, real wages again rose, and so did the wage-rent ratio. The consequences of these developments varied broadly across the regions of now-republican Mexico. We begin with the Bajío, because this was the principal theater of the insurgents, Hidalgo, and Allende, among others. We will consider the South and the far North apart.

The framework we employed for colonial New Spain depended on relative factors scarcities as an explanatory device. So it makes sense to repeat the analysis, starting with the wage-rent ratio. Working on the early nineteenth century involves certain compromises with data, since not every region has equally viable, homogeneous, or complete series.[1]

DOI: 10.4324/9781003532583-3

The best real wage series for "Mexico" in this period is based on Mexico City. For land rents, we employ an original series based on mortgage books (*libros de hipoteca*) from the state archive in Querétaro. The series spans 1818–1844 and uses a 10-percent sample of asset (property) values as a proxy for rent. This is shown in Figure 2.1. Labor is more mobile than land, so using Mexico City real wages will introduce some error, but not much in relation to an accurate sample of property values where land is, of course, immobile and prices are tied down by local conditions.

Figures 2.1 and 2.2 provide some insights into what was occurring and into its sources. One the one hand, the wage-rent ratio in Querétaro first rose into the early 1830s. But after that, it fell just as rapidly into the 1840s. As we shall see, deaths from the Insurgency and its associated evils—such as epidemic disease—produced devastating population losses and began to drive real wages up from the late eighteenth century. So studies such as Simon Miller's emphasize chronic labor shortages the region endured through the 1840s, sometimes aggravated by epidemic disease.[2] Yet this peaked soon enough; population pressure once again pushed rentals up. But at the same time (see Figure 2.2) the restoration of silver mining in Guanajuato, famously annihilated by the Insurgency, continued. By the 1840s, the recovery was almost complete. On the one hand, the demand for intermediate inputs that silver mining created grew. At the same time, mining put high-powered money back into circulation, supporting higher expenditure and, perhaps, accommodating a rise in the price level as well.[3] Other factors came into play, as the economy recovered prior to the outbreak of the War with the United States.[4]

The loss of life during the Insurgency was immense. A figure of a million souls is usually provided, which would have put the population of Mexico back

FIGURE 2.1 Wage-Rent Ratio for Querétaro, 1818–1845

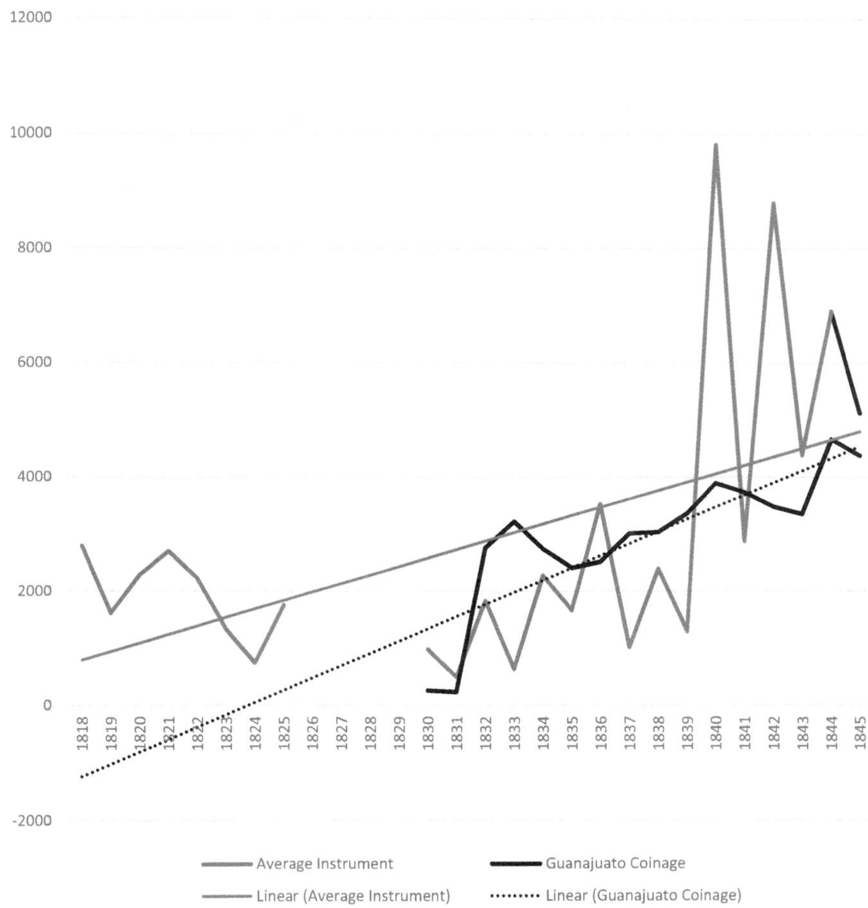

FIGURE 2.2 Average Property Instrument (*Hipoteca*) in Querétaro versus Coinage at Guanajuato, 1818–1845 (in Current Pesos)

to what it was in the 1770s or early 1780s. Figures for the city and department (state) of Querétaro are better documented. The department was said to have lost a fourth of its population "because of the war and the emigration of its people . . . because of the death of its [woollen] factories and paralysis of other sources of its wealth."—a decline from perhaps 200,000 to 140,000. As for the city, a text of 1822 puts its population at no more than 30,000; but in 1810, the city was said to have 50,000 people.[5] While some historians have minimized the destruction brought to the city and region, another spoke of "destruction inherent in a war as prolonged," especially in the mining districts of the state, a consequence of the Insurgency not normally associated with Querétaro.[6] Of course, the city and its hinterland, Querétaro's reputation as a royalist bastion notwithstanding, was the scene of open fighting throughout the 1810s and early 1820s, bloody and vicious as partisan warfare tends to be. One very detailed report from the town council of Salvatierra makes a few points explicitly. Local haciendas, the council explained, had been stripped of animals, with structures destroyed as well. The burden of forced contributions, such as 70,000 pesos to support defensive fortifications and a *cuerpo patriótico* was exhausting. Local farmers, loaded with unpayable debts, were unable to sell in Querétaro in a timely fashion. The movement of goods was not only slowed but also hit with war taxes and convoy fees. Quite accurately, the council explained prices to buyers were driven up while farmers received much less, the very definition of a deadweight loss caused by inefficiency. The haciendas were producing at half their capacity. When a garrison was moved from Salvatierra to Irapuato, draught animals, mules, and burros disappeared as well. With overall efficiency reduced, the council complained it had no idea of what to advise producers about paying the tithe.[7]

Any sort of reckoning with the "cost" of the Insurgency in the Bajío under Hidalgo and his followers is impossible. Hidalgo's ecclesiastical superior, the Bishop-Elect of Michoacán, pointedly preached that fighting under Hidalgo was a mortal sin. To die unconfessed at the cost of one's immortal soul requires a calculus we do not possess. But Abad also reckoned—considering Hidalgo's armed insurrection alone—in terms of opportunity cost, the value of lost production—which Abad estimated 10,000 pesos per day.[8] Hidalgo alone operated in Central Mexico in late 1810 and 1811 for, say, 180 days. That would be 1.8 million pesos in lost agricultural output. And the evidence for the disruption of agricultural production is widespread. Throughout the Archbishopric of Mexico, from 1810 through 1816, the net value of the tithe—a rough measure of the output of cereals and ranching—fell by more than 50 percent. By 1820, pre-insurgency levels had not been reattained. A report from Jarquillo in 1821 detailed individual "donations" of a real or two that added up to some 280 days of labor, well above Abad's estimate. That would be at least a year's output lost and more likely two as late as 1821.[9] The evidence for the disruption of agricultural production is widespread. Throughout the Archbishopric of Mexico, from 1810 through 1816, the net value of the tithe—a rough measure of the output of cereals and ranching—fell by more than 50 percent. By 1820, pre-insurgency levels had not been reattained. Well into the 1830s, a careful analysis of the tithe there concluded "the ravages of the War of Independence and subsequent armed rebellions . . . damaged certain productive entities and [resulted in] a shortage of labor."[10]

Silver production, largely from Guanajuato, fell nearly 50 percent in the 1810s, or no less than 3 or 4 percent of the total output. The cost of supporting the royalist army in Querétaro was somewhat less than 6 million pesos. Combining these imprecise and heterogeneous figures, is it completely unfounded to think that the rebellion in the Bajío and Central Mexico alone would have cost New Spain 5 to 20 percent of the output in a 200-million-peso economy? Those are large numbers, but not pulled from thin air. The Insurgency was exceptionally costly in lives, property, and current production.[11] The Insurgency was the most powerful and influential shock to hit republican Mexican in the first half of the nineteenth century, including the direct consequences of the War with the United States and the loss of Texas.

As if these estimates of lost output during the Insurgency were not enough, there were other direct fiscal costs that seem extraordinary. According to Juan Ortiz Escamilla, the costs of expelling the Spanish garrison from San Juan de Ulúa in the Port of Veracruz from 1821 through 1825 rose to an incredible 18 million pesos. This included refurbishing Mexican vessels to place the fortress under siege and other costs. When one considers that the net receipts of the London loans that Mexico raised in the early 1820s have been estimated at some 11 million pesos, one might conclude that those debts, which dogged the country through the 1880s and were the source of endless political, fiscal, and diplomatic grief, including excluding Mexico from international capital markets after default in 1827, meant the costs of the Insurgency were essentially incalculable.[12]

But even so, recovery had begun by the 1840s, much of it explained by the recovery of mining, benign climatic conditions after independence, and what is sometimes called a "bounceback" effect in areas that have been ravaged by heavy combat and loss of life. It is worth considering some of these factors in more detail.

Querétaro was in the agricultural heartland of Mexico, richly endowed in arable land. Some of its surrounding districts, such as Amealco, were poised for an expansion of cultivation. The population there grew from 703 in 1790 to 9,896 in 1822–1826, at least some of the expansion reflecting a displacement of population from Querétaro and its surrounding theater of combat as well.[13] By the 1840s, if government reports are to be believed, the problem with cereal cultivation there was not shortage, but surplus. With no natural vent for surplus because of high transportation costs in the pre-railroad era, prices tended to fall. Del Raso's exhaustive and very carefully researched study of the region—his population figures, for instance, are broadly confirmed by an examination of parish registers—showed that between 1841 and 1844, the maize crop sown in the district of Querétaro had nearly doubled. In the entire department, the increase was nearly 40 percent. By the early 1840s, agricultural supply was growing, and that was the largest share of national product.[14]

The second factor that accounted for the agricultural expansion of the Bajío was an unusually favorable turn of weather. Examining the drought index (PDSI) centered on Amealco in Figure 2.3 from the years from 1780 through 1810 (the decade of the 1790s excepted) were quite dry, with some of the worst times coming in the late 1780s. Yet after 1810, the reversal in conditions was nearly complete, save for briefly in the late 1810s. The years after 1810 (the smoothed form is a ten-year spline) makes the difference very apparent. The years after 1810 are relatively wetter. So the prospects for agriculture in the second half of the period were more favorable. This, in turn, was reflected in a series of abundant harvests, notably 1820, 1821, and 1822, even if transportation costs remained high because of the Insurgency.[15]

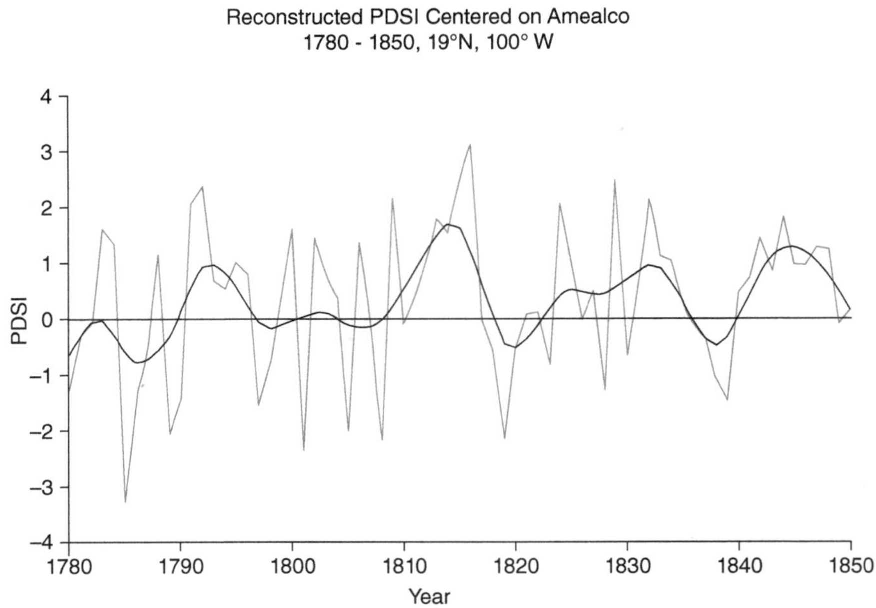

FIGURE 2.3 PSDI 1750–1850 Centered on Amealco with Ten-Year Smoothing

The fiscal and monetary impact of the recovery of the Guanajuato silver mines was basically complete by the early 1840s. Their output had fallen from 5.3 million pesos per annum in 1800–1818 to 2 million pesos per annum in 1828–1829. The decline was reversed by 1840 (see Figure 2.2). Throughout the Bajío—in Querétaro, Michoacán, and as far North as San Luis Potosí, indicators of economic recovery turned positive. It was not mining alone, but mining in conjunction with other factors that drove the recovery of Central Mexico by 1840.[16]

The notion that there was a stable relation between silver mining and the rest of Mexican output—a sort of fiscal multiplier—was well established by the beginning of the nineteenth century. A remarkable report by one of the judges of the audiencia of Mexico, José Ysido Yáñez, attempted to compute the size of the putative multiplier. That number is less interesting than his conviction that during the Insurgency, the only economic variable that mattered was mintage based on silver mining. Therefore, Yáñez concluded, the only explanation for the reduction in economic activity in New Spain was the disruption of silver mining, creating what we might term a "natural experiment." Thus a return to pre-insurgency levels of mining would, in general, restore total output to its previous levels.[17]

Recall that population recovery was accompanied by a falling wage-rent ratio (Figure 2.1). In Part One of this study, we emphasized that the extraction of ore was nothing, if not labor intensive. So labor shortages and high wages discouraged the rehabilitation of the mines, but the converse was true as well. Expensive and extensive engineering modifications were needed to drain water from mines that had flooded during inactivity. High wages would have diverted capital from such important purposes. And in Guanajuato and elsewhere, such shortages were severe obstacles to the recovery of the mines. At Real del Monte in Hidalgo, there were six labor clashes between 1827 and 1845. "Company officials complained all through the period . . . that wages paid . . . were too high." Shortages of workers were also a severe problem in Guanajuato.[18]

In the amalgamation or refining process, which was often carried out independently of the mines, "maize, straw, salt and copper pyrites represented 45 percent of costs." Since the price of mercury, the principal reagent used in amalgamation, had skyrocketed between 1827 and 1840 under the monopoly of Rothschild, some of the mines, like Real del Monte, which were at best marginally profitable, logically depended on maize, which could be purchased at low prices. Any effort at resurrecting silver production and growth more generally hinged on cheap grain and on a relative reduction in wages.

A second aspect to the recovery was the incipient push for mechanization of the cotton industry in the 1830s that began with Lucas Alamán's development fund, the Banco de Avío (1830–1842). It was hardly the most auspicious time to begin a program of industrialization, particularly with the price of British cottons falling as the Mexican net barter terms of trade improved—albeit mildly. Even if relative Mexican wages were falling, they remained high by British standards, a problem not helped by the apparent misalignment of the Mexican exchange rate under the silver standard—a case of what is now called Dutch Disease, where the exportable good, in abundant local supply (silver, Mexico's principal export) is underpriced relative to international levels.[19] Yet, at least in cottons, there was a start to industrialization. By 1844, the conventional figure given for spindles in operation was over 100,000, over half of which were then located in the departments of Michoacán and México.[20] The terms of trade deteriorated sharply around 1831, coinciding with the establishment of the Banco de Avío, which may well have encouraged Mexicans to think that industrialization was then both necessary and possible.[21]

Mexicans of this generation regarded industrialization as synonymous with prosperity, economic independence, and modernity. Textile entrepreneurs like Estevan de Antuñano secured funding from the Banco de Avío.[22] Yet that funding was always squeezed by military requirements, whose exact dimensions and accounting were, by all accounts, not only large but largely incomprehensible and probably the object of much corruption and abuse.[23] There was also the pressing but intermittent need to service both domestic and foreign creditors, although rarely simultaneously.[24] Almost as a sop to rent-seeking entrepreneurs who emerged during "Centralism," and played such a major role in finance, an array of tariffs, prohibitions, licenses, and other barriers to trade appeared in the late 1830s and early 1840s, of which the terms of trade really takes no account. An imperfect index of protection, an Implicit Index of Tariff Protection (see Figure 2.4), shows what the central government was up to clearly enough. And there were always military contracts themselves,

Year	*Percentage (%)*
1821	25
1825	32
1825–1836	46
1826–1827	47
1827–1828	30
1840	36
1841	42
1842	44
1843	55
1844	56
1845	35

FIGURE 2.4 Implicit Index of Tariff Protection, 1821–1845

primarily for outfitting the infantry and cavalry which supported the *obrajes* of Querétaro; well-connected military entrepreneurs could expect to generate millions of pesos of business one way or another.[25]

At no time in the mid- to late 1820s did the ratio of external taxes to the current value of imports fall to anything approaching its low levels of imperial "free trade" in 1821. By the early 1840s, it was nearly twice as high. The Mexican Congress, through which commercial policy was made, responded to the industrial interests in the Central Republic and to such financier industrialists as Cayetano Rubio, Manuel Escandón, the Martínez del Rio, and Manuel Julián de Lizardi, the conservative banker to Santa Anna, by extending protection to their industrial enterprises. In Rubio's case, he benefitted from substantial military contracts for uniforms as well, selling the government 500,000 pesos worth of cloth for uniforms from factories in Celaya and Querétaro.[26]

Since the Querétaro district was still struggling with the overhang from the Insurgency and the destruction of the colonial *obrajes*, it too became a target for industrialization. Del Raso's discussion is not without difficulty, but he thought nearly 13,000 families had been deprived of work, at a cost of around 170 pesos per family. This loss stemmed from the violence, capital flight, and an interval of looser trade (in the early 1820s) that had destroyed the woolen industry there that flourished as late as the 1790s. There was much to gain and little to lose from a revival of industry.[27] Let us then look more carefully at Del Raso's discussion of Querétaro because it points to an extremely important way of understanding why the growth of GDP in Republican Mexico was slow. It is a simple economic calculation based on the definition of GDP. It is, for the most part, not rooted in a particular ideology.

Del Raso's data on Querétaro's population is the best we currently have. Born in Puebla, Del Raso (1780–1848) spent nearly two thirds of his life in Querétaro. He had been the administrator of the hacienda "San Cristóbal" in nearby Acámbaro. He also held positions in the *ayuntamiento* of the city, in the departmental assembly, and in the National Congress. He briefly served as interim Governor in 1846.

He had his biases because he was a thorough liberal and anti-Santanista. In a comprehensive denunciation of José María Gutiérrez Estrada's monarchical project for Mexico, Del Raso styled himself "un republicano exaltado" and spared no effort to demonstrate that Mexico was fit material for a republic. The country had in no way retroceded morally, materially, or politically since independence.[28]

Del Raso also knew what he was talking about. He based his calculations on population data coming from nineteen parishes and vicarages in the department. Comparison with original parish registers (when available) or even documents in church archives for the tithe indicates he was reasonably careful.[29] The inadequacies and biases of the registers themselves are quite another issue, but it is them or nothing. In general, Del Raso assumes a critical attitude toward his data; he discloses his sources; and he makes the nature of his assumptions clear. This is about the most a reasonable critic could ask.[30]

From 1827 through 1844, Del Raso calculates that population growth in the department was about 3.5 percent per year. This is obviously quite high, and not true of Mexico overall. One has only to look at the neighboring state of Veracruz for comparison.[31] There population growth was extremely slow—almost flat. So we are looking at the Bajío and the Eastern portion at that time. Del Raso's are, besides, simply averages. Some parts of the department had experienced little growth since the late colonial period; others, such as Amealco, a center of *ranchero* or small farm production, had experienced an explosive increase after the 1770s. Population increase was probably driven mostly by natural increase and the redrawing of administrative boundaries. In-migration was of lesser importance.

It is probably best to begin at the beginning and to look at the overall structure of the population when Del Raso wrote. He provides ample data with which to do this, although the ages by which he defines cohorts are not ideal. Yet the results are suggestive and make historical sense. Figure 2.5 shows a basic population pyramid that we constructed from Del Raso's data.[32] The population is quite young. Nearly 44 percent of the department was 12 years of age or younger, not unreasonable for a "developing" country, if not an idealized Stage One or Stage Two population pyramid. Both birth (CBR) and death (CDR) rates are high (see Figure 2.6), but mortality is falling. Fertility is as well, but natural increase is still relatively high.

One of the truly striking features of the pyramid is the sharp contraction the cohort in the base as it passes the age of 7. Much, if not most of the loss could be attributable to deaths in the first year of life, whose rate in 1877 was calculated at 213 per thousand. Demetrio Mejía, the proximate source of the figure, adds that elevated mortality in children under the age of 10 was the rule, which corresponds to what we have here.[33] In Querétaro, where the measure was taken a third of a century earlier (1844), the death rate in the first year of life was 230 per 1000, largely caused by dysentery, fevers, respiratory ailments, and a malady called *alferercía*.

The second feature to examine is the unexpectedly large reduction in the male cohort ages 50 to 60. Males of this age were born between 1784 and 1794; in other words, they would have been between 16 and 26 years of age in 1810. The cohort

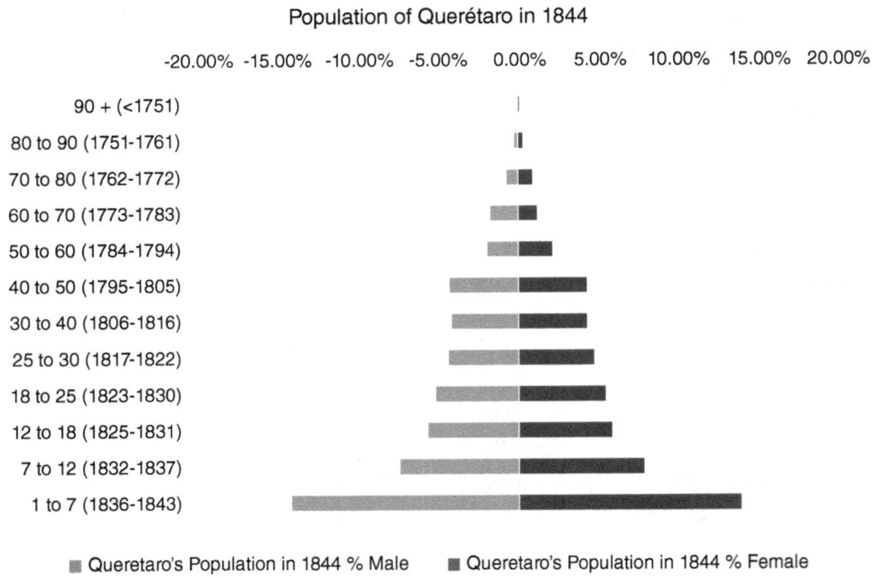

FIGURE 2.5 Age Structure of Querétaro Population, 1844

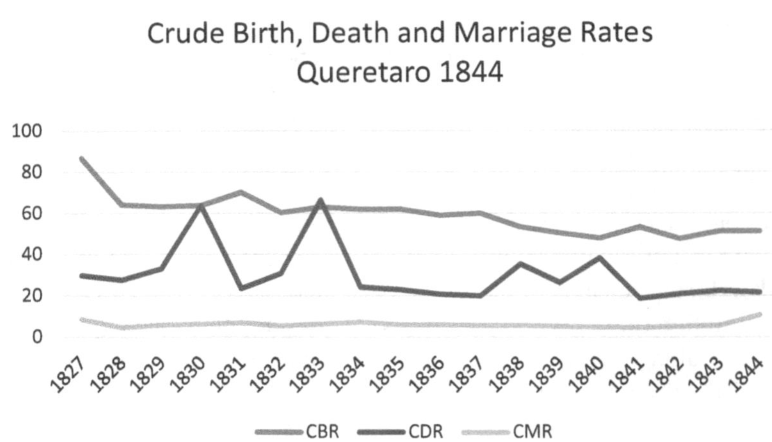

FIGURE 2.6 Crude Birth and Death Rates, Querétaro

of males aged 60 to 70 would have been born between 1773 and 1783. In. 1810, they would have been between 27 and 37. There is no point in speculating how much of an impact the Insurgency itself had because both cohorts would have passed through the "starving year" of 1786, where estimates for Michoacán conclude that as much as 15 percent of the population was carried away by famine and epidemic disease. Nevertheless, the implication that males between 16 and 37 in

1810 would have reached the ages of 36 and 57 in 1830 must have approximated much of the working population impacted by the Insurgency. The notion that these groups were decimated by war, famine, and disease is an intriguing one. It may well indicate that slow (or no) economic growth in this period was a function of a much-reduced labor force.[34] There is, to put it bluntly, no such thing as a free revolution, insurgency, or war.

The demographic effects identified in Querétaro show up elsewhere in Central Mexico. A careful analysis of census data from Toluca in the 1830s shows a similar, if not precisely identical pattern.

> [Male] age cohorts 15–19, 20–24 and 25–29 show sharp indentations. . . . Men from this group would have been born between 1805 and 1819. Their decreased numbers were likely attributable to numerous causes, including decreased fertility during the decades of the wars for independence, and increased mortality caused by the 1813 and 1833 [cholera] epidemics.

A substantial excess of the female population was in evidence as well. There was also heavy fighting in and around Toluca in 1812 between the Royal government and insurgents loyal to Morelos. The valley of Toluca must have looked much like the department of Querétaro, and with the same implications for a reduction in the labor force and output. Margarita Menegus agrees in her examination of the tithe around Temascaltepec and Tenancingo, although more because of the impact of the contraction in silver mining there than because of population effects per se.[35]

Of course, what is true for Central Mexico is not necessarily the case elsewhere. In the far Northeast, Coahuila y Texas, there was virtually no insurgency and little warfare; the factors promoting immigration and settlement had a vastly different result on the structure of a population, both free and slave, which was intended to increase the output of staples like cotton. Here the age cohorts from 16 to 40 were correspondingly growing.[36] We have already noticed that even Veracruz looks quite different. Strictly speaking, a Mexican *national* economy did not exist. The regions were like different countries.

Moreover, and this is to anticipate our major argument, the difference between the age structure of the population in Texas and Central Mexico speaks to very different rates of economic growth. As Andrew Torget has emphasized, the point of Mexican, and then Texan immigration policy—with or without slave labor—was to turn Texas into a thriving cotton republic. Demographic growth meant the growth of labor supply, and the growth of output more generally. How different in the early nineteenth century was the rest of Mexico? Is it any wonder evidence of growth was (and is) hard to find?[37] Interestingly, Del Raso suggests that political movements—he specifically mentions 1829 and 1842 when troops garrisoned in the city of Querétaro left for Jalisco and México—depressed the birth rate by impeding family formation, "A demonstration of how dangerous wars are for the progress of population and, by extension, for economic growth."[38] This would be the opposite of a "bounceback effect" on population growth after a period of warfare. Even the fiscal crises accompanying the fall of Iturbide in 1823 had echoes in the Bajío. It is just not easy to put a number on them as economic shocks go.[39]

While we have long had figures for total Mexican output based on José María Quirós 1817 figure (190 to 230 million pesos, depending on the author and attention to double counting), these have rested on estimating the consumption (C) of a representative agent and then scaling this up by population. Making suitable, if arbitrary adjustments for public expenditure (G) and private investment (I), the result (C+I+G) is an estimate for a closed economy based on expenditure. Raymond Goldsmith used this method for the Roman Empire, but the amount of guesswork involved leaves contemporary economic historians skeptical that any similarity between income and expenditure so computed is more than an accident or a coincidence rather than an accounting identity. Whether or not nineteenth-century Mexicans regarded Quirós' figures as plausible and not, say, Humboldt's or Mora's or anything else is dismissed—if it is even considered—as irrelevant.[40]

One of the great virtues of Del Raso's data is that it can, with a little modification, be used to estimate the product of Querétaro (or the Bajío) in ways more consistent with economic theory. The canonical approach in the "new" economic history was laid out in 1967 by Paul David. The key to understanding David's work is productivity change and the labor force participation rate. While there have been subsequent attempts by David and others to update his calculations, it seems appropriate to employ his original approach as the starting point for a Mexican calculation in about 1844. It is straightforward and can be summarized in the following identity:

$$\mathrm{GDP/P} = (\mathrm{LF/P})\left[\mathrm{S_a}(\mathrm{O/LF})\mathrm{a} + \mathrm{S_n}(\mathrm{O/LF})\mathrm{n}\right]$$

This means output per person (GDP/P) equals the product of the labor force participation rate and output per worker $\left[(\mathrm{O/LF})\mathrm{a} + \mathrm{S_n}(\mathrm{O/LF})\mathrm{n}\right]$. Output per worker, in turn, can be written as a weighted average of output per worker in agriculture (a) and nonagriculture (everything else!) (n) where the weights are each sector's share or proportion of the labor force.

Del Raso, an underappreciated savant, provided data that can be used to follow David's method of estimation—up to a point.[41] There are a number of tedious calculations involved, but assuming no mechanical errors creep in, the result produces a per capita income figure of 29 to 30 pesos. Considering that Ernest Sánchez Santiró reports an almost stable nineteenth-century consensus estimate of 36 to 43 pesos, what we have seems plausible enough.[42] Realistically, we are best relying on an interval rather than a point estimate, because, intuitively, the probability is much higher that we have gotten an interval rather than a point right. Nevertheless, we need to give this some thought, because there are any number of subtleties or complications.

First, of course, is that we have already argued there was no national economy in the 1840s, so any per capita income figure specific to one region—theoretically satisfying or not—is apt to be misleading. There is presently no good basis for estimating or even guessing a figure elsewhere. So, we must put the result in that perspective. For all we know, we have something falling at the mean of some probability distribution whose variance (or even whose exact shape) is unknown.

Second, David was looking at a market-embedded economy in the United States. His emphasis on "labor force" would strike a historian as anachronistic or inappropriate for Mexico because Del Raso does not consider as "employed," for instance, women who prepared tortilla for their families and are never included. This is a serious deficiency because in the nineteenth century, and not only in rural areas, the food supply depended on the daily "slavery of the metate," the laborious process by which an ear of corn was transformed into the tortilla, a staple food of the Mexican diet.[43] Since food may have comprised as much as 80 percent of the daily expenditure of the average Mexican, a failure to impute market value to food processing per se results in a major *underestimation* of product. And here we are faced with the arbitrary adjustment of the outcome of David's ostensibly unobjectionable methodology. Rather than recognizing this fact, it is hard to know precisely what to do. There are, moreover, other complications. Del Raso's overall implied output per worker in all sectors is 80 pesos, but employed people make up only 25 percent of the population! Del Raso's data for "child" labor and *alquilados*—and Del Raso claimed 4,000 children were "employed" was about 20 pesos per capita. Del Raso assumed a family size of five members, which implied that family income was about 117 pesos, suggesting that per capita income in families was lower than per capita income in general. None of this is helpful, but it does suggest that there was a wide variation in income between employed individuals, the "unemployed" (especially women household workers), family workers, and families, so income per capita was by no means the same as income per worker.[44]

Since Del Raso placed 40 percent of the labor force in agriculture and only about 8 percent in manufacturing, another source of income variation could be attributed to what Del Raso termed "rentiers" merchants, artisans, and others in urban occupations and in the priestly, bourgeois, and professional classes found in the city of Querétaro, who comprised 50 percent of the labor force. Logically, Del Raso described a department whose average was typical for the rural economy. Yet in the city and the new industrial sector, almost, but not quite unique to the eastern Bajío, productivity and incomes were higher. For example, Del Raso implies that productivity per worker in spinning, weaving, carpet-making, and tanning is about 111 pesos. Productivity in the woolen and cotton industries was different because factories (cottons) were on the rise while the *obrajes* (woolens) were on the decline. A "typical" worker in Cayetano Rubio's "Hercules" textile mill earned 178 pesos, and that mill accounted for over 75 percent of the cottons and over 60 percent of the value of textiles produced there.[45] Clearly, high variance in incomes was the rule, not the exception; thus placing much weight on averages such as per capita income is probably undesirable—other considerations, such as regional disparities, aside.

Let us conclude this discussion. The principal point is that the demographic consequences of the Insurgency, namely, an initially much-reduced labor force and then a rising, and a subsequently falling rent-wage ratio explains the economic movements of what can be observed in the Bajío and other portions of Central Mexico in the 1840s—a stagnation of output until the population can recover from what occurred. Margaret Chowning's study of Michoacán suggests a similar pattern. In general, Jan Bazant's data on clerical mortgages—not regionally specific—shows an expansion of lending during the 1830s and into the early 1850s, even as other assets of the Church came under pressure government expropriation.[46]

Potential growth in Southern Mexico, on the other hand, was also constrained by demography. The population of Oaxaca, for example, stagnated. In 1810, the state had some 596,000 people. This level would not again be seen until 1862, if then. If potential output growth is the sum of the growth of the labor force (population, crudely) and productivity, there was no obvious source. While indigenous villages were embedded in a dense network of markets, exchange took place along the lines of ecological niches, like those found in the Andean highlands. The production and export of cochineal that would have boosted demand fell steadily due to the availability of synthetic dyestuffs throughout the mid-nineteenth century. Oaxaca, and the South, were then very different in numerous sociocultural and economic ways.[47]

Manifest Destiny, Manifest Disaster?

Since the War of 1847 (Mexican American War) was a cataclysmic event in Mexican national history, it is natural to assume that it must have been important to Mexican economic history. But was it? For example, did the outbreak of the war bring an end to the incipient recovery from the Insurgency? Did physical damage from the war diminish the productive potential of the economy, just as the Insurgency had? Most importantly, did the impact of territorial losses to the United States, conventionally placed at half of Mexico's national territory, have a dramatic effect on output, present and future. Surprisingly, and to a substantial extent, the answer to these questions is "no." The effects of the war on Mexican memory, collective psyche, and culture were indeed profound. With the economy, arguably, much less so. This is not a military history, much less a conventional account of the war. Those already exist.[48] Rather, this is a kind of counterfactual thought experiment. Had the war never occurred, would Mexican economic history have demonstrably and indubitably been different? Probably not, *at least in the framework we have chosen*.

Let us first consider what economic factors may have led to Mexico's military defeat. The German general Erwin Rommel once observed, "The battle is fought and won by the quartermaster even before the shooting begins."[49] There is no doubt, however, that Mexicans observed, "Without the efficient cooperation of the states, nothing could have been done. Day by Day, it [the Mexican Army] became a smaller force."[50] Jalisco, Guanajuato, Michoacán, Querétaro, Aguascalientes, San

Luis Potosí, and the Distrito Federal had provided, it was said, men and money. Yet others had not. Some, under the pressure of the invasion, had nothing to spare, or so they said. Whatever the case, the underlying source of defeat came down to money and resources. The United States could mobilize men and resources. Mexico could not. Whether a consequence of resource endowments, institutions, or different "steady states" is a relevant question.

The US Army in the North, specifically under the command of Zachary Tylor, could and did buy what it needed on campaign. In 1847, the Quartermaster's department purchased nearly 7,000 mules and 100 horses at Tampico. The Assistant Quartermaster there disbursed $800,000. Ironically, just as the Americans were spending lavishly in Tampico, the Mexican General in the area, Urrea, was complaining bitterly that he had no resources and was forced to take drastic measures to get them since customs—no longer at his disposal—from Tampico had been one source of military supply.[51] For Scott's army in Central Mexico, forced to live off local resources after abandoning its base of supply in Veracruz, the Assistant Quartermaster spent over $200,000 which included 20,000 bushels of corn. All told, the subsistence costs for the US Army in Mexico in 1848 were estimated at over $6 million, mostly local expenditure.[52] Meanwhile, Joaquín Rea, a general of brigade trying to recapture Puebla from Scott's troops, wrote a remarkably bitter dispatch in which he blamed the state government of Puebla for failing to support the Mexican Army and the partisans he had assembled with money and materiel. He protested that he would not have laid down his sword while a Yankee soldier in Mexico drew breath. The Mexican Army's problem was not cowardice "but a total lack of resources." The War Ministry's marginal response was essentially "Not our problem. We have no money."[53]

The Mexican Army, particularly the *Ejército del Norte*, ultimately commanded by Antonio López de Santa Anna, simply had no money. It could not compete in the marketplace. And so poorly armed, outgunned, and frequently best by hunger, it was defeated. At Palo Alto, Resaca de la Palma, Monterrey, and La Angostura (Buena Vista) from the mid-1846 through early 1847, the *Ejército del Norte* was repeatedly defeated or fought to a standstill. To be sure, there were charges of poor generalship, internal divisions within the general staff, political interference, and inexplicable, untoward retreats. But if an army travels on its stomach, the stomach of the *Ejército del Norte* was empty.

In the run up to the loss of Monterrey, the presidial companies of Coahuila had no more than 50 percent of their complement of horses for Saltillo, Río Grande, and Monclova. A steady stream of distraught correspondence ultimately reached Santa Anna regarding the lack of supplies at all levels. There was an extraordinary one from the Mexican Commander in Monterrey, Pedro de Ampudia, asking for additional mules, not for combat support, but to help in the honorable withdrawal of his troops from the battleground since "supplies have run out and ammunition in scarce." A standard account of the battle mentions that Taylor "was low on supplies and ammunition" but leaves the impression that Ampudia's withdrawal was hard to credit. Ampudia may have withdrawn prematurely; it is questionable whether he was "defeated," at least by Taylor's troops.[54]

The clearest statement of this thesis was published by Manuel Balbontín, a retired artillery officer, after La Angostura: "The enemy had food, but we lacked a full ration per man. Not even our officers had anything to eat. So we couldn't wait for Taylor to be defeated by hunger. He had to be defeated by arms."[55] Santa Anna's army had begun to run out of food on the march from San Luis Potosí to La Angostura. Even though the Mexican forces outnumbered the Mexican troops and in military terms, the battle was essentially a draw, Santa Anna, like Ampudia at Monterrey, disengaged.[56] The withdrawal of the tired, hungry troops, afflicted with dysentery, was a disaster. Mexican losses were placed at 10,500, or nearly half the force brought to the battle itself.[57] La Angostura, which should have been a Mexican victory, instead turned the American General Zachary Taylor into the "Hero of Buena Vista" and catapulted him into the US Presidency. The situation on the ground for the Mexican military was chaotic, and lack of money was often the reason. Even the interim President Mariano Salas at one point ended up as an American prisoner of war.[58]

Before 1850, Mexico was chronically insolvent. In mid-1846, the institutional form of the Mexican national government was in transition or turmoil, depending on one's point of view. "Centralist" and "Federalist" are oversimplifications, but they did represent two contending views of the disposition of liquid resources at the local and national levels, always a contentious matter, who was in power notwithstanding. Beginning in the 1830s, the constitutional expressions of these tendencies were in conflict; they would remain so for most of the nineteenth century. By the 1840s, no equilibrium had been reached. On the one hand, a centralist regime had been formally established in 1837 when the First Federal Republic collapsed. On the other, an attempt to implement a centralist regime based on a direct wealth tax had broken down by 1841, when yet another "revolution" occurred ultimately leading to the reestablishment of federalism in late summer 1846. Contemporaries thought the unpredictable shifting of fiscal and commercial policy between partisan forces was the root cause of the impoverishment of the national government.[59]

Both Mexico and the United States drew heavily on customs revenues to fund their central governments; in fact, the United States did relatively more heavily than Mexico in the 1840s, on the order of 60 to 40 percent. This meant a few things. The international trade of the United States was larger than Mexico's, so other things being equal, the United States could always raise absolutely more money this way (the United States did not introduce a direct tax on income until its Civil War). Since the "federal" government in Mexico, the *Federación*—had no direct tax, it relied more on internal borrowing and the *contingente* or state payment quotas. As a result, the willingness of the states and private Mexican capitalists to finance the *Federación* was crucial. This turned a politically fraught process into a nightmare. It allowed refractory state governors to effectively hold up the *Federación* and, as we shall see, some did.

Yet a far simpler explanation is possible. Mexico relied heavily on customs duties. The United States blockaded Mexico's Gulf and Pacific ports beginning in 1846. Once the United States was in physical possession of a port, it enacted its own War Tariff and collected customs duties as a means of partially offsetting the cost of the war. Hence the only revenues upon which the *Federación* could count were those that the states provided that could be raised from internal forced loans or by appeals to citizen patriotism. Clearly, these never sufficed.[60]

The commander of the *Ejército del Norte* was the erstwhile "conservative dictator" Antonio López de Santa Anna, who had been garrisoned with his army in San Luis Potosí. Dictator or not, Santa Anna had virtually no resources at his disposal to prosecute a war. At the beginning of August 1846, the Treasury in Mexico City had a cash balance of 43,000 pesos. That was all. The Treasury's capacity to borrow had been all but obliterated by the suspension of payments to domestic creditors, a move that had brought bitter denunciations from the lenders.[61] To put this figure in perspective, consider that the *Federación* itself estimates that at bare minimum, it cost 50,000 pesos per month to prosecute the war.[62] Therefore, by one conservative estimate, the Mexican government did not have even *one month's funds* when it "began" the war. Absent the capacity to borrow heavily, which Mexico did not then have, the decision to go to war with the United States amounted to fiscal suicide. As it happened, by December 1846, the cash balance of the *Federación* was 482 pesos. The government was insolvent, and the war had barely begun.[63] And even then, Mexico planned on spending $6 million per year for the war. Within days (December 31), the Treasury was scrambling to find a way to raise a million pesos.

In the United States, on the other hand, military preparations for a war had begun nearly two years earlier, in 1844. The balance on hand in the US Treasury in July 1845 was $7.7 million. The War Department estimated that in the fiscal year 1846–1847, the cost of the war would amount to roughly $17 million. Expenses for 1846 were out at about $3 million. So, true enough, the United States would need to finance around $13 million. Yet the Treasury thought this could be financed by the issue of Treasury notes. If the war were speedily concluded, no other borrowing would be necessary.

To summarize, the United States planned to spend *three times* per year as much as Mexico, and probably without resort to anything more than note issue, which in plain language, meant a short-run inflation tax. It is difficult to suppress the thought that Mexico was out of its depth both financially and militarily before hostilities broke out on the Rio Grande.[64]

When the call went out to contribute to the support of the army, the response of the states was quite mixed.[65] While, for example, the governor of San Luis Potosí, Ramón Adame, was a santanista, his material support for the army was as much rhetorical as substantive. While the engineering battalion of the army called for Adame's support in enlisting the efforts of agricultural laborers from the surrounding haciendas and ranchos to work on military fortifications, there were discouragingly few forthcoming. Presumably the support of the local landowning class was an important part of Adame's political base; he showed himself loathe to upset them, arguing that to do so would be to drive labor out of the state. As a result, Adame may have supported Santa Anna, but the rural economy of San Luis Potosí remained surprisingly unaffected despite the garrisoning of the army in the capital in 1846–1847 and some nearby military action. There was little obvious extraction of resources from the region's haciendas, which remained prosperous.[66]

Moreover, Santa Anna had few friends in Zacatecas, whose governor refused to supply men or materiel in any form, or in Durango. The loyalty of both states under Centralism has been the subject of veiled, if pointed discussion among the military's senior officers in the North. Their concerns turned out to be well founded.[67] In Zacatecas, the Governor Manuel González Cosío questioned both the practical consequences of sending as many as 4,500 men (as well as the constitutional authority of the government) or the Commander of the *Ejército del Norte* to demand that an autonomous state do so. Santa Anna, with visible irritation, replied that he was reminded of the federalist rebellion he had been obliged to put down there in 1835 (and in Texas) by such action, but had no alternative but to fume. On the other hand, the notional cash balance of the state of Zacatecas at the beginning of fiscal 1846 was about 7,000 pesos, which may have well motivated González Cosío to refuse to provide funds he simply did not have.[68]

The state of Tamaulipas had a history of secessionist movements dating to at least 1837. These fed fears that the reluctance of its residents to support the *Ejército del Norte* signaled renewed efforts to place the region under the jurisdiction of the United States once the war had ended. In July 1847, civil authorities in the district of Tula had complained bitterly about the demands in money and materiel that Gen José Urrea had placed on them.[69] Urrea's rather astounding reply to the complaints—a kind of nineteenth-century version of Anthony McAullife's "Nuts" at Bastogne during the Battle of the Bulge in World War II—was followed by a generalized charge of the region's disloyalty. The problem, Santa Anna was advised, was that the governor of Tamaulipas was looking for a reason to place the state under the control of the United States. Political dissension rather than disparities of wealth alone had gotten in the way of paying for the war.[70]

A similar account could be given of the Federal government's attempts to place state militias under its control in 1847. In Michoacán and Guanajuato, the order to send troops to Mexico City went unheeded, buttressed by the standard answer that there were no guns, no ammunition, and no money with which to obtain them. The state of Querétaro may have sent a few hundred. Tlaxcala sent a handful. The spirit was willing, but the flesh was weak.[71] A remarkable survey of human and other resources available in the departments of Durango, Chihuahua, Zacatecas, and Nuevo Mexico in early 1846 concluded that there were fewer than *two thousand* armed men available to throw up against the advancing US forces. No money, no men, and little prospect of finding more.[72]

Once Wool's army was established in Saltillo, its provisioning was not only adequate. It was abundant. On hand were 68 days of salt meat; 44 days of bread stuffs;

26 days of coffee; 40 days of sugar; 42 days of vinegar; 72 days of salt; and 62 days of salt. "The next [mule] train out of Camargo will make up nearly 60 days of every item."[73] The Americans billeted in Monterrey paid market rents for the properties they occupied. There is no evidence that they simply requisitioned local properties without compensation. The Mexican Army frequently ran out of war materiel, but the Americans kept excess stocks. It is literally true that the Americans could have supplied both themselves and the Mexicans had they so desired. As Peter Guardino shows, after the Battle of Angostura (Buena Vista), they literally did. The American military travelled on its stomach, but the Mexican soldiers often had to desert if they wanted to eat.[74]

On the other hand, the impact of the war does show up clearly and systematically in one area: on the supply and availability of draft animals to all kinds of private users. While the figures for Nuevo León are striking, they are typical of other nineteenth-century military conflicts in Mexico as well. The Mexican Army (and others) travelled with horses and mule trains. Their control, distribution, and numbers were, at least in theory, very carefully regulated because access to mules was "assigned" as a perquisite of rank as well as a basic means of moving equipment, personal effects, and materiel. In 1847, the Mexican Army and its component militia was ostensibly at full strength with about 22,000 troops; 4,000 horses; and 1,500 mules, not to mention muleteers.[75] As a result, the United States was obliged to compete locally for available mules, or even to ship them to Mexico as "deck loads for use in the campaigns." "At the present season, I am told that mules may be had at New Orleans in great numbers from the plantations. Purchase and send forward all the well broken mules and all the harness you can obtain." Wrote the US Quartermaster General, "Almost one quadruped for each man."[76]

Typically, the assumptions historians make is that the greatest cost to the economy of warfare in an agrarian economy in the nineteenth century is lost man-hours, particularly by peasants who were dragooned into fighting for one army or another. This is a sensible approach, one which Abad y Queipo used for the Insurgency. A reduction in labor supply reduces total output, whatever else occurs to productivity. And yet the Mexican Army was relatively small, around 20,000 troops, depending on the source, and whether it is inflated by combat, or by reductions in numbers after the war was concluded. If we use the standard range of estimates for per capita income, 30 to 40 pesos, then the value of output lost (assuming an army defending a country produces nothing of value, which is dubious), with total output growing to about 300 million pesos by the time of the war, would be about 3 percent of GDP, or far less than the losses produced by the Insurgency. It is a small sum, especially when viewed in the context of the loss of half the national territory.

Yet that is also a calculation made from the assumption that productivity was otherwise unaffected by war. When we consider the impact of warfare on mules and horses, this assumption seems implausible. Mules were the backbone of the Mexican transportation system well into the nineteenth century. One inevitably wonders what the marginal impact of the war was in the areas most affected by the movements of the armies. For example, the hacienda of Guanamé, west of Venado, in San Luis Potosí, donated 200 horses to military service in 1846, a huge contribution. The hacienda Potosí in Galeana in Nuevo León donated somewhat fewer.[77] The owner of Guanamé was gracious about the gesture, but some gave the impression that work pretty much ground to a halt when livestock was taken. One irate owner of an hacienda between Matamoros and San Fernando complained because of the nearness of fighting the guerillas under General Antonio Canales had stripped the place of horses and mules, leaving the cowboys "with nothing to do." His frustration sounds more authentic than ritualized protestations of loyalty common to the genre.[78] At best, this is anecdotal evidence from a war zone, but there is a consensus that transportation costs were an "obstacle" to Mexican development in the nineteenth century. With the effect widespread, it is reasonable to wonder what the impact on productivity disruptions to transportation had. One historian of Mexico succinctly put the problem, "The complex of problems associated with the conveyance of goods (*transporte*) prejudiced the entire economy, because it reduced the circulation of merchandise, money and capital." A shortage of mules, basically, was as serious as a "bad grain harvest." The grinding famines of the 1780s may have been largely over by the 1840s, but shortages of mules induced by barracks revolts, pronouncements, "revolutions," and wars were becoming distressingly common. As a writer such as Payno suggests, in Mexico, the army, not famine, was the new plague.[79]

Precisely because the government in Mexico City was unable to furnish resources, not to mention many of the resistant states, the war had to be financed in other ways. One expedient that Santa Anna or his subordinates hit upon was the creation of a Junta Central under the direct control of the ministries of Finance and of Home and Foreign Relations in Mexico City "so that other juntas may be set up in the capitals of the states or territories in communication in the Junta Central to keep it informed of the voluntary donations that might be made." Still others should be set up in the "Districts, Departments, Prefectures or Subprefectures of the States and Territories under the control of the state capitals or territories." The objective, obviously, was to bypass the control of the state assemblies, governors—indeed, the Chamber of Deputies—while drawing on the regional patriotism and resources from which power emanated, a kind of soft "centralist" counter coup once Federalism had been reestablished in 1846. The initial heads of the Junta Central, Felipe Neri del Berrio, Antonio Ycaza, and Juan Maria Flores, all appear to have been chosen for their political reliability.[80]

This was a hand-to-mouth device and the circumstances of war and invasion did not favor a meticulous accounting. Many of the local responses are highly stylized: after pledging cooperation, the documents typically report that a rancher had donated so many horses or mules for the support of the army. In one case, the employees of the sales tax office in the capital donated 300 pesos. In another, at Mineral del Chico in the Sierra de Pachuca, the workers of the mines and haciendas "contributed" 284 pesos, but nearly 10 percent of that came from two individuals. From the haciendas, the average contribution was between two to four reales, perhaps the wages of a day or two, but how "voluntary" these efforts were is questionable.

Most of these sums were small, especially when compared to the mammoth donations that large merchants in New Spain coughed up during the Napoleonic era.[81] We might guess that if the donations from Mineral del Chico were typical, and that half the population of Mexico contributed, the result would have been at most 2 million pesos. If the annual cost of the war were 6 million pesos, under the best of circumstances, such ad hoc finance could have raised at most a third of what was required. As far as the economic effects were concerned, spending exactly what is taxed away has a multiplier of one in a modern economy—a small effect.

The direct costs of the Mexican War to the United States, including the postwar indemnity paid to Mexico, amounted to about 6 percent of US GDP at the time; we have already placed the cost to Mexico at about 3 percent of GDP.[82] But there are two far more difficult issues: valuing the loss of lives and the loss of Mexican territory, normally put at 50 percent of Mexico's territory.

Estimates of Mexican casualties are literally nearly random, ranging from implausibly small (civilian losses of 1,000 pesos) to very extensive (total losses of all sorts of 50,000pesos). Whatever the case, they were probably too small to affect the overall wage-rent ratio, the standard by which we have until now judged economic significance. So we leave them aside, tragic but inevitable casualties of war. The loss of 50 percent of a country's territory, however, would seem to be another matter. The potential output was certainly reduced, as any elementary account of production possibility would insist. But beyond this, it is difficult to say much of anything. Historians are accustomed to judging the cost of war by the value of what was lost, but oddly, they seem inclined to assume that output would have remained unaltered under Mexican sovereignty. I jokingly refer to this as the counterfactual Disneyland hypothesis: things in the lost territories would have progressed just as they did under the US rule: Disneyland would have sprung up in Anaheim under either Mexico or the United States. This seems remarkably unlikely. Let us start with the wage-rent ratio, admitting, at the outset, that it cannot be resolved with the data available. Even though land immediately became scarcer, no one finds the emergence of a strengthened landholder class in Mexico due to a reversal of factor scarcity because of the Treaty of Guadalupe Hidalgo. Historians have typically found precisely the opposite, with rancheros strengthened and hacendados struggling to retain control. Perhaps the loss of the Northern territories was so far removed from the traditional core of Mexico as to have occurred literally in another country, the Southwestern United States, at least before the railroad age. Real wages did fall in Mexico after the war to levels last seen half a century earlier but whether this reflected a notional rise in population density because of the loss of lands where few people actually lived—in the Northern territories— seems illogical.[83]

Clearly, the War was a watershed in Mexican history and in Mexican economic history as well. But a plausible counterfactual of how Mexico would have developed had the war not occurred is simply not at hand. And may never be.[84]

Steps Backward

The nineteenth century in Mexico is, in general, a difficult period for economic history. Good empirical studies are few. Some regional studies approach larger economic questions from a political perspective, but politics, especially when serious internal rebellions occurred, is difficult to reconcile neatly.[85] So it is useful to establish some standard benchmarks, such as the size of the economy. This is not easy.

There are two that we will briefly examine, both worthy of more detailed analysis. Both, not surprisingly, are linked to fiscal questions, for Mexico came out of the War of 1847 bankrupt and heavily indebted. Reorganizing the fisc was a priority because experience since 1821 had demonstrated that a bankrupt government was almost worse than no government at all.

The first attempt is of uncertain authorship, but clearly well informed. "Fifty years of mistakes and missteps in our administrative course are, without a doubt, a terrible lesson."[86] The authors look back to the 1790s for data and were familiar with Humboldt, Abad y Queipo, Mora, and, above all, Quirós. What is most striking about this effort is its critical perspective: "past estimates of production do not agree, nor are they complete."[87] This is correct, the source of endless problems in trying to estimate the volume of output. However, the authors chose Quirós as their starting point, which was wise. Humboldt, Mora, and Abad y Queipo—all are helpful but ultimately deficient, not to say misleading. Alas, it is not clear that *Breves Indicaciones* is much better. As the authors approached national income in terms of expenditure and made reasonable estimates of a representative agent, they committed elementary errors. Their estimate suffered from double counting: intermediate inputs and final output were intermingled and therefore counted twice. When pressed for industrial output, the authors admitted they were rushed, had no novel data, and seem to have arbitrarily adjusted Quirós, while admitting that Sebastián Lerdo de Tejada's industrial output was nearly twice theirs. But the major changes in industrialization, especially in cotton textiles began in the 1830s, well after Quirós wrote. By 1845, Mexico operated over 100,000 spindles for cotton in more than 50 factories.[88] Ignoring the development makes the author's estimate of output practically useless. Their final value in 1864 is over 400 million pesos, or 50 pesos per head at the estimated population of 8 million. For all practical purposes, the figure means nothing; so for now, we leave it aside.

There was an almost simultaneous attempt to produce a similar set of estimates in 1865. At first blush, this one appears far more promising. It even attempts to account for nonmarket production of maize, effectively judging that market values for maize are 75 percent of total production.[89] But once again, there are problems of double counting and total product is 580 million pesos with a per capita output of over 70 pesos. Trying to adjust for double counting reduces things to a nominal figure less than Quirós' 1817 estimate, clearly implausible. Quite probably, the source of the problem was the author's failure to normalize his individual categories of expenditure in any way, so that different fractions of the population are then assumed to account for production, but the entire population is used to produce a per capita estimate. Not very promising, and almost impossible to repair.

So then, two original attempts to get at the size of the macroeconomy around 1860 come to nothing; we are apparently no better off than before. This is very discouraging, but we can try one more approach. Both studies allow us to estimate aggregate household (final) food consumption. When we do this and adjust for nonmarket production (25 percent), we reach an agricultural (food) total of over 250 million pesos, more or less. We know from the work of Challu and Gómez Galvariato that food consumption accounts for about 80 percent of householding spending[90] in their "bare bones" real wages model. Using this, we can derive a per capita income of about 32 pesos or a total GDP of about 312 million pesos (and, again, recall that women's household labor making tortilla is not represented in this figure, so the figure is biased down.)[91]

Now, if we return to the 1840s using the "correct" (Paul David) procedure and data from Querétaro, we arrive at the same figure of around 30 pesos, although the similarity could be nothing more than chance. Nevertheless, it is still hard to escape John Coatsworth's 1978 conclusion that, at best, there was little or no real per capita growth in Mexico in the middle years of the nineteenth century. And considering what we know about economic shocks now that was still not clear in 1978, this may not be very surprising. Of course, in the interim, there was War with the United States, the Reform Wars, and the French Intervention (1862–1867). The Civil War from 1858 to 1860 was brutal and could have obliterated intervening growth between the 1840s and the 1860s. But, for now, we simply do not know.

When Antonio López de Santa Anna fell from power the last time, it was through a rebellion. Rebellions have costs and economic dimensions, and this was no different. The period following his fall, La Reforma, did not end "political instability." We are accustomed at looking at the period in largely ideological and political terms. That is not wrong but incomplete.

Ignacio Comonfort, one of the leaders of the Liberal Movement, was not a thinker. He had held political positions under Santa Anna, the last of which was as the administrator of the Customs in the Port of Acapulco. This is no coincidence. It does not mean that the Reforma began as a tax or trade revolt, but it clearly had a financial dimension. Fighting requires money, and the Reforma was no different. The usual story is that the rebels against Santa Anna in the South had run out of money. Comonfort, who could find no backers among financiers in Mexico—none of Santa Anna's financiers were about to overthrow him—went to the United States. There he found Gregorio de Arjuria, an apparently wealthy friend who selflessly agreed to lend him money. At the same time, Comonfort—or someone (*and* Santa Anna, for that matter)—had agents in New York, probably looking to raise more money or buy arms. He was apparently successful. All this was happening in the summer of 1856.[92]

Arjuria was an interesting character as well. He was a Spaniard who made his way to Mazatlán and gradually made money as a supercargo. He moved on to California and married into a wealthy family. Some speculate that he met Comonfort via business in Acapulco. Whatever the case, he agreed to lend Comonfort a substantial amount—some accounts say as much as $200,000—on the understanding that he would have an inside track in financing a Liberal government if Comonfort and his allies succeeded. He was, in other words, another *agiotista*—but not part of Santa Anna's exclusive clique. Ajuria was on the make; the ultimate failure of Comonfort himself shows this to have been a risky venture. But one clearly senses an attempt to break the monopoly over Mexican government finances and contracts that Manuel Julián Lizardi and Cayetano Rubio had enjoyed. Here was a new generation of bourgeois capitalists on the make who wanted in on the rewards of power. This, too, was an important part of the Reforma—arguably the most important part.[93]

One other point requires emphasis. While the costs of the Ayutla Revolution are unknown, they cannot have been insignificant. Anselmo de la Portilla suggests, whether correctly or not, that Santa Anna ran through 10 million pesos—the indemnity of the Mesilla purchase—well before being overthrown. The climactic siege and battle of Puebla (which had been under siege during the War of 1847 for a month!) in 1856 involved over 10,000 troops and 2,000 horses. The theater of conflict centered on Michoacán and Guerrero, but it spilled over into adjacent states as well. Santa Anna's government appears to have obtained the money to finance the battle (against Comonfort and Ajuria) from Manuel Julián de Lizardi, long Santa Anna's primary banker and *agiotista*, as well as from Manuel Escandón.[94] It may well be that the cost of the conflict was not much less, in financial terms, than the cost of the War of 1847: 2 percent of the total output would not be an unreasonable guess. If one considers the cumulative impact of such events in the nineteenth century, it is difficult not to conclude that they cost Mexico dearly. By 1856, the great bloodletting that would proceed the final restoration of the Republic in 1872, first overthrown in 1835, had scarcely begun.[95]

A key economic tenet of the incoming Liberal regime after the fall of Santa Anna was the need to vest property rights in the hands of individuals, both to create a broad class of owners and to provide correct incentives for economic development. Since the Catholic Church had historically evolved (through bequests, liens, and loans) as the Republic's largest "corporate" property owner—in Mexico City alone, the Church owned half the real estate—it was the immediate target of legislation. This law, the famous Ley Lerdo of June 25, 1856, was not an expropriation but an attempt to refashion the Church as a mortgage banker with the tenants of its properties as prospective purchasers, as well as the prospective consumption-driven backbone of a bourgeoisie. The details have been amply demonstrated by Bazant, and they are quite complex.[96]

While it may be tempting to make sweeping generalizations about the effects of the Ley Lerdo, in the short run, the creation of voluminous paperwork apart, little happened. In fact, as Bazant observes, the practical effect of the legislation after 1856 was to create massive uncertainty in the disposition of property rights. "The immediate results were rather chaotic. Many tenants did not pay rents, buyers could not pay interest and the corporations could not meet their commitments. In this sense, the economy was paralyzed." The Ley Lerdo did not produce an enormous boost to demand and growth in the short run. Indeed, precisely the opposite occurred. And when the Civil War broke out between the Liberals and Conservatives in 1858, the Ley Lerdo was cancelled where the Conservatives retook control. Since we are talking about 100,000,000 pesos of real estate, the result must have been utter chaos. Even Bazant is cautious in his conclusions about the transformative effect of the Reforma regarding the distribution of ecclesiastical urban properties. For the most part, it did not happen. And where it did, such as in Mexico City, an infinitesimally small proportion of the population was involved—perhaps one-tenth of 1 percent. Perhaps the bulk of ownership of clerical properties, such as *vecindades* (roughly apartment blocks), was concentrated mostly in the center of large cities such as Mexico, at least if the 1848 census of properties is representative.[97]

On the other hand, once the Reform War (1858–1860) broke out, the nationalization of clerical properties by the Liberals began in earnest in July 1859. The violence of the conflict was appalling, although it is difficult to put another estimate on what the costs of sustained instability may have been. On the one hand, an econometric study of the cotton textile industry finds no reason to think that industrial output was much affected. But there is so little evidence in the paper for 1858 through 1860 that it is difficult to know what to think. Worse the prefect in Orizaba in Veracruz explicitly complained about the paralyzed state of the important Cocolapam factory due to a shortage of cotton.[98] A detailed study of the agrarian economy of Querétaro during the war finds that maize prices shot up during the period. Haciendas there complained of demands affecting them from both Liberal and Conservative sides. Yet fluctuations in maize output may have been as much determined by a sharp drought as by anything else. Spending by Conservatives, financed primarily by the Catholic Church (to whom the Liberals were indeed a mortal threat) reached over 4.6 million pesos in 1858 alone that makes no allowance for output lost. By late 1859, the Liberal government was openly fulminating against the Church for a kind of "stripping of the altars," selling the Church jewels and chalices to support the Conservatives "turning them into infamous resources of vengeance and death."[99]

The abridgement of property rights was, ironically, established *by law.* "It is the duty of the inhabitants of the Republic to quarter troops on haciendas, ranchos, taverns and private buildings."[100] Thus, for example, the hacienda "Vaquerías" in Veracruz was commandeered as an outpost for 120 troops in July of 1860 "because it was useful for many military operations." Of course, such requisitions were to last only three days and be indemnified, but that was pure theory. Even great estates owned by politically powerful families such as the hacienda "Arroyozarco" in Aculco, an enormous producer of maize, wheat, and barley, were affected. The Constitutionalist (Liberal) general Zaragoza had to remind his commanders to "pay attention to the [owners'] rights under law and take only what was absolutely indispensable" and properly documented. It is unlikely that an ordinary property would be afforded such consideration.[101] The military then could shift the costs of war to the private sector. The effect on capital formation and productivity can only be imagined, whether it affects existing output figures or not. This is a reduction in *potential* output and not simply, and deceptively, an effect visible on realized production alone.

As to the human costs of the fighting, lives lost and cut short, there appears to be no comprehensive estimate for the Reform War. We might however give some account of lives lost in campaign, if for no other reason than to provide a sense of losses to which the contending forces were accustomed. In early 1859, the Liberals attempted to wrest control of Mexico City from the Conservatives. There are eyewitness accounts which put the size of the Liberal attacking force at 6,000 who "suffered grievous losses [and] such was the state of things that only 300 men of those who fought at Tacubaya returned to Tulancingo.[102] But all too often, the dead simply went uncounted: "Everyone who passed through the ravine in the days of the battle [of Atenquique between Guadalajara and Manzanillo] said the dead fusilier, covered the battlefield so thickly that all you could see was red and green, not to mention those who fell distant and could be carried away."[103] Body counts lay in the future.

We know too that fighting placed a heavy demand on human resources everywhere. An account of men and materiel supplied by Tamaulipas and the Huasteca for operations in the capital is revealing, and no doubt typical of what could be found elsewhere. From Tamaulipas: "A thousand armed men including two batteries of mountain artillery. Ammunition and arms for five thousand men. Food and Clothing for the same. All the resources that can be spared from the Aduana of Tampico." All told, Tamaulipas and villages in the Huasteca were expected to provide 5,580 men and their corresponding supply for two months. Since this was one of the more sparsely populated areas of the Republic at the time, the burden could have well amounted to between 2 percent and 2.5 percent of the total population, and presumably, a much larger fraction of the able-bodied men and resources required to provision them.[104]

Another approach to the problem of human costs is to examine what would happen to the wartime cohorts as they aged, in this case, using the Census of 1895. This was the first "modern" national census. While no one makes many claims for the accuracy of the results, the pattern that emerges in Figure 2.7 is, at least, plausible. The effects of the War of 1847 and the Reforma, if they had anything like the effects of the Insurgency, should have raised mortality and lowered fertility and possibly stimulated outmigration as well. All should be visible in the population pyramid to some degree, and they are, with "holes" for the "Generation of 1845" and for the "Generation of 1860 and Before." The point is that people who die, leave, or are never born neither produce nor consume. And these demographic effects of instability and warfare in the nineteenth century are everywhere visible. Small wonder the economy did not grow. The argument that political instability

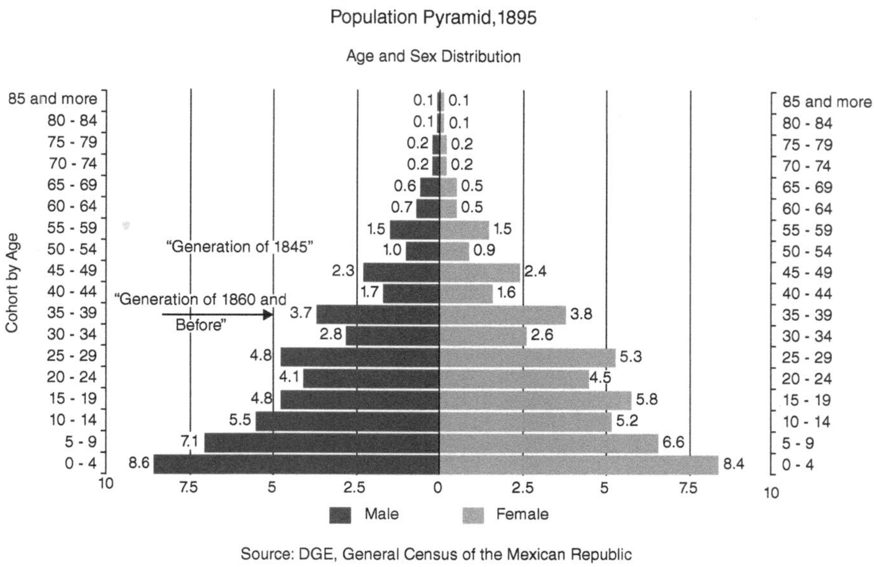

FIGURE 2.7 Mexico Population Pyramid, 1895

would have little effect on the real (or on the financial economy, as it turned out) is simply not tenable.

It is only too evident that continuing economic shocks produced by wars from the 1840s through the 1860s affected the potential output. Nor did the end of the Reform War bring a lasting peace, much less a settlement between Liberal and Conservative factions. Benito Juarez' moratorium on servicing the foreign debt in July 1861 brought a new round of conflict, this time provoked by the invasion of France, Spain, and Britain in 1862. While the British and Spanish soon withdrew, the French mounted a serious military campaign, ultimately dispatching an "expeditionary" force that reached over 30,000 foreign troops. French ambitions in Mexico included a sustainable source of Mexican silver—a goal of French imperial diplomacy since the eighteenth century—as well as blocking the hemispheric ambitions of the rising Anglo-Saxon power of the United States.[105]

The romantic tales of Maximilian and Charlotte and Cinco de Mayo notwithstanding, the French intervention turned into an extraordinarily violent affair, a guerilla war in which much blood was shed, and in which, after 1863, neutrality was simply impossible. And yet substantial human casualties, hardly the least of it, were once again not all. As during the Insurgency, trade and commerce throughout Mexico was badly disrupted. It was necessary for goods to move only with political authorization to keep them from falling into the "wrong" hands; so once again, exchange was disrupted. For example, a permission was granted to Chabot Brothers, merchants in Querétaro, to send 200 bundles of raw cotton to wherever it suited them, including the occupied territory, without interference.[106] Similar documents were issued to Chabot and other houses for paper, *mantas del país,* and cocoa to various destinations throughout the interior, an attempt to regulate internal trade similar to 1810. Alas, it did not always work. Manuel Julián de Lizardi, the owner of a textile mill in Celaya, "Cempoala," found one of his shipments seized by the Conservative General Tomás Mejía. It is not clear whether this was simply a mistake or an instance of Lizardi trying to sell to Liberals and finding his wares in the hands of his erstwhile conservative allies instead. This was how business was typically conducted during the French intervention, which lasted until 1867.[107]

The financial consequences of the French intervention were substantial. In 1864 and 1865, Mexico "borrowed" a nominal sum of 534 million French francs, very little of which ended up in Mexico. Most of the debt principal was ultimately repudiated by Mexico, so if we use $30 million, that amounts to about 10 percent of the output. If so, the French intervention ranks with the Insurgency as one of the costliest political shocks of the nineteenth century. Anyone who doubts this should read Manuel Payno's bitter conclusion to his account of French finances in Mexico during the Intervention. Payno was a partisan, true enough, and foreign financiers tended to dislike him intensely, but he rarely reached the palpable tone of anger and indignation that he did here (it has been periodically reprinted in Mexico). He knew looting when he saw it, unlike some modern economic historians.[108]

One question remains.[109] Did the shocks of the Reforma and the French intervention change the wage-rent ratio in any material way? In particular, the Ley Lerdo has been traditionally associated with the wholescale loss of indigenous "communal" lands, something that would have presumably mattered one way or the other. Yet historians in Mexico no longer regard this story as remotely accurate, looking instead to ecology, geography, social structure, and commercial accessibility as yielding a more convincing story about what transpired with corporate holdings in the long run. We take this up in our account of the Porfiriato, where changing land tenure and its causes and consequences are considered. For now, we can simply reject the "traditional" story of villages turning into large private holdings because of the Ley Lerdo as unfounded. As Romana Falcón observed, "The reality was far more complex than issuing laws or judicial resolutions" in the state of Mexico. In Oaxaca, Antonio Escobar Ohmstede found that the outcome was "a bit of everything."[110]

"Relative" Deindustrialization in Porfirian Mexico?

The name Antonio Peñafiel (1830–1922) in unlikely to appear in many histories of Porfirian Mexico. He was not an important banker, soldier, politician or diplomat. He was, by training, a medical doctor. But in his way, he was a polymath who typified the professional class of Porfirian society. From 1883 until 1910, he was the head of the statistical service (*Dirección General de Estadística* or DGE) within the Ministerio de Fomento, or Ministry of Development. An account of his work simply states, "With him, the era of uniform, systematized information began."[111] We can begin with some account of population and vital rates, selective to be sure, and incomplete. Peñafiel and his associates were under no illusions." It is regrettable that the tables in this *Anuario* [1893] are not complete; some of the responsible authorities do not submit the different classes of data requested, or they do so too late, once the publication was in press." (1893, vi). The First Census conducted by Peñafiel was in 1895; there is no question it is inaccurate. Yet for practical purposes, we can say that Mexico grew from about 9 million people in 1876 to 15 million in 1910, which is a (geometric) growth rate of 1.5 percent per year. This is in accordance with Robert McCaa's careful analysis of the nineteenth century.[112] Whether that represents a substantial discontinuity or not depends largely on whether one accepts what McCaa terms the "conventional" or "new" population estimates. By the "conventional" estimate of 1 percent a year, of course, the increase, while numerically small, is relatively large. But if we measure the interval between 1830 and 1870 using McCaa's "new series," the rate increases on to 1.1 percent, which is not negligible, but hardly earthshattering. And whether we compare 1.5 percent to 1.0 or 1.1 percent, the jump during the Porfiriato is still relatively impressive.

The natural question is the source of the increase. McCaa is impressed by the impact of war on mortality in Mexico City by drawing on Celia Maldonado's pioneering work. It is not much more than a strong impression at this point, but the increase is plausibly attributed to a decline in mortality and to a rise in the birth rate, both familiar products of warfare. It is difficult to underestimate the disruptiveness of civil strife on everyday life—perhaps not so much on the destruction of physical capital, although this was not trivial. Yet both the draft and the departure of soldiers from garrison towns impeded the normal frequency of sexual relations, a fact to which Del Raso in Querétraro obliquely alluded in 1829 and 1842. One suspects that the much maligned "Porfirian Peace," born of repression and oppression or not, had a positive spillover. Moreover, the economically active share of the population, which Del Raso pegged at a very low 25 percent in the Bajío, had risen to 39 percent in 1895, if INEGI estimates are to be credited.[113] The implications of these demographic changes are significant. Most people survived into their prime work years because of the reduction in the frequency of wars and invasions. They provided a larger labor force which could not only produce more but produce it more efficiently as well. Again, from INEGI data, the total real output doubled from 1877 through 1896 at about 3.5 percent per year. If population growth accounted for 1.5 percent of that, the remainder, 2 percent, was productivity increase. This, then, is the principal issue with which we must deal. What were the sources of productivity increase during the Porfiriato?

The change in the age structure of the population that the *Pax Porfiriana* brought undoubtedly contributed to the increase in productivity, although with the advent of the railroad, this could have scarcely been the principal source. It is simply a matter of numbers: the addition of even a few hundred thousand souls whose marginal productivity was significantly higher as they survived to a more productive age because widespread fighting ceased. It is not that this was trivial. But how large could it have been *relative* to the gains from railroads—both social savings and the dynamic gains from reallocation that changing regional comparative advantage brought. Since Summerhill places the social savings alone in Mexico at between 8 percent and 17 percent of GDP, it is difficult to think of *anything* that could produce comparable gains. A careful study by Simon Miller of the regional economy of Querétaro shows that the arrival of railroads there in 1882 opened new markets to hitherto purely local production; augmented land values; and provided a spur to mechanization—a development perceived in the region as nearly revolutionary and associated with commercial and financial modernization *tout court.* More evidence for this was the increasing presence of corn from the United States in Mexican markets, some 5 million bushels between 1883 and 1885 alone.[114]

How to capture these effects and to explain them is the challenge. Since railroads reduced transportation costs, they opened new lands to cultivation. This, in turn, coincided with a dramatic increase in the production of commodities such as henequen, rubber, chicle, dyewoods, coffee, beans, fresh fruit, hides, and chickpeas. Not all increased to the same extent; some of the increase was for the home market. Yet the composition of Mexico's exports, hitherto confined largely to precious metals, especially silver, was now decisively altered. Falling transportation costs make the conveyance and export of bulkier, low-value commodities possible, something literally impossible in the earlier nineteenth century when the price of wheat flour in Philadelphia had more to do with its price in Havana, even though wheat farmers in the Puebla-Tlaxcala basin could produce surpluses. Yet there was, until the 1880s, no point in increasing supply. It would simply encounter a regionally inelastic demand and drive, down prices, revenues, and profits. This phenomenon was one of the fundamental obstacles to Mexican development.[115]

Thanks to the efforts of Sandra Kuntz Ficker, it is now possible to analyze the reallocation of resources systematically.[116] In Table 2.1, we display a standard autoregressive model that uses kilometers of railroad built during the Porfiriato to "explain" the share of Mexican exports that are, essentially, something other than silver, the "traditional" colonial export. It is true there is no specific theory behind

TABLE 2.1 Railroad Mileage versus Share of Nontraditional Exports

Dependent Variable: Share of Nonmetallic Exports
$R^2_{(adjusted)} = 0.791$
D = 2.07
SER = 0.07
F = 21.477 (sig. 99 percent)
C = 0.536
Dependent Variable
RR kilometers (–1) = –1.32 ($\times 10^{-5}$)
RR kilometers (–2) = –2.79 ($\times 10^{-5}$)
RR kilometers (–3) = 6.57 ($\times 10^{-5}$) (sig. 90 percent)

this, but the results are consistent with what one might expect. The left-hand variable, non-silver exports, is explained by additional railroad kilometers, but only with a lag of three years. It took time for the economy (here using the period 1879–1906 because of data constraints) to adjust to changing transportation costs and relative prices as the railroads were built. As the adjustment occurs over time, the share of "nontraditional" exports begins to increase: regional specialization and comparative advantage begin to appear as markets become better integrated due to the growing railroad network. The result, one thinks, was something out of Adam Smith.[117]

We stated earlier that in terms of a model of factor endowments, the changes that occurred during the Porfiriato were truly revolutionary—in more sense than one. The expansion of the nontraditional export sector driven by Mexico's "transportation revolution" was merely one aspect of a far more complex set of changes. We need to examine these to understand why and how the country descended into Revolution in 1910, just as it had a century earlier. Again, Sandra Kuntz Ficker's work enables us to understand the features of these changes.

First, not only did the composition of Mexican trade change during the Porfiriato. Equally important, the volume and value of trade literally exploded from 1876 through 1910. Mexico was, in essence, transformed from an economy with very little international trade to one with a substantial external component. As Kuntz Ficker demonstrates, from 1870 to 1890, merchandise trade per capita was about $2 per head. By 1910, it had multiplied to $11 per head. From 1870 to 1920, the share of trade in GDP doubled.[118]

The most dramatic effect of the large-scale construction of railroads was to lower transportation costs and therefore to enlarge the commercially feasible proportion of the Republic.[119] In one case, the Mexicano, which was the initial line, constructed in 1873 between the capital and the Port of Veracruz, the reduction in cost per kilometer was on the order of 65 percent. On the Central, which ran between Paso del Norte (Ciudad Juárez) and Mexico City, the reduction was smaller, but still a substantial (nearly) 50 percent. This takes no account of the explosive branching that took place between 1898 and 1910 in the Center West, Center, and Center South of the Republic, although, according to Kuntz Ficker, the largest share of the fall took place before 1892. While historians disagree about the relative impact of the railroads on the growth of domestic versus exportable production—Kuntz Ficker is firmly in the camp of the "domestic" market—even the growth of internal trade led to the unification of hitherto unintegrated regional markets. In any case, while the areas sewn with maize and beans, staples of the popular diet, remained constant or even fell slightly between 1880 and 1910, exportables such as chickpeas, coffee, and henequen increased dramatically. Between 1900 and 1910, the area sewn with wheat also declined, but the production of exportable hardwoods increased, as did that of ordinary timber or mesquite, which was hardly an exportable. In other words, there is no doubt that the railroads led to an increase in "land" that far outstripped the growth of "labor" in Porfirian Mexico. The modification of exportables in favor of resource-based commodities certainly makes sense in terms of a Ricardian model of factor endowments, but it is also a model that finds the sources of growth and development—or their absence—in international trade. Domestic, monetary, and institutional factors figure less prominently, which is far from the current consensus in Mexican economic history, insofar as there is a consensus at all.

There are, moreover, other complications. Moramay López Alonso's work on the height of Mexican soldiers during the Porfiriato, a reliable indicator of popular well-being, concludes that "the dictatorship of Porfirio Díaz did not improve the biological standard of the working classes." The distinction drawn between the wealthy upper classes—mostly property owners—and the working class is supported by anthropometric evidence.[120]

An effort at applying a Human Development Index to Porfirian Mexico finds substantial regional inequality, some persisting from the early nineteenth century, if not before. There is evidence that the North gained, but that the Center did not. And finally, Javier Arnaut's work on disaggregated real wages tells much the same story: real wages in the North rose. Elsewhere, they stagnated.[121] Mexico's internal economy grew substantially during the Porfiriato, but there were clear winners and losers, if only in a relative sense. And it is not as if they were any mechanism—or political desire—for the gainers to compensate the losers, which only added to the potential combustibility of the situation. The real question is to what extent these divergences were tied to an expansion of export growth.

Jeffrey Williamson's Ricardian trade model argued that early nineteenth-century Mexico did not deindustrialize because the improvement in the net barter terms of trade was modest (with British cottons as the principal import). With some modification—the deliberate use of domestic spending to encourage industry, particularly by military contracts—this argument is acceptable. However, after 1870, as Sandra Kuntz Ficker (and Jeffrey Williamson and Gómez Galvarriato) observed, the net barter terms of trade fell by 40 to 50 percent, depending on whose calculations one prefers.[122] The importance of cotton textiles in the import basket fell as capital goods and industrialization rose and as import substitution in cotton textiles expanded, as Gómez Galvarriato has emphasized. So Mexico certainly did not deindustrialize in any *absolute* sense. The dramatic depreciation of the Mexican peso because of the fall of the price of silver relative to gold starting in the late 1870s was substantial. Between 1882 and 1902, the peso, measured in US dollars, fell by 62 percent, and this alone was enough to provide a dramatic stimulus to agricultural commodity exports and a substantial measure of compensation against an equally sharp fall in the level of tariff protection (as measured by the implicit tariff level) over much of the same period. Finally, falling transportation costs should have raised the prices that exporters received for their output—particularly in agriculture, as shown in Table 2.1—even as they worked to lower effective tariff protection to Mexican industry. Out of this complex vector of offsetting and sometimes confounding forces, a striking result occurred. While the aggregate data are, at best, uncertain, it is fair to conclude that industrial production in Porfirian

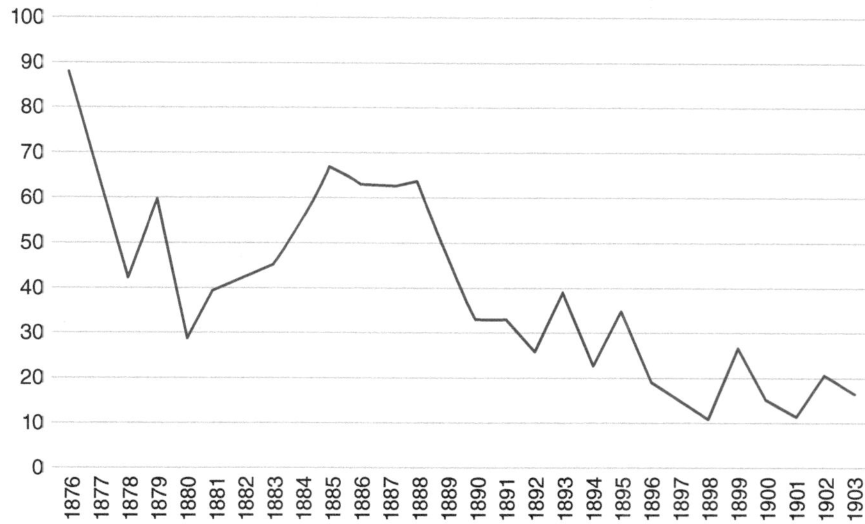

FIGURE 2.8 Wage-Rent Ratio in Porfirian Mexico

Mexico rose absolutely but *declined* somewhat as a share of total output as agricultural exportables surged. This is what Williamson terms *relative* rather than absolute deindustrialization. It is supported by Coatsworth's calculation of output shares in Porfirian Mexico in which manufactures declined.

But more importantly, our calculation of the wage-rent ratio in Porfirian Mexico provides even more striking evidence of the inequality of results, much as does López-Alonso's anthropometric data. In Figure 2.8, we show the wage-rent ratio for Mexico. For Porfirian Mexico between 1876 and 1903, years for which we have data. From1876 to 1880, undoubtedly driven by the depreciation of the silver peso, the ratio declines sharply, by nearly 70 percent, only to recover somewhat through the late 1880s. But another sustained decline begins around 1888 and continues until 1903, with another decline of nearly 70 percent. This is about what one would expect in a land-rich country, which, effectively, the development of the rail network had done: it raised the commercially viable portion of the Republic significantly and produced a boom in commodity exports like coffee, sugar, henequen, tropical wood, and similar goods. This in turn, drove up land rents relative to wages, produced an increased share of agricultural output, and even, if one examines the available data for maize prices from places like Querétaro, coincided with a rise in prices that implied a rise in nominal wages in manufacturing. These results are consistent with Jeffrey Williamson's "Ricardian" work, but with a distinctly Mexican turn.[123]

There can be only one conclusion to the analysis. Porfirian Mexico was indeed marked by a return to economic growth, the first such sustained period in the nineteenth century. But the bulk of the gains in productivity went to landowners and capitalists rather than to workers. And so, just as in 1810, a political crisis in 1910—the overthrow of Porfirio Díaz by Francisco Madero—became the catalyst for the convulsive unwinding of social inequality that had marked Mexico since the Conquest, if not before. The one period of progressive redistribution and growth since the 1840s would now be decisively undone. Intermittent episodes of violent instability had cost Mexico dearly after Independence, holding the country back. The cycle was about to be repeated.

These are, of course, highly tentative findings. Walter Scheidel has considered the question of war and inequality in traditional agrarian societies; his answers are hardly straightforward. Mexico may well have been one of those cases where cycles of reduced and then recovering inequality stretched across the nineteenth century from the Insurgency to the Porfiriato and then, in the Revolution, back again. Calls for additional research are clichés, but the answer to this most important question lies in the archives, and not in some ideological formulation about the inevitable impact of one particular economic system or another. Scheidel admits that "civil war rarely functioned as a source of leveling, except under exceptionally persistent circumstances, such as an intentional social and economic revolution." In Mexico, this remains to be seen.[124]

Notes

1 Amilcar E. Challu and Aurora Gómez-Galvarriato, "Mexico's Real Wages in the Age of the Great Divergence, 1730–1930," *Revista de Historia Económica. Journal of Iberian and Latin American Economic History* 33 (2015): 83–122. Also see Elías Gaona, "Real Wages Index of a Mining Family in Real del Monte 18th and 19th Century," *América Latina en la Historia Económica* 29 (2022), https://doi/org.10.18232/20073496.1230.

2 Simon Miller, "Agrarian Capitalism in Central Mexico: From Hacienda to Rancho in the State of Queretaro, 1845–1900" (PhD thesis, Durham theses, Durham (UK) University, 1983), accessed May 20, 2024, http://etheses.dur.ac.uk/view/creators/Miller=3ASimon=3A=3A.html.

3 Statements like these are subject to much uncertainty. The fall in coinage from the mint and other shocks to trade may have actually pushed prices down in some places, i.e., monetary forces may have produced deflation (via a premium on pesos from the mint in Mexico City,) while a fall in the supply of real goods would have worked in the other direction. It is simply impossible to know what the net effect would have been, other than to note that they sparked loud protests from merchants in Jalisco as late as the elevation of Iturbide to Emperor. See the Ayuntamiento of Guadalajara to The Emperor, Guadalajara, August 3, 1821, Archivo de la Secretaría de Defensa Nacional (SEDENA henceforth), exp. 199.

4 Seignorage (money creation) is associated with the campaign against Texas. See El Gobernador del Departamento de Querétaro, Querétaro, January 5, 1837, and other documents in F1331H5, v. 17, Fondo Fernando Díaz Ramírez, Capilla Alfonsina, Universidad Autónoma de Nuevo León, accessed July 9, 2024, http://cdigital.dgb.uanl.mx/la/1020004042/1020004042.html.

5 José Martín Hurtado Galves, *El Ejército Realista en la Ciudad de Querétaro, 1810–1826*, 2 vols (Querétaro, Mexico: Poder Ejecutivo, 2019), 1: 698, with much on 257–66 on troops fighting.

6 M. Gutiérrez, *Apuntes para servir a la estadística minera del Estado de Querétaro* (Mexico City: Jens y Zapiain, 1875), 8.

7 Ayuntamiento of Salvatierra to Agustín Iturbide, May 7, 1821, SEDENA, exp. 100.
8 "Edicto instructivo que el ilustrísimo don Manuel Abad y Queipo, obispo electo de Michoacán, dirige a sus diocesanos," Valladolid, September 30, 1810, in *Colección de Documentos para la Historia de la Guerra de Independencia de México, 1808–1821*, 6 vols, ed. Juan E. Hernández y Dávalos (Mexico City, 2010). de Alfredo Ávila y Virginia Guedea, ed., *CD ROM* (Universidad Nacional Autónoma de México), 3: 159.
9 "Lista que presenta el Ayuntamiento de Jarquillo . . . de los individuos que han satisfecho el dinero de donativo," October 21, 1821, SEDENA, exp. 100.
10 Carlos Alberto Ortega González, *El Ocaso de Un Imperio. El Diezmo en el Arzopbispado en México, 1810–1833* (Mexico City: Instituto Mora, 2015), 9, 174.
11 For the cost of the royalist army in Querétaro, see José Martín Hurtado Galves, "El Ejército Realista en la Ciudad de Querétaro, 1810–1821," in *Nómadas. Revista Crítica de Ciencias Sociales y Jurídicas* (Universidad Complutense De Madrid, 2012), accessed May 21, 2024, https://doi.org/10.5209/rev_NOMA.2012.41787.
12 "Seminario de la Historia de la Armada Mexicana" (Lecture of October 13, 2021), accessed May 21, 2024, https://youtube/Cqsa5Z2UR5w.
13 José Antonio Del Raso, *Notas Estadísticas del Departamento de Querétaro* (Mexico City: Mariano Lara, 1848), 97, 99.
14 Del Raso, *Notas Estadísticas*, 36.
15 Formally, a Unit Root with Break Test on the PDSI locates the break at 1814, significant at 99 percent. For harvests, see Archivo Histórico Arzobispado de Mexico, Fondo Cabildo, Sec. Haceduría, Ser. Jueces Hacedores, and Caja 4, "Instrucción de la Colecturia de Querétaro," Querétaro, May 17, 1823.
16 Margaret Rankine, "The Mexican Mining Industry in the Nineteenth Century with Special Reference to Guanajuato," *Bulletin of Latin American Research* 11 (1992): 29–48, esp. 29. Alfonso Luis Velasco, *Geografía y Estadística de la República Mexicana: Guanajuato* (Mexico City: Secretaría de Fomento, 1890), 156–57 for mining data and the post-Insurgency slump.
17 José Joaquín de Eguía, *Memoria sobre la utilidad é influjo de la minería en el reino; necesidad de su fomento y arbitrios de verificarlos* (Mexico City: Oficina de don Juan Bautista Arizpe, 1819).
18 Robert W. Randall, *Real del Monte. A British Silver Mining Venture in Mexico* (Austin, TX: University of Texas Press, 1972), 170. Rankine, "Mexican Mining," 34.
19 Challu and Gómez Galvarriato, "Mexico's Real Wages," 103. Jeffrey Williamson, *Trade and Poverty. When the Third World Fell Behind* (Cambridge, MA: MIT Press, 2013), 119–43. R.J. Salvucci, "Algunas consideraciones económicas. Análisis mexicano de la depresión a principios del siglo XIX." *Historia Mexicana* 55 (1836; 2005): 67–97, accessed May 21, 2024, https://historiamexicana.colmex.mx/index.php/RHM/article/view/1501.
20 Mexico Dirección General de la Industria Nacional, *Memoria sobre el Estado de la Agricultura e Industria de la República, en el año de 1844: que la Dirección General de estos ramos presenta al Gobierno Supremo en cumplimiento del Artículo 26 del decreto orgánico de 2 de diciembre de 1842* (Mexico City: Imprenta de Lara, 1845), accessed July 11, 2024, https://cd.dgb.uanl.mx/handle/201504211/15725.
21 Robert Crichton Wyllie, *México. Noticia Sobre Su Hacienda Pública Bajo el Gobierno Español y Después de la Independencia* (Mexico City: Ignacio Cumplido, 1845), Sec. VI, "Sobre Si el Establecimiento en la República Mexicana de Fábricas de Hilados y Tejidos de algodón promueve o retarda su prosperidad. . . ." See also Aurora Gómez Galvarriato, "Ni Sur, ni Norte: la industria textil mexicana en la historia global del algodón," *H-industria*, accessed June 28, 2024, https://ojs.econ.uba.ar/index.php/H-ind/article/view/3031/3899.
22 Evelyne Sánchez, *Las élites empresariales y la independencia de Mexico. Estevan de Antuñano o las vicisitudes del fundador de la industria textil moderna (1792–1847)* (Mexico City: Plaza y Valdés, 2013).

23 Rafael Mangino, *Observaciones del Contador Mayor de Hacienda sobre la cuenta . . . del año 1825* (Mexico City: Secretaría de Hacienda, 1826). Biblioteca Nacional de España, Colección Digital, Mss 13255, paragraphs 181–86. Taking the published military spending figures literally in this period requires a willing suspension of disbelief, to put it mildly. If you take Mexican budget figures for this period literally, especially for the military, you are asking for trouble. They are literally incredible according to this careful report written by the long-time civil servant Rafael Mangino.

24 Richard J. Salvucci, *Politics, Markets and Mexico's "London Debt," 1823–1887* (Cambridge, UK: Cambridge University Press, 2009), passim.

25 See the 3-million peso contract awarded in 1832 in SEDENA, exp. 1871.

26 Rubio to Gen Mariano Paredes, August 20, 1845, in *La situación política, militar y económica de la República Mexicana al iniciarse su guerra con los Estados Unidos* (1989; Mexico City: Ignacio B del Castillo, 1913), 136–37.

27 Del Raso, *Notas Estadísticas*, 61–62. Under conventional assumptions of family size, this implies a per capita income of somewhere in the low 30+ peso range, which is consistent with Del Raso's other data.

28 [José] Antonio del Raso, *Refutación del Proyecto monárquico extranjero de Don José María Gutiérrez Estrada* (Mexico City: Imprenta de Galván, 1840), 13–14.
Everyone is aware of the deficiencies of parish records. And they go far beyond whether or not some vital event was recorded to the more basic question of *who* had the right or duty to maintain the record. Accounting for this second-order problem is not usually considered, but it was there from the eighteenth century onward. See Marcela Dávalos, *Los letrados interpretan la ciudad: Los barrios de indios en el umbral de la Independencia* (Mexico City: Instituto Nacional de Antropología e Historia, 2009), 18–29.

29 There are some inconsistences. Some sources point to a large population loss in the state in 1833–1834 due to the cholera morbus epidemic. This is not reflected in del Raso. See David Carbajal López, *Epidemias en el Obispado de Guadalajara: la muerte masiva en el primer tercio del siglo xix* (Zapopan, JAL: Editorial Página Seis, 2017), 122.

30 Frankly, the difference between lost parish records and incomplete records is observationally equivalent. One is as big a problem as another when a researcher tries to allow for deficiencies. There is no reason to assume the inaccuracy is either greater or reduced.

31 Sebastián Camacho, *Estadística del Estado Libre y Soberano de Veracruz* (Jalapa, VER: Oficina del Gobierno, 1831), 127.

32 Del Raso, *Estadísticas*, 114.

33 Demetrio Mejía, *Estadística de la mortalidad en México* (Mexico City: Impreso de Ignacio Escalante, 1879), 19. Also see Carbajal López, *Epidemias en el obispado de Guadalajara,* Chapter I.

34 The customary age for the leva for males was between 16 and 50. This is just another way of saying the army would pass through, seize likely looking males, and impress them into the ranks after shaving their heads. See Anselmo de la Portilla, *Historia de la Revolución de México Contra la Dictadura del General Santa Anna, 1853–1855* (1856; Mexico City: Fondo de Cultura Económica, 1993), 74.
By definition, GDP is (hours of work*labor productivity). Growth is the sum of the growth in the labor input plus growth in productivity. Among other factors, the age composition of the population is related to the growth of the labor input (excluding those too old or young). A smaller working-age population—absent productivity change—implies reduced production, or, at least, potential production.

35 Mark Joseph Mairot, "Mexican Provincial Society During the Age of Revolution: A Social and Economic History of Toluca, 1790–1834" (PhD diss., UCLA, 2013), 131. Ortega González, *Ocaso de un impuesto*, 174.

36 *Memoria en que El Gobernador del Estado Libre de Coahuila y Texas Da Cuenta De Los Ramos De Su Administación* (Monclova: Imprenta del Supremo Gobierno del Estado,

1834), "Plan Que Manifiesta La Población del Estado según los censos remitidos por los Ayuntamientos en el año de 1833," accessed May 22, 2024, https://id.lib.uh.edu/ark:/84475/do2832r6040.

37 Andrew J. Torget, *Seeds of Empire. Cottom, Slavery, and the Transformation of the Texas Borderlands (1800–1850)* (Chapel Hill, NC: University of North Carolina Press, 2015), 57–96, 179–218.
Texas was entirely another matter. The demand for labor there was so strong that in the 1830s and 1840s, there was a clandestine slave trade from Cuba. Evidence: For one thing, the Law of One Price operates: the ratio of slave prices in Cuba to Texas dropped from 1.74 (1837) to 1.07 (1845). For another, the British Consul at Galveston admitted to 200 African slaves imported from Cuba ("the Havana") in 1832–1842, but acknowledged he really had no precise information; the convergence of prices suggests quite another story. See Charles Stuart to the Foreign Secretary, Galveston, July 25, 1843, FO 84/479, National Archives, Kew, Middlesex, United Kingdom. For Cuban slave prices (fieldhands) see Laird Bergad, Fe Iglesias García, and María del Carmen Barcia, *The Cuban Slave Market* (New York, NY: Cambridge University Press, 1995), 77. For Texas slave prices, see Randolph B. Campbell, *An Empire for Slavery. The Peculiar Institution in Texas, 1821–1865* (Baton Rouge, LA: Louisiana State University Press, 1989), Table 2. There are references to the slave trade with Cuba throughout the volume that make the 200 number very doubtful, convergence of prices apart.

38 Del Raso, *Estadística de Querétaro Relativa a la Población* (Querétaro: Imp. Francisco Frías, 1846), 8. Formal attempts to measure through appropriate regression dummies produced correct signs, but at less than customary levels of significance. But del Raso did not think that instability did not matter.

39 Archivo Histórico Arzobispado de México, Fondo Cabildo, Sec. Haceduría, Ser. Jueces Hacedores, to the Contaduría Nacional de Diezmos, Caja 3, Exp. 3, July 9, 1823 and Juan José García and Sabás Antonio Domínguez to the Secretary of the Diputación Provincial de Querétaro, June 30, 1823, discussing seizures of funds in San Juan del Río and Cadereyta to pay the Army.

40 Raymond Goldsmith, "An Estimate of the Size and Structure of the National Product of the Early Roman Empire," *Review of Income and Wealth* 30 (1984): 263–88, accessed May 23, 2024, https://doi.org/10.1111/j.1475-4991.1984.tb00552.x.

41 Del Raso, *Notas Estadisticas,* 78 is my source.

42 Through the mid-1840s, the common figure for the consumption of a "typical" Mexican was 1 real per day, or about 45 pesos per year. See *Observaciones imparciales acerca de administración financiera en la época del gobierno provisional* (Mexico City: J.M. Lara, 1845), 15. To vote under the Bases Orgánicas of 1843, the required property income was 200 pesos per year, which is far from an elite income.

43 Aurora Gómez-Galvarriato, "Una breve historia de la tortilla de maíz," September 30, 2019, Secretaría de Economía México, accessed May 23, 2024, www.youtube.com/watch?v=LVFa36cy20w. Also see Elizaberth Schillingo, "Las jardines flotantes de Xochimilco (1938) in Rojas Rabiela, *La agricultura chinampera,* 134.

44 All are calculated from Del Raso, *Notas Estadísticas*, 44, 45, 38, 88.

45 See José Oscar Ávila Juárez, *Cayetano Rubio y la Compañía Hércules y la Industrialización Queretana en el siglo XIX* (Querétaro, MX: Universidad Autónoma de Querétaro, 2018), 43–74.

46 Margaret Chowning, *Wealth and Power in Provincial Mexico. Michoacán From the Late Colony to the Revolution* (Stanford, CA: Stanford University Press, 1999), 122–200. Jan Bazant, *Alienation of Church Wealth in Mexico. Social and Economic Aspects of the Liberal Revolution, 1856–1875* (Cambridge, UK: Cambridge University Press, 1971), 35.

47 Carlos Sánchez Silva, *Indios, comerciantes y burocracia en la Oaxaca poscolonial, 1786–1860* (Oaxaca, MX: Instituto Oaxaqueño de la Culturas, 1998), 45–46, 77–79, 101–4, 218.

48 Most recently, Peter Guardino, *The Dead March. A History of the Mexican American War* (Cambridge, MA: Harvard University Press, 2017).

49 Curtis F. Morgan, Jr., "Nathaniel Greene as Quartermaster General," *Journal of the American Revolution* (November 8, 2013), accessed May 24, 2024, https://allthingsliberty.com/2013/11/nathanael-greene-quartermaster-general/.

50 Ramón Alcaraz et al., *Apuntes para la historia de la Guerra entre México y los Estados Unidos* (1848; Mexico City: Secretaría de Cultura, 2005), 115.

51 "Partes del Gral. José Urréa, Comandante General de los Edos internos de Oriente . . . dando cuente de la falta de recursos de la División de su mando, así como del desembarque de fuerzas norteamericanas en Tampico (1847)," SEDENA, Exp. 2742.

52 These were consistently reported sums. See *Duties, Revenue and Public Expenditure*, US Congress, House, 30th Congress, 1st session, Executive Document 82, August 12, 1848, 218, 238. Also see George Gibson to the US Sec of War, Washington, DC, November 9, 1847, and following tables *Estimations of Appropriations. Letter From the Secretary of the Treasury*, US Congress, House, 29th Congress, 1st session, Executive Document 2, December 6, 1847, 91–94.

53 Joaquín Rea to the War Ministry, Atlixco, October 24, 1847, SEDENA, Exp. 2734. Paul G. Pierapaoli, Jr., "Joaquín Rea," in *The Encyclopedia of the Mexican-American War*, 3 vols, ed. Spencer C. Tucker (Santa Barbara, CA: ABC-CLIO), 2: 439–42, 546.

54 SEDENA, Mexico, Exp. 2335. The communication containing Ampudia's request was dated the night of September 25, 1846, but did not reach Santa Anna until September 30, by which time the engagement was over. Steven E. Siry and Spencer C. Tucker, "Battle of Monterrey," in *Mexican-American War*, ed. Spencer C. Tucker (Santa Barbara, CA: ABC-CLIO), Jr., 2: 439–42. For what it's worth, the *Encyclopedia* is a good reference work, but it does not seem to have included much from the Mexican archives. Mexican commanders inevitably discussed resource constraints in graphic terms in their communications and typically did not hold back. The same could also be said of the discussion of Rea in Puebla.

55 Manuel Balbontín, *La invasión Americana, 1846–1848: Apuntes del subteniente de artillería Manuel Balbontín* (Mexico City: Ignacio Cumplido, 1888), 84.

56 Samuel Chamberlain, *My Confession [1846–1848]* (New York: Harper and Brothers, 1956), 114–30.

57 See Alcaraz et al., *Apuntes para la historia de la Guerra,* 139–65, 165 for the loss figure. There are contemporary archival records in SEDENA of Mexican battle losses and prisoners of war, but some were inaccessible for technical reasons.

58 Relación de los Generales, Jefes y Oficiales que en su calidad de prisioneros están en esta Ciudad, Querétaro, November 4, 1847, SEDENA, exp. 2679.

59 Javier Torres Medina, *Centralismo y reorganización. La Hacienda pública y la administración durante la primera república central de Mexico, 1835–1842* (México: Instituto Mora, 2013), 219, 235. *Observaciones imparciales de la Administración financiera en la época del gobierno provisional* (Mexico City: J.M. de Lara, 1845), 12–18.

60 Harold N. Boyer, Sr., "Naval Blockade," in *Mexican War*, ed. Spencer C. Tucker, 1: 72–73. *Tariff Duties in the Ports of Mexico*, US Congress, House, 30th Congress, 2nd session, Executive Document 20, 2–7. A lengthy series of Executive Orders beginning in March 1847 clarified duties, procedures, authorities, etc. See, for example, "All Ports held by U.S. may remain subject to duties payable to U.S. to finance cost of war. The Secretary of Treasury to set up tariff schedule," March 23, 1847, accessed August 31, 2020, https//:congressional.proquest.com/congressional/docview/t67.d72.1847-17-23?accountid=7103.

61 *El Monitor Republicano,* August 12, 1846. Also see *Dos palabras al Ecsmo. Sr. Presidente de la República sobre la suspensión general de pagos* (Mexico City: 1846).

62 "Presupuesto," in Ministro de Guerra y Marina, *Decreto del supremo gobierno de la República sobre arreglo del ejército* (Querétaro, MX: J.M. Lara, 1847), 45.

63 *El Monitor Republicano*, January 4, 1847.

64 *Messages From the President of the United States. Communicating Information Relating to Military Preparations in Anticipation of War*, US Congress, Executive, 28th Congress, 1st session, May 15, 1844; *Report of the Secretary of the Treasury on the State of Finances*, US Congress, 29th Congress, 1st session, December 1845, 2; *Message of the President of the United States . . . Relative to the Mode of Raising Funds for Carrying on the War with Mexico*, US Congress, 29th Congress, 1st session, June 16, 1846, esp. 4, 11. Even allowing for disparities in the number of troops deployed Mexican estimates were based on a force of 20,000; the United States assumed 30,000. Disparity in spending could not simply be attributed to differences in the size of the army.

65 For the best survey on the department level, see Josefina Vázquez, coord., *Mexico al tiempo de su Guerra con los Estados Unidos* (México: Fondo de Cultura Económica, 1997), esp. 104–33.

66 Jan Bazant, *Cinco haciendas mexicanas. Tres siglos de vida rural en San Luis Potosí (1600–1910)* (Mexico City: El Colegio de México, 1975), 49, 69. Also see María del Carmen Salinas Sandoval, *Política interna e invasión norteamericana en el Estado de Mexico, 1846–1847* (Toluca, MEX: 2000), 38–39. Adame may have got payback when the war was over. He was arrested, ostensibly for plotting with Genl Paredes, to continue the war. Juan S. Amadaor to the Minister of War and Marine, San Luis Potosi, March 4, 1848, SEDENA, exp. 2781. Also see Announcement from the Governor of San Luis Potosí, Ramón Adame, to his fellow citizens, August 25, 1847, accessed May 24, 2024, https: digital.lib.uh.edu/collection/1969_027/item/556/show/554.

67 Mariano Paredes y Arrillaga, *Contestaciones habidas entre los Exmos. Señores Generales de División D. Mariano Paredes de Arillaga, D Mariano Arista y el Supremo Gobierno por las que solo falta cualquiera clase de recurso por mesquinos que hubieran sido para que todo el Ejército de reserva marchara al norte . . .* (San Luis Potosí: Imprenta del Estado, 1845), esp. 5.

68 González Cosío to the Minister of Home and Foreign Relations, Zacatecas, May 25, 1847, Legajos Encuadernados 1089, exp. 7, Archivo de la Secretaría de Relaciones Exteriores, México (hereafter, ASREM).

69 Francisco V Serra and Yldefonso Castillo to the Minister of Home and Foreign Relations, Ciudad Victoria, July 8, 1847. Also see "Memoria que presenta el Teniente Colonel don Ángel Miramón al Excelentísimo Presidente de la República," México, June 24, 1847, both in Legajos Encuadernados 1090, exp. 3, ASREM.

70 Andrés Reséndez, "Política transnacional entre Texas y Tamaulipas en el siglo xix o las peripecias del general José María de Jesús Carvajal," in *El territorio disputado en la guerra de 1846–1848*, coords. Danna A. Levin Rojo and Martha Ortega (Mexico City: Miguel Ángel Porrúa, 2007), 47–73.

71 Legajos Encuadernados, 1089, exp. 7, ASREM. "Sobre Defensa de Aquel Estado [Guanajuato]," Guanajuato, April 9, 1847, SEDENA, Exp. 2458.

72 A remarkable survey of human and other resources available in the departments of Durango, Chihuahua, Zacatecas, and Nuevo Mexico in early 1846 concluded that there were fewer than 2,000 armed men available to throw up against the advancing US forces. No money, no men, and little prospect of finding more.

73 "Memo for General Wool," Monterrey, March 11, 1848, John E. Wool Papers (1810–1869), Box 28, folder 13, New York State Library, New York, http://nysl.nysed.gov/msscfa/sc15361.htm, and folders 10–14 more generally for much useful quartermaster data.

74 Guardino, *Dead March*, 154–55.

75 "Presupuesto," in *Decreto del supremo gobierno de la República: sobre arreglo del ejército*.

76 Daniel Wilson to Magoun and Co., New Orleans, December 16, 1846, Col. 230, Deputy-Quartermaster General, New Orleans, LA, July 18, 1846, in "Mexican War Correspondence," 598. T. Cross to Lt Col T F Hunt, Corpus Christi Camp, March 6, 1846, 652.

77 José Dios Pérez Gálvez, Mexico City, September 18, 1846, 1ª sección, AGNM.
78 One's impression is that the Mexican Army was more likely to simply appropriate things than were the Americans, for which money was never an issue. Recall the scene in Manuel Payno's canonical *Bandidos of Río Frío* where the Mexican Army simply devastates the lawyer's Lamparilla's ranch, consuming the maize crop or slaughtering literally any edible animal. This may have simply reflected a liberal intellectual's distaste for the army because we know there were contratistas who supplied the Mexican Army. Yet there was an element of "winning hearts and minds" to the Americans' approach, at least among its General Staff in the North, where political loyalties were suspect. Which, of course, did not mean that material atrocities did not take place—only that they were not policy.
79 Clara Elena Suárez Argüello, "Sequía y crisis en el transporte novohispano en 1794–1795," *Historia Mexicana* 44 (1985): 400. See also "La quiebra de una casa de conductos Novohispana en los inicios del siglo xix: Sus causas," *Historia Mexicana* 56 (2007): 836.
80 Manueletto de Sandoval to the Minister of Home and Foreign Relations, Mexico City, October 13, 1846, Legajos Encuadernados, 1085, exp. 25. ASREM.
81 *See Carlos Marichal, Bankruptcy of Empire. Mexican Silver and the Wars Between Spain, Britain and France, 1760–1810* (New York, NY: Cambridge University Press, 2007), 223–24.
82 The 6-percent figure excludes war pensions. Adding them would drive the cost to 8 percent in terms of nominal GDP of 1847, although strictly speaking, later payments should be reduced to the present value. The figures are derived from James William Cummings, "Financing the Mexican War" (PhD diss., Oklahoma State University, 2003), 279. Also Emory Upton, *The Military Policy of the United States During the Mexican War*, US Congress, House, 63rd Congress, 2nd session, 1914, 220–21.
83 A guesstimate might place the total loss of population because of territorial loss and casualties in 1848 at a quarter of a million. Mexico lost half of its territory. But it did not lose half of its population. Hence, strictly speaking, the ratio of population to land rose. Also see John Tutino, "The Revolution in Mexican Independence: Insurgency and the Renegotiation of Property, Production and Patriarchy in the Bajío, 1800–1855," *Hispanic American Historical Review* 78 (1998): 367–418. Challú and Gómez Galvarriato, "Mexico's Real Wages," 102.
84 Perhaps still best captured in spirit by R. Preston McAfee's "American Economic Growth and the Voyage of Columbus," *American Economic Review* 73 (1983): 735–40.
85 It might be helpful to continue to follow Querétaro into the 1850s and 1860s, but the standard treatment describes fluctuations in the nature and size of landholdings unhelpfully. See María Eugenia García Ugarte, *Breve historia de Querétaro* (Mexico City: Fondo de Cultura Económica, 1999), 157–71.
86 Secretaría de Hacienda y Crédito Público, *Breves indicaciones que manifiestan la urgente necesidad de establecer un nuevo sistema de hacienda que reemplace al que actualmente rige en el Imperio Mexicano* (Mexico City: Imprenta Literaria, 1864), 22.
87 *Breves indicaciones*, 45.
88 Potash, *Banco de Avío*, 148.
89 José Sánchez Trujillo, *Proyecto sobre productos y recursos de Hacienda* (Mexico City: M. Murgía, 1865), 48. Both Sánchez Trujillo and *Breves indicaciones* may owe their agricultural figure to Sebastián Lerdo de Tejada's *Cuadro sinóptico de la República Mexicana en 1856* (Mexico City: Ignacio Cumplido, 1856), 25 which provides similar data.
90 Challú and Gómez Galvarriato, "Mexico's Real Wages."
91 Compare with Carlos de Jesús Becerril Hernández, "La Legislación Tributaria del Segundo Imperio Mexicano, 1864–1867" (Unpub. Master's thesis, Instituto Mora, 2012), 157, which comes to roughly the same conclusion.

92 (?) Report of Consul of Mexico City in New York (reservado), México, June 16, 1856, SEDENA, Exp. 5376. "Another Revolution in Mexico," *New York Times,* June 9, 1856; Anselmo de la Portilla, *Historia de la Revolucion en México Contra la Dictadura de Santa Anna 1853–1855* (1856; México: Fondo de Cultura Económica, 1993), 157–60; *El Universal*, March 24, 1855 for Santa Anna's weapons purchases.
93 On Ajuria, see Maria del Carmen Reyna and Jean Paul Krammer, *La familia Ajuria* (México: INAH, 2014). Also see Andrés Molina Enríquez, *Los grandes problemas nacionales*, repr. ed. (1909; Mexico City: Ediciones Era, 1978), 433. Bazant, *Alienation of Church Wealth,* Makes a similar point, 67–68.
94 See Guillermo Prieto's commentary in *El Siglo XIX,* October 27, 1856, 4. Nicole Girón, "Manuel Payno: El Ir y Venir por la Secretaría de Hacienda," in *Los Secretarios de Hacienda y sus Proyectos (1821–1933)*, 2 vols, coord., Leonor Ludlow (Mexico City: Universidad Nacional Autónoma de México, 2002), 1: 379–80.
95 Foldout in Portilla, *Historia de la Revolución,* "Ejército de Operaciones sobre Puebla," March 6, 1856. The claim that the government had spent about 70 percent of the Mesilla indemnity by April 1855 appears on p. 143. The full 10 million pesos would have been about 2 percent of GDP at that point, very crudely. Manuel Payno said much less, a million pesos. See Bazant, *Alienation of Church Wealth,* 41n. Payno's estimate is, however, implausibly low. From March through October 1854, Manuel Escandón advanced the government over 750,000 pesos. In November alone, 400,000 pesos. *El Siglo XIX,* March 18, 1855, 2. The cost of suppressing just the Revolt of Zacapoaxtla in December of 1856 has been put at $1.2 million. Robert J. Knowlton, *Church Property and the Mexican Reform, 1856–1910* (DeKalb, IL: Northern Illinois University Press, 1976), 23.
96 Bazant, *Alienation of Church Wealth,* 52–56, and 95 for ownership in Mexico City. Also in general, Knowlton, *Church Property and the Mexican Reform.*
97 Bazant, *Alienation of Church Wealth,* 13, 114, 133, 135–44, 287–90. I calculate the percentage of buyers in Mexico City from Bazant's Appendix XVI, relative to a population of perhaps 200,000. Also see María Gayón Córdova, *1848: Una ciudad de grandes contrastes* (Mexico City: Instituto Nacional de Antropología e Historia), 143–46.
98 *Diario Oficial del Supremo Gobierno*, June 4, 1858. It is easy to dismiss the complaints of contemporaries on the ground as mere anecdote, while econometric specification and testing require data. Be that as it may, to paraphrase the famous economist George Stigler, the singular of data is anecdote. If the results of econometric testing of the data do not square with the everyday observations of the participants, one may fairly ask where the problem really lies.
99 Circular by the Ministry of Justice and Public Instruction, Veracruz, October 24, 1859, SEDENA, exp. 7413.
100 Santa Anna, decree of December 29, 1853. (via the ministry of War and Marine) in SEDENA, exp. 4036. For "Vaquerias," see Manuel Zamora to the Minister of War and Marine, Veracruz, October 3, 1860, SEDENA, exp. 4359.
101 Ignacio Zaragoza to the "chiefs of Constitutional forces" [Sierra de Puebla], September 1, 1861, SEDENA, exp. 8205.
102 The account, by a merchant from Mexico City, was dated April 26, 1859, and is found in SEDENA, Mexico, exp. 6942. This was about two weeks after the unsuccessful assault which witnessed perhaps the worst atrocity of the entire conflict, the so-called Tacubaya Martyrs of April 11, 1859. This matter, and much more, is documented here. See also Galindo, *La gran década nacional o relación histórica de la Guerra de Reforma, intervención extranjera y gobierno del archiduque Maximiliano, 1857–1867*, 3 vols. (Mexico City: Fondo de Cultura Economica, 1987 [1904]), 1, 233–35, and Appendix.
103 *Diario Oficial del Supremo Gobierno*, July 27, 1858. An interesting attempt to provide just this is Will Fowler, *La Guerra de Tres Años, 1857–1861*, kind. ed. (Mexico City: Crítica), 11–12.

104 Requisition signed by Dario Baladino, Tampico, October 14, 1858, SEDENA, exp. 6057. Base population figures from *Nuevo Atlas Nacional de México* (Mexico City: Universidad Nacional Autónoma de México, 2007), MAPA H IV 21.

105 Salvucci, Politics, Markets and Mexico's "London Debt," 237–54. Shirley J. Black, "Napoléon III et le Mexique: un triomphe monetaire," *Revue Historique*, no. 259 (1978): 55–73. Benoit Haberbusch, "L'emploi de la gendermerie au Mexique (1861–1867): force prévotale ou force de sécurité intérieure," *Revue historique des armées* [En ligne], o. 2, accessed September 13, 2020, http://journals.openedition.org/rha/6910.

106 Authorization signed by J.A. Gamboa, San Luis Potosí, October 7, 1863, SEDENA, exp. 12012.

107 "Reclamación presentada por Manuel J. Lizardi, para que se le cobre el adeudo por efectos entregados al General Tomás Mejía de la 'Brigada Mejía' SEDENA," exp. 14245.

108 The French model of colonialism was consistent. And it is called looting. For a Haitian comparison, see www.nytimes.com/2022/05/20/world/americas/haiti-history-colonized-france.html, "The Ransom," *New York Times*, May 20, 2022. Spencer C. Tucker, ed., *The Encyclopedia of the Mexican-American War*, 3 vols (Santa Barbara, CA: ABC-CLIO), 667, 669. The franc was pegged at .290322581 grams of gold in 1865, with 31.1 grams to the troy ounce of gold. Hence FR 2.06 to USD 1.
Manuel Payno, *Cuentas, gastos, acreedores y otros asuntos del tiempo de la intervención francesa y del imperio: Obra escrita y publicada del gobierno constitucional de la república* (Mexico City: Ignacio Cumplido, 1868).

109 See especially Emilio Kouri, "Sobre la propiedad comunal de los pueblos, de la Reforma a la Revolución," *Historia Mexicana,* no. 66 (2017).

110 Antonio Escobar Ohmstede, Romana Falcón, and Martín Sánchez Rodríguez, coords., *La Desamortización Civil Desde Perspectiva Plurales* (Mexico City: El Colegio de México, 2017), 99, 113.

111 Instituto Nacional de Estadística e Geografía, *Precursores de las Estadísticas oficiales en México* (Aguascalientes, MX: Instituto Nacional de Estadística, y Geografia, 2011), 4.

112 Mexico Dirección General de Estadística, *Anuario estadístico de la República Mexicana formado por la Dirección General de Estadística*, accessed May 28, 2024, https://catalog.hathitrust.org/Record/008923807 provides the complete series by searching annually. Unless otherwise specified, it is to this series I make reference.

113 Maldonado and McCaa seem to be supported by the Census of 1895, although its reliability is questionable. Nevertheless the proportion of the population ages 10 to 59 (.66) comes very close to a theoretical, smoothed proportional distribution (.67) calculated by Eduardo Arriaga, the standard reference. See Eduardo Arriaga, *New Life Tables for Latin American Populations in the Nineteenth and Twentieth Centuries* (1968; Westport, CT: Greenwood Press, 1976), 165.

114 Richard J. Salvucci, "Export-Led Industrialization," 271. A simple thought experiment might help. Suppose railroad social savings in 1910 were 8 percent of GDP. INEGI statistics put GDP per head in 1910 (at 1970 prices) at 3,104 pesos. The total GDP was 47,054,000,000 pesos. 3,764,620,000 is 8 percent of that or 250 pesos per head. But we are thinking about fewer people than total population, perhaps 300,000 additional survivors. This would require an increased income per head of multiple thousands of pesos—far more than per capita income itself. And the larger the social savings, the larger the required jump in income. One can think of no plausible explanation for such an increase in productivity to occur from any learning-by-doing (aging). Technology—the railroads—must have therefore accounted for the great bulk of productivity increase in Porfirian Mexico.

115 Richard Salvucci, Linda Salvucci, and Aslán Cohen, "Politics of Protection: Interpreting Commercial Policy in Late Bourbon and Early National Mexico," in *The Political Economy of Spanish America in the Age of Revolution, 1750–1850*, eds. Kenneth

J. Andrien and Lyman L. Johnson (Albuquerque, NM: University of New Mexico Press, 1994), 105–6. Stephen Haber, "Assessing the Obstacles to Industrialisation: The Mexican Economy, 1830–1940," *Journal of Latin American Studies*, no. 24 (1992): 1–32. Joaquín Casasus, *La Reforma Monetaria en México: Informes Presentados a la Comisión Monetaria* (Mexico City: Imprenta de Hull, 1905), 25–30.

116 Sandra Kuntz Ficker, *El comercio exterior de México en la era del capitalismo liberal, 1870–1929* (Mexico City: El Colegio de México, 2007). Sandra Kuntz Ficker, *Las exportaciones mexicanas durante la primera globalización, 1870–1929* (Mexico City, 2010). The analysis here is based on *Comercio Exterior*, 47–68, 82, 475.

117 For further support, see Rafael Dobado and Gustavo A. Marrero, "Corn Market Integration in Porfirian Mexico," *Journal of Economic History*, no. 65 (2005): 103–28.

118 Kuntz Ficker, *Comercio Exterior*, 76.

119 Kuntz Ficker, *Comercio Exterior*, 130, with my estimates. I draw heavily on *Atlas Historico de Mexico*, 2nd ed., ed. Enrique Florescano (Mexico City: CONAFE, 1984), Láminas 63–65. Also see Teresa Rojas Rabiela and Ignacio Gutiérrez Ruvalcaba, *Cien ventanas a los paisajes de antaño: fotografías del campo mexicano de hace un siglo* (Mexico City: Conacyt, 2013), 37–52, which is largely based on the work of Francisco Calderón and Karl Kaerger. All data on production and cultivation are taken from *Estadísticas Historicas de México, 2009*, Table 8.

120 Moramay López Alonso and Raúl Porras Condey, "The Ups and Downs of Mexican Economic Growth: The Biological Standard of Living and Inequality, 1870–1950," *Economics and Human Biology* 1 (2003): 169–86.

121 Javier Arnaut, "Mexican Real Wages Before the Revolution: A Reappraisal," *Iberoamericana*, no. 47 (2018).

122 Aurora Gómez Galvarriato and Jeffrey Williamson, "Was It Prices, Productivity or Policy? Latin American Industrialisation After 1870," *Journal of Latin American Studies*, no. 41 (2009): 663–94.

123 Williamson, *Trade and Poverty*, 162.

124 Walter Scheidel, *The Great Leveler. Violence and the History of Inequality From the Stone Age to the Twenty-First Century* (Princeton, NJ: Princeton University Press), 174–209, and especially quote, 209.

Bibliography

Archival Sources

Archivo Histórico Arzobispado de México, Fondo Cabildo, Sec. Haceduría, Ser. Jueces Hacedores
Caja 3, Caja 4.

Archivo Historico del Estado de Querétaro, Querétaro, QRO.
Libros de Hipoteca, 1818–1844.

Archivo de la Secretaría de Defensa Nacional, México (Please see Data Appendix for caveat regarding *legajo* numbers) (legajos).
100, 199, 1871, 2450, 2679, 4359, 5376, 6057, 6942, 12012, 14245.

Archivo de la Secretaría de Relaciones Exteriores, México (legajos encuadernados).
1085, 1089, 1090.

Biblioteca Nacional de España, Madrid, Spain.
Ms. 13255.

National Archives, Kew, Middlesex, United Kingdom.
FO 84/479.

New York State Library, Albany, New York.
John Ellis Wool Papers.
Box28.

Universidad Autónoma de Nuevo León, NL, México, Colección Digital.
http://cdigital.dgb.uanl.mx/la/1020004042/1020004042.html.
http://cdigital.dgb.uanl.mx/la/1080012866_C/1080012866_C.html.

University of Houston Libraries, Special Collections, Mexican Documents Collection, Hispanic Research Collections, Houston, TX.

Secondary and Published Primary Sources and Newspapers

Arnaut, Javier. "Mexican Real Wages Before the Revolution: A Reappraisal." *Iberoamericana: Nordic Journal of Latin American and Caribbean Studies*, no. 47 (2018): 45–62. https://iberoamericana.se/articles/10.16993/iberoamericana.421.

Arriaga, Eduardo. *New Life Tables for Latin American Populations in the Nineteenth and Twentieth Centuries*. Repr. ed. Westport, CT: Greenwood Press, 1976. First published 1968.

Ávila Juárez, José Oscar. *Cayetano Rubio y la Compañía Hércules y la Industrialización Queretana en el siglo XIX*. Querétaro, QRO: Universidad Autónoma de Querétaro, 2018.

Balbontín, Manuel. *La invasión Americana, 1846–1848: Apuntes del subteniente de artillería Manuel Balbontín*. Mexico: Ignacio Cumplido, 1888. http://cdigital.dgb.uanl.mx/la/1080012385/1080012385.PDF.

Bazant, Jan. *Alienation of Church Wealth in Mexico. Social and Economic Aspects of the Liberal Revolution, 1856–1875*. Cambridge, UK: Cambridge University Press, 1971.

Bazant, Jan. *Cinco haciendas mexicanas. Tres siglos de vida rural en San Luis Potosí (1600–1910)*. Mexico City: El Colegio de México, 1975.

Becerril Hernández, Carlos de Jesús. "La Legislación Tributaria del Segundo Imperio Mexicano, 1864–1867." Unpub. Master's thesis, Instituto Mora, 2012. https://mora.repositorioinstitucional.mx/jspui/bitstream/1018/251/1/MOR01000095335%20%20LA%20LEGISLACI%C3%93N%20TRIBUTARIA%20DEL%20SEGUNDO%20IMPERIO%20MEXICANO%2C%201864-1867.pdf.

Bergad, Laird, Fe Iglesias García, and María del Carmen Barcia. *The Cuban Slave Market*. New York, NY: Cambridge University Press, 1995.

Black, Shirley J. "Napoléon III et le Mexique: un triomphe monetaire." *Revue Historique*, no. 259 (1978): 55–73.

Campbell, Randolph B. *An Empire for Slavery. The Peculiar Institution in Texas, 1821–1865*. Baton Rouge, LA: Louisiana State University Press, 1989.

Carbajal López, David. *Epidemias en el Obispado de Guadalajara: la muerte masiva en el primer tercio del siglo xix*. Zapopan, JAL, MX: Editorial Página Seis, 2017.

Casasus, Joaquín. *La Reforma Monetaria en México: Informes Presentados a la Comisión Monetaria*. Mexico City: Imprenta de Hull, 1905. http://catalog.hathitrust.org/Record/008604897.

Challu, Amilcar, and Aurora Gómez-Galvarriato. "Mexico's Real Wages in the Age of the Great Divergence, 1730–1930." *Revista de Historia Económica. Journal of Iberian and Latin American Economic History*, no. 33 (2015): 83–122.

Chamberlain, Samuel. *My Confession [1846–1848]*. New York, NY: Harper and Brothers, 1956.

Chowning, Margaret. *Wealth and Power in Provincial Mexico. Michoacán From the Late Colony to the Revolution*. Stanford, CA: Stanford University Press, 1999.

Cummings, James Williams. "Financing the Mexican War." Unpub. PhD diss., Oklahoma State University, 2003.

Dávalos, Marcela. *Los letrados interpretan la ciudad: Los barrios de indios en el umbral de la Independencia.* Mexico City: Instituto Nacional de Antropología e Historia, 2009.

de Eguía, José Joaquín. *Memoria sobre la utilidad é influjo de la minería en el reino; necesidad de su fomento y arbitrios de verificarlos*. Mexico City: Oficina de don Juan Bautista Arizpe, 1819.

De la Portilla, Anselmo. *Historia de la Revolución en México Contra la Dictadura de Santa Anna 1853–1855.* Repr. ed. México: Fondo de Cultura Económica, 1993. First published 1856.

Del Raso, José Antonio. *Refutación del Proyecto monárquico extranjero de Don José María Gutiérrez Estrada.* Mexico City, 1840. http://cdigital.dgb.uanl.mx/la/1020002877/1020002877.htm.

Del Raso, José Antonio. *Notas Estadísticas del Departamento de Querétaro.* Mexico City: Mariano Lara, 1848. http://cdigital.dgb.uanl.mx/la/1020003998/1020003998.PDF.

Dirección General de Estadística. *Censo general de la República Mexicana verificada el 20 de octubre de 1895.* Mexico City: Oficina Tipografica de la Nación, 1899.

Dobado, Rafael, and Gustavo A. Marrero. "Corn Market Integration in Porfirian Mexico." *Journal of Economic History,* no. 65 (2005): 103–28.

Duties, Revenue and Public Expenditure. US Congress, House, 30th Congress, 1st session, Executive Document 82, 1848.

Escobar Ohmstede, Antonio, Romana Falcón, and Martín Sánchez Rodríguez, coords. *La Desamortización Civil Desde Perspectiva Plurales.* Mexico City: El Colegio de México, 2017.

Estimations of Appropriations. Letter From the Secretary of the Treasury US Congress, House, 29th Congress, 1st session, Executive Document 2, 1847.

Florescano, Enrique, ed. *Atlas Histórico de México.* 2nd ed. Mexico City: CONAFE, 1984.

Fowler, Will. *La Guerra de Tres Años, 1857–1861.* Mexico City: Planeta, 2020. E Book.

Galindo y Galindo, Miguel. *La gran década nacional, ó relación histórica de la Guerra de Reforma, intervención extranjera y Gobierno del Archiduque Maximiliano 1857–1867.* 3 vols. Mexico City: Oficina Tip. de la Secretaría de Fomento, 1904–1906. http://cdigital.dgb.uanl.mx/la/1080012866_C/1080012866_C.html.

García, Genaro. *Documentos Inéditos o Muy Raros Para la Historia de México. Repr. ed. Mexico* City: Editorial Porrua, 2006. First published 1905–*1911.*

García Ugarte, Maria Eugenia. *Breve historia de Querétaro.* Mexico City: Fondo de Cultura Económica, 1999.

Gayón Córdova, María. *1848: Una ciudad de grandes contrastes.* Mexico City: Instituto Nacional de Antropología e Historia, 2013.

Girón, Nicole. "Manuel Payno: El Ir y Venir por la Secretaría de Hacienda." In *Los Secretarios de Hacienda y sus Proyectos (1821–1933).* 2 vols, edited by Leonor Ludlow. Mexico City: Universidad Nacional Autónoma de México, 2002.

Goldsmith, Raymond. "An Estimate of the Size and Structure of the National Product of the Early Roman Empire." *Review of Income and Wealth,* no. 30 (1984): 263–88. https://doi.org/10.1111/j.1475-4991.1984.tb00552.x.

Gómez Galvarriato, Aurora, and Jeffrey Williamson. "Was it Prices, Productivity or Policy? Latin American Industrialisation After 1870." *Journal of Latin American Studies,* no. 41 (2009): 663–94.

Gómez-Galvarriato, Aurora. Lecture at the Secretaría de Economía México, "Una breve historia de la tortilla de maíz," September 30, 2019. www.youtube.com/watch?v=LVFa36cy20w.

Guardino, Peter. *The Dead March. A History of the Mexican American War.* Cambridge, MA: Harvard University Press, 2017.

Gutiérrez, M. *Apuntes para servir a la estadística minera del Estado de Querétaro.* Mexico City: Jens y Zapiain, 1875.

Haber, Stephen. "Assessing the Obstacles to Industrialisation: The Mexican Economy, 1830–1940." *Journal of Latin American Studies,* no. 24 (1992): 1–32.

Hurtado Galves, José Martin. *El Ejército Realista en la Ciudad de Querétaro, 1810–1826.* 2 vols. Querétaro, QTO: Poder Ejecutivo, 2019.

Instituto Nacional de Estadística e Geografía. *Cien Años de Censos de Población.* Aguascalientes, AGS: Instituto Nacional de Estadística, y Geografía, 1996.

Instituto Nacional de Estadística e Geografía. *Estadísticas históricas de Mexico, 2009.* 5th ed. Aguascalientes, AGS: Instituto Nacional de Estadística, y Geografía, 2009.

Instituto Nacional de Estadística e Geografía. *Precursores de las Estadísticas oficiales en México.* Aguascalientes, AGS: Instituto Nacional de Estadística, y Geografía, 2011.

Knowlton, Robert J. *Church Property and the Mexican Reform, 1856–1910.* DeKalb, IL: Northern Illinois University Press, 1976.

Kuntz Ficker, Sandra. *El comercio exterior de México en la era del capitalismo liberal, 1870–1929.* Mexico City: El Colegio de México, 2007.

Kuntz Ficker, Sandra. *Las exportaciones mexicanas durante la primera globalización, 1870–1929.* Mexico City: El Colegio de México, 2010.

Lerdo de Tejada, Sebastián. *Cuadro sinóptico de la República Mexicana en 1856.* Mexico City: Ignacio Cumplido, 1856. http://catalog.hathitrust.org/Record/008399213.

López Alonso, Moramay, and Raúl Porras Condey. "The Ups and Downs of Mexican Economic Growth: The Biological Standard of Living and Inequality, 1870–1950." *Economics and Human Biology*, no. 1 (2003): 169–86.

Mairot, Mark Joseph. "Mexican Provincial Society During the Age of Revolution: A Social and Economic History of Toluca, 1790–1834." Unpub. PhD diss., UCLA, 2013.

Mangino, Rafael. *Observaciones del Contador Mayor de Hacienda sobre la cuenta del Sr. Secretario del Despacho del mismo ramo, respectiva a los ocho primeros meses del año de 1825*. Mexico City: Secretaría de Hacienda, 1826. http://catalogo.bne.es/uhtbin/cgisirsi/0/x/0/05?searchdata1=biam0000009831.

Marichal, Carlos. Bankruptcy of Empire. Mexican Silver and the Wars Between Spain, Britain and France, 1760–1810. New York, NY: Cambridge University Press, 2007.

McAfee, R. Preston. "American Economic Growth and the Voyage of Columbus." *American Economic Review,* no. 73 (1983): 735–40.

Mejía, Demetrio. *Estadística de la mortalidad en México.* Mexico City: Impreso de Ignacio Escalante, 1879. https://repositorio.unam.mx/4240.

Miller, Simon. "Agrarian Capitalism in Central Mexico: From Hacienda to Rancho in the State of Querétaro, 1845–1900." Unpub. PhD thesis. Durham theses, Durham (UK) University, 1983. http://etheses.dur.ac.uk/view/creators/Miller=3ASimon=3A=3A.html.

Molina Enríquez, Andrés. *Los grandes problemas nacionales*. Repr. ed. Mexico City: Ediciones Era, 1978. First published 1909.

Observaciones imparciales de la Administración financiera en la época del gobierno provisional. Mexico City: J.M. de Lara, 1845.

Ortega González, Carlos Alberto. *El Ocaso de Un Imperio. El Diezmo en el Arzobispado en México, 1810–1833*. Mexico City: Instituto Mora, 2015.

Ortiz Escamilla, Juan. Seminario Histórico de la Armada de México y Presentación de Libro Conmemorativo, "El Teatro de la Guerra en Veracruz y la Guerra de la Independencia en México," October 13, 2021. www.youtube.com/watch?v=Cqsa5Z2UR5w.

Paredes y Arrillaga, Mariano. *Contestaciones habidas entre los Exmos. Señores Generales de División D. Mariano Paredes de Arillaga, D Mariano Arista y el Supremo Gobierno por las que solo falta cualquiera clase de recurso por mesquinos que hubieran sido para que todo el Ejército de reserva marchara al norte . . .* San Luis Potosí: Imprenta del Estado, 1845.

Ramón, Alcaraz, et al. *Apuntes para la historia de la Guerra entre México y los Estados Unidos*. Mexico City: Secretaría de Cultura, 2005. First published 1848. https://libros-mexico.mx/.

Randall, Robert W. *Real del Monte. A British Silver Mining Venture in Mexico.* Austin, TX: University of Texas Press, 1972.
Rankine, Margaret. "The Mexican Mining Industry in the Nineteenth Century with Special Reference to Guanajuato." *Bulletin of Latin American Research,* no. 11 (1992): 29–48.
Reséndez, Andrés. "Política transnacional entre Texas y Tamaulipas en el siglo xix o las peripecias del general José María de Jesús Carvajal." In *El territorio disputado en la guerra de 1846–1848*, coordinated by Danna A. Levin Rojo and Martha Ortega. Mexico City: Miguel Ángel Porrúa, 2007.
Reyna, Maria del Carmen, and Jean Paul Krammer. *La familia Ajuria.* Mexico City: Instituto Nacional de Antropología e Historia, 2014.
Rojas Rabiela, Teresa, and Ignacio Gutiérrez Ruvalcaba. *Cien ventanas a los paisajes de antaño: fotografías del campo mexicano de hace un siglo.* Mexico City: Conacyt, 2013.
Salinas Sandoval, María del Carmen. *Política interna e invasión norteamericana en el Estado de México, 1846–1847.* Toluca, MEX: El Colegio Mexiquense, 2000.
Salvucci, R.J. "Algunas consideraciones económicas. Análisis mexicano de la depresión a principios del siglo XIX." *Historia Mexicana*, no. 55 (2005): 67–97. First published 1836.
Salvucci, Richard J. "Export-Led Industrialisation." In *The Cambridge Economic History of Latin America.* 2 vols, edited by Victor Bulmer-Thomas, John H. Coatsworth, and Roberto Cortés Conde, 1, 249–92. Cambridge, UK: Cambridge University Press, 2006.
Salvucci, Richard J. *Politics, Markets and Mexico's "London Debt," 1823–1887.* Cambridge, UK: Cambridge University Press, 2009.
Salvucci, Richard J., Linda Salvucci, and Aslan Cohen. "The Politics of Protection: Interpreting Commercial Policy in Late Bourbon and Early National Mexico." In *The Political Economy of Spanish America in the Age of Revolution, 1750–1850*, edited by Kenneth J. Andrien and Lyman L Johnson. Albuquerque, NM: University of New Mexico Press, 1994.
Sánchez Silva, Carlos. *Indios, comerciantes y burocracia en la Oaxaca poscolonial, 1786–1860.* Oaxaca, OAX: Instituto Oaxaqueño de la Culturas, 1998.
Sánchez Trujillo, José. *Proyecto sobre productos y recursos de Hacienda.* Mexico City: M. Murgía, 1865.
Scheidel, Walter. *The Great Leveler. Violence and the History of Inequality From the Stone Age to the Twenty-First Century.* Princeton, NJ: Princeton University Press, 2018.
Suárez Argüello, Clara Elena. "Sequía y crisis en el transporte novohispano en 1794–1795." *Historia Mexicana*, no. 44 (1985): 385–402.
Suárez Argüello, Clara Elena. "La quiebra de una casa de conductos Novohispana en los inicios del siglo xix: Sus causas." *Historia Mexicana,* no. 56 (2007): 817–62.
Tariff Duties in the Ports of Mexico. US Congress, House, 30th Congress, 2nd session, Executive Document 20, 1848–1849.
Torget, Andrew J. *Seeds of Empire. Cottom, Slavery, and the Transformation of the Texas Borderlands (1800–1850).* Chapel Hill, NC: University of North Carolina Press, 2015.
Torres Medina, Javier. *Centralismo y reorganización. La Hacienda pública y la administración durante la primera república central de Mexico, 1835–1842.* México: Instituto Mora, 2013.
Tucker, Spencer C., ed. *The Encyclopedia of the Mexican-American War.* 3 vols. Santa Barbara, CA: ABC-CLIO, 2013.
Tutino, John. "The Revolution in Mexican Independence: Insurgency and the Renegotiation of Property, Production and Patriarchy in the Bajío, 1800–1855." *Hispanic American Historical Review*, no. 78 (1998): 367–418.
Upton, Emory. *The Military Policy of the United States During the Mexican War.* US Congress, House, 63rd Congress, 2nd session, 1914.
Vázquez, Josefina, coord. *Mexico al tiempo de su Guerra con los Estados Unidos.* Mexico City: Fondo de Cultura Económica, 1997.

Velasco, Alfonso Luis. *Geografía y Estadística de la República Mexicana: Guanajuato.* Mexico City: Secretaría de Fomento, 1890.
Williamson, Jeffrey. *Trade and Poverty. When the Third World Fell Behind.* Cambridge, MA: MIT Press, 2013.
Wyllie, Robert Crichton. *México. Noticia Sobre Su Hacienda Pública Bajo el Gobierno Español y Después de la Independencia.* Mexico City: Ignacio Cumplido, 1845.
Anuario Estadístico de la República Mexicana, 1893–1908
Diario Oficial del Supremo Gobierno
El Monitor Republicano
El Siglo XIX
El Universal
New York Times

3

A CENTURY OF REVOLUTIONS AND "MIRACLES"

Economy and Revolution

In 1910, Mexico (the entire country) had a population of about 15 million souls. A century later, the population of the *metropolitan zone of the Valley of Mexico*—admittedly, an area larger than Mexico City itself, counted over 20 million people. There were as many inhabitants in the City of Mexico (CDMX, in current Mexican usage) and adjacent portions of the state of Hidalgo and Mexico in 2010 as there had been in the entire country itself a century earlier.[1] In other words, in 1910, Mexico was sparsely populated and mostly rural. Within a century, Mexico was far more densely populated and urban. If land and resources had previously been abundant and the source of comparative advantage, labor was now (by the turn of the twenty-first century) the abundant factor of production. In theory, it should have become the source of Mexico's comparative advantage. Mexico should have industrialized in the twentieth century and entered the international economy on that basis. Attempts to circumvent comparative advantage and market signals, even if the product of good intentions, rarely end well. As we shall see, they did not in Mexico, although the "false dawn" of "stabilizing development" led most to think otherwise by the 1970s. To develop this argument is now the burden of the narrative.

Some would argue, and not unfairly, that the central fact of the twentieth century (we are but barely into the twenty-first) would be what is commonly known as "The Mexican Miracle," the extraordinary and perhaps singular economic expansion that ran from the mid-1950s to the mid- or late 1970s (these dates are flexible, and some would say starting during the 1940s and ending in 1982). Per capita product grew at about 3.7 percent per year. Inflation averaged 3.7 percent. And the public sector deficit was less than 2 percent. transformation of the structure of national output—called

DOI: 10.4324/9781003532583-4

"The Mexican Miracle," the extraordinary and perhaps singular economic expansion that ran from the mid-1950s to the mid- or late 1970s (these dates are flexible, and some would say starting during the 1940s and ending in 1982). Per capita product grew at about 3.7 percent per year. Inflation averaged 3.7 percent. And the public sector deficit was less than 2 percent.[2] Others might point to the transformation of the structure of national output—called economic development—as the central reality of the century. In 1900 (in prices of 1970), how things looked from a modern perspective, agriculture (value added in prices of 1970) as a share of total product was about 25.7 percent. By 2000, these shares were almost precisely reversed at 6 percent for agriculture and 25 percent for manufacturing.

Standard practice is to begin with some account of the Mexican Revolution under Francisco Madero that (1910–1920) overthrew the long government of Porfirio Díaz (1876–1910). Since the events, conflicts, underlying causes, triggers, battles, and apparent outcomes have been rehearsed in so many places, there is no point in repeating them here. Suffice it to say that whatever middle, working class, and peasant strains there were to the Revolution in the early years, the victors, in the long run, the so-called Sonoran Dynasty, were capitalist modernizers, not social revolutionaries. More than anything else, this accounts for the shape the Mexican economy ultimately assumed: a mixed regime, with a significant private sector and strong elements of state direction and planning, if not outright control. It is a much-contested legacy and the source of considerable ideological confusion.[3]

For our purposes, we focus on demographic change and on agricultural "reconstruction" and reform. While the industrialization of Mexico and its relation to state direction is of paramount importance, we begin with agriculture. Not only does the choice have a basis in the theory of economic development—people must eat before they do much else. It is also at the heart of some of the most radical and thoroughgoing reforms brought by the Revolution, agrarian reform beginning in 1915.

There is also a sense in which demography and demographic change are vital. The population losses from the Revolution have generally been severely underestimated. This, in turn, suggests the economic impact of the Revolution, at least in the short run, is apt to be misunderstood, not to say, to be underestimated. Second, the relation of factor endowments to subsequent economic development cannot be understood if the true extent of population losses is not appreciated. The Revolution of 1910 was, in this sense, somewhat analogous to the Insurgency of 1810. Both had substantial human losses whose consequences were evident sooner (in the short run) or later (in the long run).

It has long been customary to put the human losses from the Revolution at about 1 million people (that number turns up with suspicious frequency in Mexican history when revolts, rebellions, and revolutions are concerned). This is far too small.[4] For one thing, the Revolution coincided with the Pandemic of 1918, which Odorico and Lezama argue "was the single most important factor in the decline of the population between 1910 and 1921." They speculate that demographic losses in the countryside were severe in the cities, but even so, in 1918, over a million died in Mexico City alone.[5] The Odorico and Lezama figure, which includes mortality (49 percent); births that did not occur because of social disruption (38 percent); and emigration (12 percent), principally to Texas and California, is nearly 3 million people (i.e., triple previous "estimates"). If the population of Mexico was about 17 million in 1921 (a very uncertain figure because the census was not only late but highly defective), that is, a loss of over 16 percent of the population—comparable to the losses of the Insurgency of 1810.

While the gross numbers are themselves remarkable, some consideration as to age and gender-specific mortality are in order. Márquez and Molina del Villar point to the age cohort of 20–45 as the most seriously affected. Moreover, as Odorico and Lezama speculate, the involvement of children as young as 10 years of age is scarcely unknown. While mortality was primarily male, women were affected as well, not only by disease and the interruption of fertility but also by an active presence in combat. Again, the result was a considerable shock to the economically productive portion of the labor force. So, we are faced by a circumstance analogous to 1810. If there was a macro shock based on the consequences of the Insurgency—at least through the 1840s—then what of the Consequences of 1910, at least in this restricted sense?

The short answer is that the Revolution had precisely the same effect on real wages that the Insurgency did. If we look at the data of Challú and Gómez Galvarriato, their calculations show that for Mexico City, the last time that any index of real wages had been as high as the period 1900–1930 was in 1825–1849, and prior to that, 1775–1779, after having fallen from 1750–1774, the peak of the eighteenth century. So, once again, as labor temporarily grew scarce relative to capital (including resources), what was the result?[6]

To repeat, our argument is that factor endowments and relative prices explain much about Mexican economic history. This discussion started in the same spirit. When real wages rise, activities that are labor intensive tend to shrink in favor of those that are not. At a general level, if economic theory makes any useful contribution, there should be some evidence here, because, at least in the short run, and at a critical time in the history of its industrialization, Mexico was affected by a substantial demographic shock.

The Revolutionary period, especially 1910 through 1920, is enormously complex. There are multiple confounding influences arising from the outbreak of World War I in Europe (1914–1918), Civil War in Mexico (1914–1915), and hyperinflation in Mexico related to political turmoil (1915–1916), so that finding, much less telling a straightforward story—stylized or not, is not easy. Nevertheless, we might illustrate the results of this shift in Mexico by a tale of two industries: textiles and crude oil. It is important to recall that reality matters: real industries, especially by the twentieth century, had political actors whose pressures in response to economic forces shaped specific responses. So, for example, the factual story of cotton textiles was made by capitalists, workers, unions, and the revolutionary government, not to mention international events and largely impersonal economic forces whose result was inevitably subject to chance. Looking at these industries in this way is simply thinking about what underlying long-term forces—what French Annaliste historians once called *structures*—could have been at work in shaping a specific outcome. When we look at the matter in detail, it is complexity that is apparent, to which we offer only a kind of radically simplifying qualification, but one without which the story would have probably turned out differently. It is a bit of a thought experiment, but hopefully a useful one.[7]

While Gómez Galvarriato points to many factors that set wages in the Orizaba textile industry, one thing is clear.[8] They did, in fact, rise sharply after 1916. While flat in the early 1920s, they basically continued to do so until 1929. Rising real wages should, other things constant, induce a substitution of capital for labor. Using the relatively comprehensive measure of looms per shift worker, this also increases from 1913 through 1930 relative to the Porfiriato, although the increase is uneven from 1913 to 1920 (1.55) and from 1921 to 1930 (1.46). Moreover, from a different approach to the question, the capital-labor ratio in cotton textiles in the 1930s was about 50 percent higher than it had been at the end of the Porfiriato.[9] A rising real wage did induce a substitution of capital for labor: at bottom, this rising wage could not have taken place without some degree of restriction in the growth of the labor force, which, at least into the 1930s, the Revolution accompanied.

Another industry that flourished during the Revolution was crude oil. It too has a most complicated history beginning during the Porfiriato, and hardly ending with Lázaro Cárdenas' historic nationalization of foreign companies (principally American, British, and Dutch) following another heated confrontation with organized labor in 1938. Here, too, the goal is not to repeat that story, which has been discussed in detail elsewhere.[10] Aside from the obvious fact that Mexico hit the "commodity lottery" at a time when the internal combustion engine was sweeping away older forms of propulsion—particularly the horse—and required refined hydrocarbons as fuel, two things are said to account for its success during the Revolution (and its decline thereafter). First, the industry was held to be too valuable to be destroyed by all factions, whose common need for finance via oil exports enforced restraint. Second, the decline of the industry was not primarily attributable to political reasons, much less to fiscal policies advocated by nationalist Revolutionary regimes, but to natural factors such as saltwater seepage into reservoirs.[11] The plain fact was that by the 1920s Mexico was the largest oil producer in Latin America and second only to the United States internationally, a position it held until the late 1920s, when it was surpassed by Venezuela. Again, the emergence of the industry was, if nothing, consistent with factor endowments. If ever an industry's costs were basically "sunk" with a marginal cost (labor or variable costs) of nearly zero, it was Mexican oil. As a contemporary put it, "The entire cost of producing Mexican oil is practically in the purchase of the property and the drilling. . . . The operation after that is practically nothing. . . . We are informed that oil can be produced in Mexico profitably at 11 cents per barrel."[12] Thus in some ways, the outbreak of the Revolution often obscures the fact that the Mexican economy, on the basis of factor endowments, had become export-led from 1880 through 1929. The puzzle is why this tendency did not eventually affect the products of light industry, such as textiles, as well, and why Mexico turned to import substitution instead, especially as population began to recover from the shock of the Revolution.[13]

It is true that the Revolution, in demographic terms, carried its impress, one way or another, on the Generation of 1910, but the context in which the consequences were realized was quite different from 1810 or subsequent conflicts. Once again, the "rebound effect" from war occurred as the Crude Birth Rate (CBR) rose during the 1920s before falling back to more accustomed levels in the 1930s. Because of improvements in sanitation, public health, and education, life expectancy at birth rose from 25.4 years in 1910 to 31.5 in the 1920s and to 36.7 in the 1930s. Between 1920 and 1960, male life expectancy at birth basically doubled. Rather than slow growth or stagnation, some speak of the "rejuvenation" of the Mexican population with the onset of the demographic transition in the 1930s. So, the "costs" of a reduced labor force that followed 1810 were never really evident after 1910, especially in the long run, even if there is some indication in the Census of 1940 of the losses that the Generation of 1910 suffered.[14]

In the long run, the population of Mexico doubled between 1910 and 1950 and subsequently doubled again between 1950 and 1975. Again, under these circumstances, one would have expected a growing substitution of labor for capital in the Mexico economy and perhaps a growing labor share of national income, not to mention to the growth of labor-intensive exports. This, we are told, emphatically did not happen (although there are a variety of opinions) and the possible reasons for it is a topic to which we shall return.

Agrarian Reform: Way Out or No Exit

While historians have argued for the last century about what the Revolution sought to achieve, here we concentrate on the agrarian aspect. Contemporary writing in Mexico focuses on it, and we do so as well.

In many ways, the course of subsequent developments was an outcome of the agrarian reform. Not exclusively, of course. Politics, finance, and even international economics played a part. But as Mexico and its leaders sought to develop in the twentieth century, the principal constraint was agricultural. As the countryside evolved, at least until the 1990s, a major goal of the Revolution was to reconstitute a peasantry—real or imagined—as the basis for rural political stability. Because of the institutional basis of the peasantry, something Mexicans call "social property" or the *ejido*, much peasant agriculture remained subsistence agriculture, especially in the Central and Southern portions of the country, where the *ejido* figured (in general) most importantly as a unit of agricultural production. Because the *ejidatarios* (beneficiaries of the *ejido*, but, initially, not owners) were largely outside the market—at least insofar as their principal crop, maize, was concerned—they remained poor and an obstacle to further economic development. The transformation that occurred (industrial and urban) was in many ways forced, and heavily subsidized both at home and, in the end, by foreign lenders. While the economy and population of the country remained small, the negative consequence—insufficient aggregate demand from the countryside—remained mostly latent. But in the face of population growth, urbanization, and, finally, globalization of trade and finance, the implications became obvious.[15]

It is impossible to establish a consensus about how and when the hacienda became such a problem, although there was no shortage of opinion that it was. And, perhaps, some consensus about what could be done about it.

In 1909, an intellectual and public servant, Andrés Molina Enríquez, published what must be counted as one of the most influential books in Mexican history, *Los Grandes Problemas Nacionales*. Molina Enríquez, who was a notary raised in Central Mexico, had extensive acquaintance with the hacienda *and* with the characteristically Mexican form of small landholding, the *rancho*. Molina Enríquez's conviction was that the problems of the countryside—and by extension, Mexico itself, was the hacienda. The large estate was cultivated unproductively, largely as a means of securing an adequate, if marginally productive labor force. The truly productive farmers were the *rancheros*, small farmers, who could produce a surplus that the hacienda did not. Their owners were thus able to enter the market with their surplus and to consume goods. His was an almost Smithian view of the way small farmers created a commercial society that ultimately accumulated wealth. Molina Enríquez also decorated his analysis with an elaborate social account of how small farmers were authentic Mexicans, *mestizos*, and not simply an offshoot of the colonial creole oligarchy. The book thus became a tract for revolutionary times.

Virtually all accounts of the Mexican Revolution ascribe a large part of its origins to the countryside and to the dominance of the hacienda or great estate. Indeed, Frank Tannenbaum's classic account calls the hacienda and the ensuing uneven distribution of land "the chief cause of the Revolution of 1910."[16]

Because Molina Enríquez was at least a kind of intellectual author of Article 27 of the Constitution of 1917, the document that came to embody and codify the institutional basis of the revolutionary settlement, his ideas were enormously influential.[17] Beginning in the mid-1910s, when the very beginnings of the agrarian reform were enacted, they would involve the creation of a class of small farmers whose property would be carved out of the existing haciendas. As the reform took shape, the embodiment of the idea was the *ejido*. This was not necessarily a collective property (although there were a few famous collectives), but it is better understood as a grant of land to a community in which individual members had both political rights and the beneficiary right to work a small portion of the land. This was not private property, and, originally, could not be sold or used as collateral. Rights to work the land were transmissible through familial inheritance, but ordinarily, that was the sole vehicle of conveyance. There were no individual property rights per se; ownership of land and resources were vested in the Mexican state, just as they had been under the Spanish Crown. So, the *ejido* was revolutionary only in the sense that it restored the *ancien regime* in land before the Liberals and the Porfiriato had altered it, i.e., revolutionary in conception, but not per se. The concept went back to the creation of "Indian" villages under the Hapsburg *composiciones de tierra* at the end of the sixteenth century.

To be sure, the existence of the *ejido* depended upon the political sympathies and activity of the sitting Mexican President and his administration. Some were supporters, and some—especially Northerners—were not. A society of rural pseudo-smallholders was not created at the stroke of a pen by virtue of the existence of the agrarian reform laws. Existing hacendados frequently opposed the agrarian reform because it was their land (technically anything more than 100 hectares or 50 acres) that was the subject of confiscation; however, it had been acquired since the colonial period. In many cases, rural workers, especially those who lived on the haciendas (known as *acasillados*) regarded the estates as their homes, a source of security and sustenance. They too could be mobilized against agrarian reform.[18]

So, the road to agrarian reform was scarcely a smooth one, proceeding by fits and starts. The most active program of redistribution was undertaken by Lázaro Cárdenas (1934–1940), who redistributed more land than all his revolutionary predecessors combined, and did, in fact, occasion considerable productive upheaval. His successors were distinctly less enthusiastic about social property, and redistribution largely stalled until the *sexenios* of Gustavo Díaz Ordaz (1964–1970) and Luis Echeverría (1970–1976) when significant activity again took place. Nevertheless, the reasons appear to have been largely political: to purchase political support for the regime in the countryside, or in the peculiar case of Baja California, to "Mexicanize" lands so as to prevent a massive influx of real estate investors from the United States who represented a potential threat to Mexican sovereignty in a politically sensitive frontier area.

The *ejido* became the basis for rural agricultural life. In 1940, 56.8 percent of landholdings were in possession of *ejidatarios*. Private or individual holdings, ostensibly small farms, represented 43.2 percent.[19] These proportions remained more or less stable over the next 70 years. According to the IX *Censo Ejidal* (*Censo Agropecuario 2007*), the proportions were 54.1 percent and 35.7 percent private property. Even the total area under cultivation expanded from 29 million hectares to 106 million hectares with roughly the same shares. It would be an oversimplification to say that the agrarian reform and the configuration of the *ejido* and private land was over by 1940, but at least in an elementary sense, it was.

The economic problems associated with the *ejido* are so numerous that it is a wonder the *ejido* functioned at all. Property rights should be at the top of the list. If farmers, by definition, produce crops ahead of demand and sale, they require credit in advance of production. The *ejidatarios* were not landowners and had no collateral to pledge. The state stepped in to fill the gap. It created a lending institution known as the BNCE (Banco Nacional de Crédito Ejidal), although its lending policies were often criticized as subject to political influence and favoritism.

Equally important—a simple issue as well—was that the beneficiary grant of land (*parcela*) was barely adequate to support a family. It is very difficult to determine how much cultivable land each *ejidatario* possessed, but if we use the *Censo*

Ejidal 1940, we come up with about 3 hectares, or about 1.5 acres, of cultivated land. That is not much land; not enough, clearly to support a family.[20] *Ejidos* frequently lacked productive capital, such as tractors, or access to superior strains of seed (what became known in Mexico in the 1940s and 1950s as the "Green Revolution") so productivity, however measured, tended to be low. Many failed to reach even subsistence levels in staples like maize, forcing the peasants on the market to purchase it. Those who did so based on credit were, in essence, "eating their loans," and had no viable means of repayment. Over time, with the growth of population, especially after 1950, the *ejido* became associated with "minifundismo" or atomized landholding and rural impoverishment. To the extent that many ended up concentrated in Oaxaca, Veracruz, Guerrero, Jalisco, and Michoacán, *ejidos* also became synonymous with concentrated rural impoverishment.[21]

Rather than forming the backbone of a prosperous rural peasantry that could produce *and* consume, enlarge the market, and contribute to long-term economic development (the vision of Molina Enríquez),[22] the *ejido* created impoverished wards of the Mexican state whose principal ability, as anthropologist Arturo Warman put it, was to organize for political demonstrations in support of the PRI (Partido Revolucionario Institucional), the dominant political party rather than to produce (and, equally important, consume).[23] If this was to be, as Eyler Simpson called it, "Mexico's way out," one on which the country could then build a prosperous industrial structure, it was not much of a foundation. Sooner or later, it would fail. It was less of a way out than a blind alley of no exit.[24]

Still, it would be incorrect to label everything that emerged from the agrarian reform as a failure. To the contrary, one measure of agriculture growth known as total factor productivity (TFP) increased substantially in Mexico from the 1940s to the late 1970s (see Table 3.1). By international standards, the increase was reasonably good. But it did not come from the revolutionary project of the *ejido.* It is worth quoting Kirsten Appendini in full to summarize the essence of the situation.

From the 1950s to the mid-1980s, domestic production sustained Mexico's cheap food policy. In the early years, as the agricultural frontier expanded and more staple

TABLE 3.1 Total Factor Productivity Change in Agriculture, 1940–2019

Year	*Percentage Growth Rate*
1940–1965	2.00 percent
1961–2019	1.35 percent
1940–1953	1.7 percent
1954–1965	1.9 percent
1961–1978	2.7 percent
1978–1989	–2.0 percent
1989–2019	1.8 percent

crops were sown, productivity shot up with the application of the green revolution technology. Mexico was self-sufficient in food until 1970.

Modernization, however, meant that the subsidies to accelerate the green revolution were channeled to areas that could quickly adjust to policy incentives, that is, commercial farms and irrigated lands. From the 1940s to the late 1960s, private landholdings became the dynamo of agricultural development. Small and medium-sized farms, consisting mainly of peasants with land distributed under the agrarian reform (ejidos), were marginalized and deprived of policy benefits. Hence, most Mexican farmers remained in peasant economies that supplied cheap labor to the economy and produced marginal agricultural surplus. The outcome was a highly polarized farm landscape. In 1970, 13.4 percent of farms produced 58 percent of farm output, while 55.7 percent of farms did not even make subsistence income and only contributed 11.7 percent of the output.[25]

What makes this long-run performance so surprising is that it is not as if the *ejido* were the only obstacle to agricultural development. Since agriculture was to provide cheap inputs, including food, to the economy, prices were controlled starting in the 1930s. By the 1950s, controlled prices were an established feature of producing maize, wheat, and beans. While acting as a possible floor for rural incomes, price controls often had perverse effects. Real prices (inflation-adjusted prices) could easily decline, which not only subsidized urban consumers of beans and tortilla but also resulted in a transfer of wealth out of the rural sector, perhaps as much as 2.3 percent of the accumulated value of agricultural output in 1942–1960. By the early 1980s, the real price of maize had fallen to only 62 percent of what it had been in 1962.[26] For beans, the corresponding figure was 79 percent, and for wheat, it was 43 percent. Not surprisingly, production stagnated and agricultural imports, which were not unknown in the 1950s had started to rise after falling to relatively low levels by 1960. Particularly in the late 1960s, the growth of maize imports was substantial. By the mid- to late 1970s, they had reached high levels and remained elevated, in part because of rapidly increasing population.[27] This would not have much mattered if external balances could be settled by exporting, but the problem with the established industrial model was intractable. With population growth and declining real wages, light industry (like textiles, with a significant history back to the late 1830s) could have become a substantial source of exports. But as Gómez Galvarriato points out, incentive to modernize the industry was lost as a protective tariff regime was reintroduced after the Revolution.[28] There were satisfactory profits in supplying the domestic market, but textiles (among others) were in no position to compete internationally as a fixed exchange rate made Mexican goods increasingly expensive abroad. There were many elements that undermined the regime of "stabilizing" (and latterly, "shared") development in the 1970s, of which some, but certainly not all, were of Mexico's making. Growing population, declining agricultural productivity in the late 1970s, and growing imports caused a considerable reassessment of agriculture in 1980 under President José López Portillo.

The SAM (Mexican Food System) began to divert revenues from Mexico's recently revitalized oil production into agricultural subsidies to Mexican farmers. But the program proved enormously expensive (necessarily, to reverse the previous transfer of resources out of agriculture), even if it achieved "self-sufficiency." The SAM was effectively abandoned by 1985. Clearly, the agrarian reform that had produced a bifurcated system of subsistence and commercial agriculture was no longer adequate to sustain a country whose population had grown to nearly 70 million by 1980 from a mere 15 million in 1910.[29]

In part of a broader series of "market oriented" government reforms during the *sexenio* of Carlos Salinas de Gortari, the formal, legal basis (established by the Constitution of 1917) came to an end in 1993.[30] *Ejidos* were given the legal basis to regularize land titles through a state program (PROCEDE) that ultimately—but under restricted conditions—allowed the sale of *ejido* lands. While there has been considerable speculation on how and if the "end" of social property would affect the *ejido*, in practice, the results have been visible but not sweeping. Some property has been absorbed by urban areas and the number of *ejidatarios* has declined in recent years, but the *ejido* itself has by no means disappeared. Moreover, the intention of the change: to create a legal market in what had been ejido lands, has not been fully realized, if at all. The illegal exchanges that preceded the 1993 law have continued and may very well swamp the effects of the Salinas reform. It is still too soon to forecast the results.[31]

Far more important was the ratification of the North American Free Trade Agreement (NAFTA) involving Canada, Mexico, and the United States in 1994. While much remains to be said about the Agreement and its subsequent revision (effective 2020) as the United States-Mexico-Canada-Agreement (USMCA), in the long run, its objective was to permit managed trade in goods and capital between the three countries. As far as agriculture was concerned, the sensitive nature of corn as a kind of totemic crop—"sin maíz, no hay país," is a Mexican saying (no maize, no Mexico)—that a phase-in period was envisioned at the time of the ratification of the Treaty (corn liberalization was to be complete by 2008). Given the association of small farmers, *ejidos*, and corn, the impact of NAFTA on agriculture is of some interest. Both the United States and Mexico were (and are) among the largest producers of corn (albeit of different varieties, yellow and white). They are grown under different conditions. Mexico draws on a large component of small farmers, and, indeed, subsistence producers. In the United States, corn is produced on large, capital-intensive farms. Costs of production were much lower in the United States, and yields commensurately higher. There were also differences in corn produced for food consumption (white corn in Mexico) and for feed and industrial uses (yellow corn in the United States). There was concern about how the two economies would be integrated.

In theory, at least, the economy with comparative advantage in one commodity specializes in its production. The other leaves off production, releasing resources to sectors in which it can produce and trade profitably. This was the expectation, at least of economists, in the United States. In other words, inefficient maize producers in Mexico, concentrated in the Center and South, would switch to more profitable crops or move out of agriculture entirely. Growth, based on greater predictive efficiencies in alternatives, would raise income and employment.

This optimism was not completely shared in some circles in both countries. It became apparent relatively quickly that small farms and *minifundios* in Mexico were left relatively exposed. Especially in places like Oaxaca and Guerrero, small producers, affected by a variety of concurrent credit, pricing, and agricultural support changes, failed to adjust. As a result, peasant farmers were required to migrate elsewhere in Mexico, or even to the United States, although no such increase had been envisioned. Indeed, a lone headline in the United States remarked, "NAFTA should have stopped illegal immigration, right?"[32] Predictably, this did not happen. While maize production grew in Mexico under NAFTA, the biggest change was the "migration" of large-scale maize production to Sinaloa, which became the center of white corn production.[33] Meanwhile, corn exports from the United States (and corn-based derivatives) increased in both volume (by a factor of 4.5 between 1994 and the present) and value (by a factor of 7). These were well beyond the expected the results. At two decades from the original NAFTA agreement, the failure of productive models to get international trade right has become an open secret.[34] As of now, the Mexican government under Andrés Manuel López Obrador has reestablished guarantee prices for agricultural commodities and made a point of shifting government-financed support to small and medium farming.

The most honest, if tentative assessment of the results of the agrarian reform of the Mexican Revolution would have to be "very mixed" since neither unqualified failure—let alone success—would be an adequate characterization of a century of change.

Stabilizing Industrialization?

While many people assume that the industrialization of Mexico was a matter of the twentieth century and of "stabilizing development" (the program of government-"guided" private sector industrialization that began in the 1950s), this is a misconception.[35] With a history of factory-type industrialization dating to the early nineteenth century, the amount of "industry" that New Spain developed was neither insignificant nor trivial.[36] It was, as Adam Smith observed, "both the clothing and the household furniture of the far greater part of the people and the produce of their own industry . . . [particularly] in poor countries." Smith understood that the theory of mercantilism notwithstanding, colonies could not live on imported manufactures. It was a matter of transportation costs. As Jeffrey Williamson observed, in the Atlantic world, those costs did not begin to fall steadily until the 1840s.[37] For most of the colonial period, Mexico and Latin America more generally were compelled to feed, clothe, and house themselves. It was principally (although *not* exclusively) the affluent upper classes who could afford Asian or European imports.

Things began to change in the 1840s, even as other places may have witnessed "deindustrialization" due to falling transport costs and British industrialization. As mentioned, Mexico spent heavily on military supplies, such as uniforms, and these came from the textile factories of Querétaro, such as the famous "Hercules" owned by Cayetano Rubio. The uses of tariffs and prohibitions to prevent imports was part of the "centralist" political economy that arose in the late 1830s.[38] Moreover, high transportation costs, far from being an "obstacle" to industrialization as some have suggested, promoted an inefficient degree of regional specialization[39] The fragmentation of markets meant that spinning and weaving, albeit technologically backward, were widespread and the beneficiaries of further "protection." Commercial policy was often perverse, taxing or excluding inputs and thereby lowering the effective protection of the nominal tariff schedule. But the distance and transport costs remained, offsetting commercial policy. Much of what economists like Williamson characterize as "industrialization" in Mexico may well have been what an earlier generation called "cottage industry" which lacked both internal production economies and even nonpecuniary external economies—the creation of large numbers of trained mechanics who grew up around early factory industrialization in the United States.[40] Early Mexican industrialization, in the nineteenth century, not to say its colonial variant, was *sui generis* and easily misunderstood by scholars seeking to find precocious examples of development around the world before Western Europe and the Industrial Revolution.[41]

Industrialization, understood in the sense of technologically sophisticated concentrations of fixed capital, not all of them "heavy," such as steelmaking, began in the Porfiriato. It was then that an industrial sector marked by concentration, imperfect competition, and monopolistic production with excess capacity emerged.[42] If, as Haber has remarked, "it didn't start with [Raúl] Prebisch," we may fairly ask whether there was anything about Mexican industrialization that made it inherently unstable when severe international shocks occurred in the 1970s, not to say earlier in the 1930s when the Great Depression occurred.

Mexican industry has always tended to some degree of concentration, especially in colonial industries like woolens (Puebla and Querétaro, for instance) because of external economies (neighborhood effects that lowered costs) in production, distribution, and supply.

In the nineteenth century, industry, especially textiles, was considerably more dispersed because of transportation costs and internal tariffs. By the 1880s, Mexico produced nearly 60 million square meters of cotton cloth and supplied an estimated 60 percent of the national market.[43] Due to the outbreak of the Revolution, spindles, looms, and workers had grown more than 3 percent per year during the Porfiriato, only to fall significantly during the revolutionary period of 1912–1925. For reasons that reflected local resources (water), the availability of imported raw cotton through the Port of Veracruz, and the presence of a tightly knit community of immigrants, the so-called Barcelonnette, from the Valley of Ubaye in France, much of the industry and two of the principal firms, CIDOSA and CIVSA, set down in the state of Veracruz. They were creations of the nineteenth century, not a legacy of the colonial industry as in Puebla and Querétaro, as some have speculated. This was not "protoindustry."

While productivity had increased considerably for cotton textiles during the Porfiriato anywhere from 1.6 to 4.5 percent per year, the Revolution had a considerable impact. The competitiveness of the cotton textile industry probably reached its peak during the late Porfiriato as costs rose. This was, in part, a consequence of the rise and incorporation of trade unions into the revolutionary state, who exercised more control over hours worked, which was to be expected. The industry was characterized by a sizeable degree of oligopoly and made a deliberate choice to dissipate its rents by choosing not to modernize looms. With an aging stock of capital, costs rose, and profits fell. An oligopoly, one sheltered by tariff protection, had little incentive to do otherwise. If these plants covered their operational costs, they were profitable, if less so than before. But it is one thing to say textiles were less profitable and quite another to say that all manufacturing was. As Donald Keesing's data on employment clearly shows, employment in textiles between 1895 and 1930 may not have grown, but *all* manufacturing was larger. Employment in newer, technologically advanced skill-intensive industries such as chemicals or machinery would grow. Investment capital migrated to those industries in search of higher returns. Even employment in textiles grew from 1930 to 1950. It is possible that other entrants took up the slack from long-established Porfirian firms like CIDOSA and CIVSA.[44]

Of the more general impact of the Revolution on manufacturing (see Figure 3.1), specifically between 1910 and 1922, there can be little doubt. The volume of output (obviously a very crude measure because it has no controls) was reduced by about 8 percent on average relative to its Porfirian trend. This is not insignificant, but less than some long-standing indices had maintained. While there was an extremely sharp fall in volume during the early years of the Great Depression (1932–1935), the 1940s and World War II brought considerable prosperity to the sector. Between 1900 and 1948, overall, the trend growth in manufacturing volume was about 1.6 percent per year (see Figure 3.2).

In general, the Great Depression apparently had less an effect on Mexican industry than elsewhere in Latin America. This may be because the secular downturn in the economy began in the 1920s. It was led by the decline in oil exports, the overall role of which had steadily diminished on an international scale. Due to the Great Depression, Mexican authorities began to discern another problem that would ultimately be crucial in the development of the postwar economy.

It was an issue for the long run, but nonetheless significant for being so: the problem of domestic markets. In late 1933, one analyst said the following:

> The fundamental problem of the country is a problem of markets. [The] average salary of the Mexican worker barely reaches $0.50 (pesos) daily. This yields an

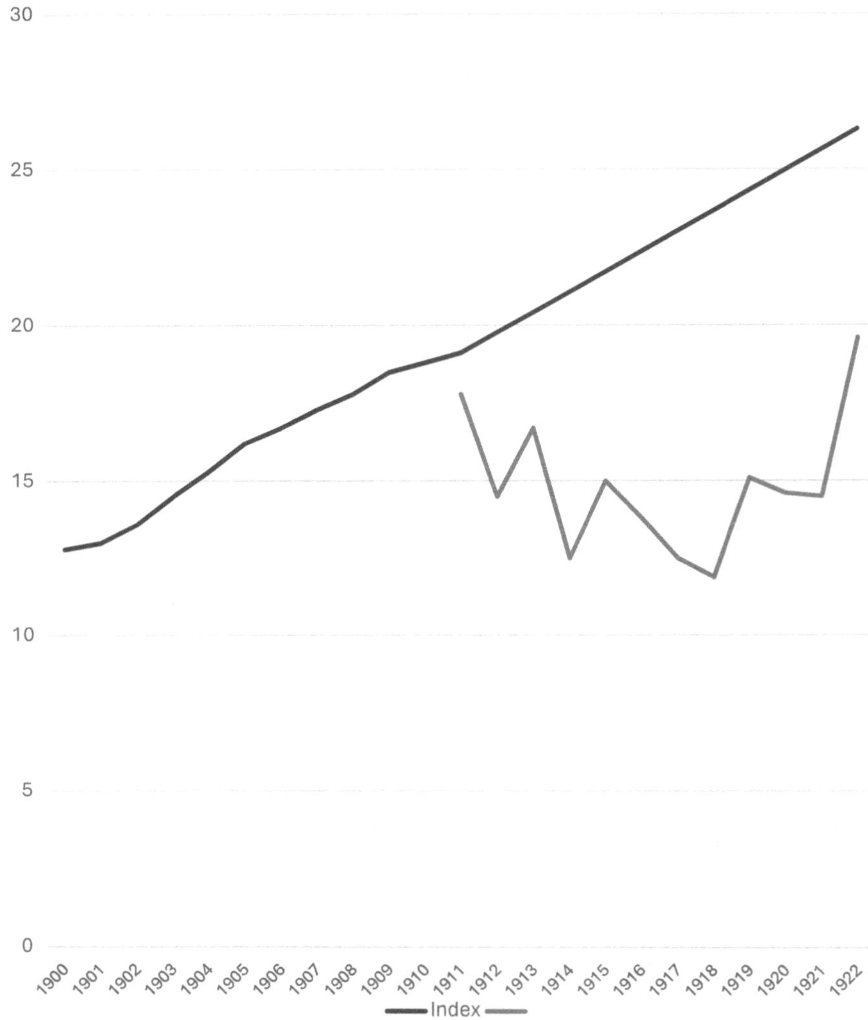

FIGURE 3.1 Secular Trend versus Realized Output

average income, per family, of $1.60. . . . The biggest share is spent on maize; the rest on a meagre nutritional component. Only a small portion is destined for clothing, composed, as everyone knows, of cotton cloth.

The remainder of the population is the effective base for a demand capable of sustaining European-style industry. It is only a small number, perhaps 4 or 5 million people [out of a census population in 1930 of around 16.5 million]. That presently means very little, since the income of the middle class and the profits of the capitalist [salaries, rents and profits, or, essentially, national income] have diminished because of the [Depression]. . . . The country is subject to a congenital

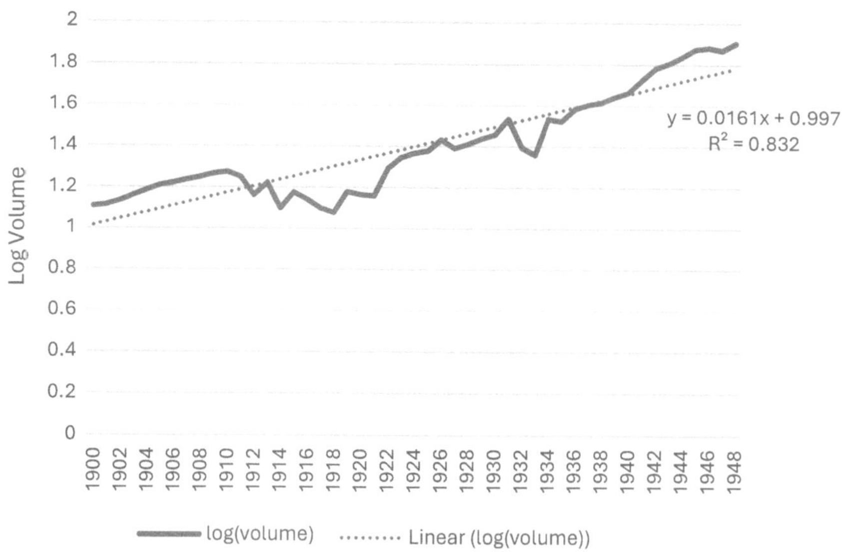

FIGURE 3.2 Trend Growth in Manufacturing, 1900–1948

> weakness. Its development proceeds with extraordinary slowness—desperately so—and is dogged at every step by its ability to consume.[45]

Here, in elegant summary, was the problem that postwar Mexico would face. With a commercial market that was effectively 25–30 percent of the population (could the colonial period or the nineteenth century have been that much lower?), the constraints on the Mexican economy were, as a first approximation, inadequate aggregate demand. This was nothing new—there were important supply issues, as we have emphasized as well. But in a nutshell, this was the situation Mexico faced when the demand-side stimulus of World War II had abated.

For just this reason, and by no means perversely, Mexico regarded the approaching war in Europe in 1939 not as a threat but as an opportunity. It was precisely a matter of aggregate demand. The probable consequences, in Mexican minds, would be very different from 1914 and World War I. Raw materials to supply the combatants would be in heavy demand and prices and export incomes would rise, as would the balance of trade.

The prospect of making money from a peso that had fallen because of the demonetization of silver in 1935 and the expropriation of foreign oil companies in 1938 under Lázaro Cárdenas in 1938 also beckoned in 1939. For certain, financial and industrial interests, among others, saw the transformative possibilities of another global conflict.[46]

As it happened, the authorities were prophetic. During World War II (1940–1947), the volume of manufacturing which had previously grown at a nearly uniform trend of 1.6 percent per year now grew 54 percent in eight years. The labor force participation rate (all sectors) grew by 7 percent between 1940 and 1950. Roads of all types (in kilometers) doubled between 1940 and 1947, from 9.9 to nearly 20,000, most of them paved.[47] The proportion of the labor force in the primary sector dropped 12 percent between 1940 and 1950. In current pesos, federal spending grew by a factor of 4.5 between 1940 and 1950. Would it be much of an exaggeration to say that the prewar expectations of the government—in 1939—had been given a significant impetus by 1950? As Rosemary Thorp points out, industry as a share of GDP in 1940 was 17 percent. By 1945, it had risen to 19 percent. Among the economies of the region, that was one of the larger relative increases.[48]

In part, the expansion occurred not simply because of the expansion of wartime demand, but because of the fiscal incentives provided by the Mexican government. Whole segments of industry were exempt from taxation during the conflict, and heavy industries such as steel and light industries such as cotton textiles also benefitted. While there were some shortages of raw materials and rising input prices, the overall impact of the war on Mexican industry was quite salutary. Agriculture, on the other hand, was considerably more subject to the vagaries of rainfall, and some, such as electricity, would require considerably expansion if industrialization were to continue smoothly.[49]

Before continuing to the postwar era, it is worth asking whether the wartime transformation of Mexico was good for everyone—shared equally. This is a difficult question to answer. Different indicators of economic welfare tell us different things, and different authors are inclined to view questions from different perspectives, ideology aside. For example, one recent synthesis that incorporates novel data tends toward a relatively optimistic view overall, well into the postwar period, while allowing that Mexico may not conform terribly well into any standard model of development.[50] A study of prices and wages shows prices rising sharply between 1939 and 1944, probably more than 100 percent. Jeffrey Bortz concludes that the share of Mexican income received as wages declined by about 13 percent, at least to judge from what we shall hereafter term the "formal sector" of the economy.[51] On the other hand, data on stature from the period analyzed by Moramay López-Alonso for members of the military shows a slight increase, somewhat at a variance with wage data.[52] The military may well have received more resources at the time, which was reflected in the divergence. On the other hand, improvements in public health and sanitation measures undertaken in the 1920s and 1930s began to take effect, regardless of what happened to the real income of, say, industrial workers. There are no easy or straightforward answers to the question of how to measure equality or inequality of result when so many different sources of change are afoot.

Nevertheless, by 1970, problems had slowly made their presence felt, especially in terms of equitable development. Population had grown to nearly 50 million, nearly half of which was under 15 years of age, and therefore not considered at maximum productive age. Life expectancy at birth had reached about 64 years of age. The net reproduction rate stood at 2.5, implying that the total population would continue to grow. Still, Mexico had reached a point in the "demographic transition" when the maximum rate of population increase had been reached.[53]

As far as industry and manufacturing were concerned, the rapid demographic growth between the end of the Revolution and 1970 again meant that the balance between "land" and "labor" in Mexico was once more in flux, with labor again becoming the abundant factor of production. That this occurred during a transition to industrialization had important implications for the shape industry assumed, as well as for the share of national income that ultimately accrued to labor.

If the growth of manufacturing is accompanied by a growth in labor productivity—and under any plausible assumption about technological change, it will inevitably be—the ability of industry to absorb a growing population into its labor force will ultimately be constrained. It soon became clear that industry would be unable to absorb the rapidly growing population, especially as development shifted from consumer goods to capital-intensive industries such as automobiles, whose demand for labor was relatively smaller. And, indeed, this is precisely what occurred, giving rise to a large and growing "informal" sector of the labor market, not just in manufacturing per se but across the economy. Labor is presumed to be "released" to other opportunities for employment, but what if they are deficient? One definition of "underdevelopment" as once understood was that markets—especially labor—did not automatically clear.

At the outset, around 1970, the share of the informal sector in the Federal District and the state of Mexico was estimated around 20 to 30 percent of the labor force.[54] Contemporary (2020) estimates placed the share at nearly twice as much. "Informality" refers to undeclared wage work, unpaid taxes, lack of compliance with health and safety regulations, and more generally (although not as straightforward), a lack of social security and its associated benefits. While informality can simply refer to people setting up business for themselves, it can also refer to small, low productivity enterprises that may or may not have links to the formal sector. These businesses keep people afloat, but not much more.

Rapid population growth depressed wages in the formal sector as well. In the 1970s, Mexico capitalized on labor abundance in manufacturing to create an industrial sector known as "maquila" or colloquially known as "border industrialization" because roughly half the employment came in the border states of Chihuahua, Baja California, and Tamaulipas as of 1998.[55] Intended to promote employment as well as technology transfer, the industry included car parts, clothing, appliances, and even plants that manufacture for Apple Computer. In 1970, employment was about 20,000 but as of March 2022, it had reached 2.8 million in some 5,200 active business, not all of them in border regions.[56] The average worker's compensation was 19,263 pesos per month, or less than 1,000 per month at current market exchange rates. As a result, in Ciudad Juárez, an important center of maquiladoras, nearly 40 percent of the population lived in poverty in the metropolitan zone, although conceivably in the absence of the maquiladoras, things could have been worse.[57]

Manufacturing, like agriculture, really consisted in part of a capital-intensive sector, productive and enjoying economies of scale. But then there was a large sector, much less productive, much of it, but by no means all, informal. In effect, this was a drag on the standard of living and a source of widespread impoverishment. Jaime Ros believed that it was possible that low wages in the "informal" sector acted as ceiling on the growth of wages in the "formal" sector, especially with less skilled labor. Indeed, growing informal employment is a reaction to economic slowdowns in Mexico, which could have simply aggravated their overall effect in aggravating poverty.[58] Formal measures of poverty, such as those provided by the National Commission for the Evaluation of Social Development Policy (CONEVAL), are not easy to come by. The "Mexican Miracle" and "stabilizing development" notwithstanding, when measured solely by the criterion of income, half the population was impoverished. Surprisingly, that figure had not changed all that much since the 1930s and 1940s, other measures notwithstanding.[59]

The results of stabilizing development in Mexico, taking not only industry and agriculture but everything into account, were disappointing. Historical measures of impoverishment are always tentative. Yet based on the best data—coming from the Economic Commission for Latin America (CEPAL), the proportion of households that received less than half the average family income—"relative poverty" in 1970—was 48 percent. The strictly urban figure was 44 percent, and the rural would have been higher. While this was by no means the worst in Latin America, it was far from the best.[60] Considering that this reflected 25 years of postwar growth and development, it was problematic. The standard measure of inequality (the Gini Coefficient: values 0 through 1, where values closer to 1 represent more inequality) was about .50 in 1950. By 1972, it had increased to .52 by "official" accounts with a CEPAL-adjusted figure of .59.[61] By any standard during the era of stabilizing development, inequality had increased and poverty (measured by income) remained widespread.

One way of considering the problem is by looking at the share of labor compensation in Gross Domestic Income (the income equivalent of GDP). In the early 1950s, estimates ranged from 42 percent (probably too high) to around 25 percent (certainly too low). Stabilizing development produced pervasive inequality. This, in turn, could never sustain the rate of growth registered in the postwar years down to 1970. Agriculture was not sufficiently prosperous (overall) to support domestic demand. The diversion of rapidly growing population into low productivity (and income) informal employment elsewhere in the economy could only make an unsustainable situation worse.

As a result, after 1970, the Mexican government turned from "stabilizing" development to "shared" development, an effort to ease political tensions that appeared in the highly volatile atmosphere accompanying the 1968 Olympic Games in Mexico City, when student protests were met by violent repression in the so-called Tlatelolco massacre of October 2, 1968. At the same time, broadening the base of economic growth would presumably enlarge consumer demand, since transferring purchasing power to the poorer classes inevitably meant increased consumer spending (on food) out of income, known as Engel's law.[62] How exactly to accomplish this was one of the factors that ultimately destabilized the entire political system and brought the 70-year hegemony of the PRI to an end in 2000.

There were various ways of increasing consumer demand, but the one chosen ultimately backfired by relying heavily on public sector spending. The problem was not government spending per se, but the kind of spending that took place: consumer subsidies rather than productive investment. It is not hard to see why the Luis Echeverría (1970–76) and José López Portillo (1976–82) *sexenios* (six-year presidential administrations) did what they did, but it is also not hard to understand (in retrospect) why their policies brought the Mexican Miracle to an end. For sure, the Mexican postwar boom came to an end because the world economic boom ended *everywhere*, the so-called Bretton Woods international trade regime (1944–1971), but the collapse occurred in Mexico with force.[63]

Growth in Mexico was sensitive to domestic demand, so the implications of a declining share of wage income were serious. Under ordinary circumstances, an effort to expand exports might well have been expected. Yet there was a strong conviction among the architects of stabilizing development that the country was particularly constrained by the balance of payments. As a result, an expansion of exports was thought to bring about an even larger increase in imports, thereby rendering the effort self-defeating. This may sound odd to modern ears, but it was a strong belief among economists influenced by structuralism and CEPAL. In fact, the concern may have been well founded.[64]

While public spending, in the long run, could also impact the balance of payments, the mechanism was indirect, the danger less apparent, and the risk more easily ignored. Some spending could be financed domestically, at least initially, although at some point, in the late 1960s, this would begin to change.

There has been a long evolution of public welfare in Mexico, beginning with the Catholic Church, moving to private charity, and ultimately, starting in the 1930s, to the public sector.[65] The means of doing so (among others) were quasi-state (*paraestatal*) entities that typically linked up the activities of the productive (private) sector to public management, ownership, and control. While a wide variety of these quasi-state entities had evolved to serve different functions (as varied as producing sugar, marketing coffee, or building diesel busses), there were some whose function was clearly directed to income maintenance and subsidies to consumption.

One of these that might serve as a representative example was CONASUPO (*Compañía Nacional de Subsistencias Populares*), which was involved with price supports for tortilla, wheat, and rice or in subsidizing milk and in operating direct retail outlets to the public that provided household products such as soap and detergent. Of course, CONASUPO was one of the ways in which the poorer parts of the population were kept in the economy. But in some ways, CONASUPO was one of the most significant initiatives. By the end of the 1970s, an estimated 70 percent of the low-income households consumed CONASUPO goods. The period from 1970 through 1982 was viewed as the "golden age" of CONASUPO, "marking its transformation from mere welfare to a fundamental component in national development." By the early to mid-1970s, CONASUPO accounted for about 20 percent of quasi-state entity spending.[66] By conservative calculation, CONASUPO and quasi-public entity spending probably accounted for about 2 percent of GDP, and more if all consumption subsidies were included. By the time Luis Echeverría took office, himself a key figure in "shared development," 2 percent of GDP was approximately the size of the public sector budget deficit. So, to put everything in its proper context, what was frequently criticized as a loss of fiscal discipline—the end of balanced federal budgets—characteristic of stabilizing development was ended by an attempt to address growing inequality without fundamentally disturbing the nature of power, the distribution of productive resources and endowments, or even the fundamental structures of the Mexican state that had evolved out of the Revolution. This was the end of the "Mexican Miracle," a severe financial crisis in 1982, of which the collapse of the Mexican peso in August 1976 (stable since 1954) was a harbinger.

The consequences of inequality are real. Peoples' lives are impacted, including the overall standard of living and nutrition. Studies of body size—in particular, of stature—have suggested that the benefits of the Revolution have been distributed unequally. Lopez-Alonso's long view of 1850–1950, especially of the post-Revolutionary period, finds that working-class people, at best, faced a stagnating standard of living, or even a deterioration. People from upper class backgrounds fared much better. After 1950, there *was* a generalized improvement, but it was not equally shared. Whatever the official history of the Revolution maintained, there were substantial and systematic differences in outcomes by gender, class, education, and region.[67]

These inequalities only reflect more basic ones in healthcare, sanitation, and nutrition. The differences in nutrition were especially stark, as between rural and urban diets. Rural people were able to consume less protein—significantly less (20 percent) and 60 percent of the calories people consumed came from maize and beans. Urban diets were more varied and generally included meat and milk. But even there significant variations appeared. Looking at the country, divided broadly into North and South, there were large disparities too, with parts of Guerrero, Yucatán, and Oaxaca, not to mention Puebla, Tlaxcala, and Hidalgo poorly served. If anything, the Revolution principally brought prosperity to urbanized areas, with most of the countryside—not to say the country—trailing well behind.[68]

The End of All Good Things

The US Treasury Secretary William Simon went on to characterize the fiscal situation in Mexico as one of "severe economic mismanagement": an increase in budget deficits of 7 percent of GDP; unrestrained money creation of about 20 percent; and a recklessly large increases in public sector wages. After much discussion between the Treasury, Mexico, and the International Monetary Fund, there was an agreement that a huge devaluation of the Mexican peso—perhaps 40 to 50 percent—would be needed.[69]

On August 31, 1976, the peso was devalued. At one point during initial trading, it reached over 20 to the dollar (from 8, fixed since 1954) Reassurances that public reaction had been mild notwithstanding, this was by no means the case. As one of the first issues of a weekly news magazine *Proceso* announced on the cover: "The Balance of a Sexenio: Gigantic Debt, Tiny Peso" (November 13, 1976, No. 2).[70]

The shock to the Mexican financial system to the end of the "era of 12.50" (referring to the peso as the equivalent of 12½ US cents) was severe. How had matters reached this stage? The situation that Simon outlined in his memo was correct. Mexico could no longer offer to redeem its pesos in dollars at the former rate, which resulted in devaluation. But why then, and why under these circumstances?

We previously argued that the underlying problem was growing inequality that constrained demand. As a result, at least in real terms, GDP growth had begun to slow as early as 1971—a full five years before the devaluation (see Table 3.2).

The 1971 date was hardly coincidental, coming as it did when the United States suspended convertibility of its dollar into gold at a fixed parity—the end of the so-called Bretton Woods exchange regime (August 15, 1971).[71] Mexico, and indeed, the entire Western economy, had prospered under a postwar regime of fixed exchange rates, tariff reductions, and the promotion of internal investment, but as John Maynard Keynes observed about the pre-World War I internal regime, it was

TABLE 3.2 Annualized Growth Rate of GDP, 1966–1982

Year	*Annualized Growth Rate*
1966	6.1
1967	5.9
1968	9.4
1969	3.4
1970	5.5
1971	3.8
1972	8.2
1973	7.9
1974	5.8
1975	5.7
1976	4.4
1977	3.4
1978	9.0
1979	9.7
1980	9.8
1981	9.6
1982	0

Source: Prices of 2015, https://data.worldbank.org/indicator/NY.GDP.MKTP.KD.ZG?locations=MX

a "delicate organization."[72] The Bretton Woods regime was different, but perhaps no less finely balanced. In Mexico, it had facilitated development, albeit development with inequality and a sense of control over secular economic developments that required both domestic political and international (and therefore internal) economic stability. When that was lost, Mexico's own version of a delicate balance fell severely, and perhaps, irreparably apart. Mechanically, if the dollar was no longer fixed to gold, then the Mexican peso, fixed to the dollar, was, in essence, no longer tied to gold either. It was only a matter of time before rising prices in Mexico would become the bearer of bad news, a sharp appreciation of what is termed the "real" exchange rate.[73] For a brief period after 1976, the resurgence of oil exports because of rising international petroleum prices (the so-called OPEC shocks of the 1970s) concealed the extent to which the model had become unsustainable and deceptively strong growth reappeared. But even that respite ended with the severe financial crisis and peso devaluation of 1982. In 1982, there was no growth, that is, 0 percent.

So much has been said about the collapse of the Miracle, mostly ex post, and mainly as a justification for dismantling the apparatus of postwar development, that it is easy to lose sight of just what was successful or just why it occurred.[74] In some ways, Mexico was a free rider to Bretton Woods, its policies viable as long as the system endured but doomed once Bretton Woods ended. That is an altogether too complicated story to be recounted here.[75] There were, certainly, uniquely Mexican elements in the failure of the system, signaled by the crisis of 1982. But as Colin Lewis has argued, there were considerable achievements to the program of import substiution that were essentially ignored by critics in light of the Crisis of 1982.

Import substitution industrialization (ISI) was not conceived in a vacuum, and there is an enormous literature, pros and cons, about it.[76] In the most general sense, the pursuit of development along orthodox lines was simply a recognition of the principle of comparative advantage, or relative least cost. Under a regime of free trade, individuals (and, by extension, countries) did best when producing what they did most efficiently, and therefore profitably. The exchange of the surplus of profitable production for goods produced less efficiently was axiomatic to an improvement in wealth and welfare, under the "correct" conditions, at least in the long run, when all markets (and their existence in all trading partners was, implicitly, an assumption as well) could adjust. While this may have been an oversimplification (it is), it supplied a justification for commodity specialization and export liberalism down to the Great Depression and World War II. Extreme specialization in sugar, rubber, coffee, hides, beef, cereals, and even precious metals inevitably led to vulnerability to large shocks in international trade produced by wars, even weather. Experience since the mid-nineteenth century had proved disappointing: it was difficult to point to a successful example of a country in Latin America that had developed by commodity exports alone. The most famous reason adduced for this was the Prebisch-Singer thesis of falling relative prices ("declining terms of trade") for commodities. Few are convinced by the argument *per se* any longer.[77]

The lived experience of World War II, in which the victorious allies (especially the United States) and the defeated Axis powers could hardly have left their fates to "the market." The United States demonstrated in graphic terms what a "controlled" economy could do under conditions of near total mobilization and price controls. The role of economics and economists in facilitating the remarkable wartime transformation of productive capacity, turning plowshares into swords, as it were, was by no means limited to John Maynard Keynes. Nevertheless, his emphasis on demand-side recovery from the Great Depression both meshed with wartime industrialization and the (temporary) disregard for fiscal and monetary orthodoxy violated the rules of the classical gold standard economies even more than the behavior of Great Britain or the United States. By the end of World War II—and certainly by the time of the so-called Chapultepec Conference (Mexico, DF, 1945), Mexico had more room for maneuver in the emerging postwar order. The US Ambassador in Mexico explicitly stated that any efforts by Mexico to increase the protection of domestic industry "do not contravene any provisions of the trade agreement of 1942 between Mexico and the United States."[78] In other words, this is a brave new world. Better get used to it.

Moreover, the idea of ISI did not really exist until 1950; even by 1960, discussions of it as a coherent economic strategy were limited. It did not become fashionable to regard the policy as an "error" until the 1980s, post hoc (see Figure 3.3). In Figure 3.3, which is a Google N-Gram with variant capitalizations, the top line matters most. The left axis is a kind of crude index number. Details apart, one thing is clear. Discussions of import substitution first peaked in the 1970s (favorable) and then again in the 1980s (unfavorable). What a difference a decade makes!

And by the mid-1980s, international economic conditions had changed so much since the late 1940s that the world was scarcely recognizable. In the wake of the 1982 financial crisis, the emphasis in Mexico was on somehow returning to the status quo ante, at least as far as growth and price stability were concerned, but this presupposes there was something successful to return to. For this reason, Clark Reynolds' landmark study of the Mexican economy, published in 1970, could effectively look on the postwar experience as a success. Much of the discussion that followed on the problems of the economy in 1982 was, at best, ahistorical, and, for the most part, exaggerated and dogmatic. Hindsight, of course, is an easier exercise than prediction.

One of the very few efforts made to measure the share of manufacturing growth that could plausibly be assigned to import substitution *per se* was made by Jaime Ros.[79] In 1960–1970, Ros calculated that import substitution accounted for 10.3 percent of manufacturing growth (far less than the growth of domestic demand). Since manufacturing grew approximately 15 percent as a share of GDP in the decade, this implies that import substitution accounted for 1.5 percent of the growth of GDP. This is hardly trivial, but far inferior to the growth of domestic demand itself. Population growth and changes in real income and relative prices were a far larger source of growth. Population (natural increase) itself was growing at more than 3 percent per year by the mid-1970s.[80]

Moreover, after 1982, there was no returning to the status quo ante. As Felipe Meza (and others) have emphasized, 1982 was a turning point in Mexican financial

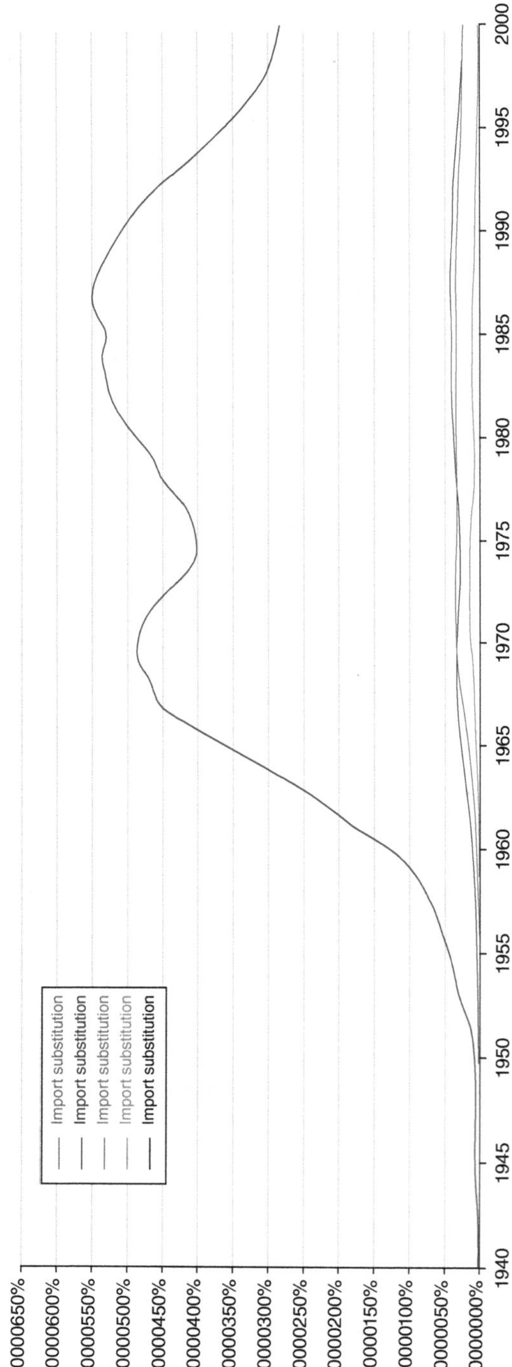

FIGURE 3.3 N-Gram Using “import substitution” as a Search Term

and economic history.[81] Prior to 1982, real GDP per capita had grown well above a 2-percent trend (3.3 percent) since1960. After 1982 and until 1995, growth steadily declined to about 0.7 percent, throwing Mexico into what some have simply termed a "great depression." Growth resumed after 1995 but at rates well below earlier levels—and was essentially flat. By 2017, "Mexico had still not recovered" from 1982 in some broader sense. Moreover, from 1982 through 1988, inflation reached levels as high as 140 percent per year, not hyperinflation by strict definition, but wildly beyond levels that had been registered under stabilizing or even shared growth. If the entire program did not simply collapse in 1982—how could it have, realistically?—the question must then be asked, but then what happened? By 2000, the point at which we have chosen to end this account, 70 years of the PRI in power was over, mostly, one supposes, because of the "great depression," as Vicente Fox of the Partido Acción Nacional (PAN) assumed the Presidency. From the perspective of the 1970s, just when Clark Reynolds was characterizing the post-revolutionary economic program as an economic success, this result was almost unthinkable.[82] But, nevertheless, the unthinkable had happened. The hard question is why. There is no simple answer.

There is a saying that if something is unsustainable, it will stop. A country's response to an international shock, or a succession of them, may or may not be sustainable. Conventionally, the argument depends on whether the shock is temporary or permanent, a one-off thing, or a change in the state of the world. In the 1970s, Mexico was affected by two major oil price shocks the so-called OPEC (Organization of Petroleum Export Countries) shocks. These were especially difficult for countries that imported crude oil. The first raised the price of oil (Heavy Crude 31° API, specifically) from $3 to $11 per barrel when Mexico was still an oil importer becoming self-sufficient in 1974 (www.opec.org/opec_web/en/index.htm).

No one lives in the future. It was as reasonable in 1973 to regard the OPEC shock as temporary as it was to regard it as permanent. And that uncertainty conditioned the Mexican fiscal response. Foreign borrowing had already begun as early as the 1960s, but in a limited way, and for reasons we have discussed.[83] Borrowing to support demand in the face of a temporary shock is hardly unreasonable because things will get back to "normal" sooner or later. Of course, the duration of "sooner or later" is an integral part of the uncertainty, particularly when a sovereign has embarked on a course of action for entirely different reasons. But Mexico's status as an oil importer changed precisely because the dollar price of oil skyrocketed.[84] Previously uneconomical sources of supply, such as rich underwater fields in the Gulf of Mexico, now became commercially feasible. Thus, "proven" oil reserves also rose dramatically. When the second OPEC shock drove the price from $15 to $34 per barrel in 1978–1979, Mexico's status as an oil exporter was virtually assured. The President of Mexico assured the public that the problem would now become one not of financing a more costly resource (technically, accommodating a price shock) but of "administering the abundance" that dramatically increased. It was, literally, a brave new world.

At the beginning (1970) of the Echeverria sexenio, the debt of the central government was a manageable 12.52 percent of GDP. By the end (1976), that share had nearly doubled to 22.35 percent, a compound rate of nearly 10 percent per year. Crude oil prices finally began to fall in 1982 just as interest rates started to rise with the implementation of the anti-inflation monetary policy of Paul Volker, the head of the US central bank in 1979. Short-term rates rose from 10 percent to 19 percent by the mid-1981, raising Mexico's costs of repayment (debt service) enormously. By August 1982, the Mexican government, caught between rising debt service and falling oil income was no longer able to maintain payment and so informed the US government. The so-called Lost Decade of the 1980s and the Debt Crisis were on. The peso, quite naturally, had to be sharply devalued to reflect a now reduced standard of living. Whereas in June of 1982 the peso traded at 46 to the dollar, by December, it had fallen to 148.[85]

The 1980s in Mexico were not called a "Lost Decade" for nothing. Virtually every meaningful measure of the standard of living in what had grown into a middle-income country in the 1970s fell, ranging from real per capita income to price stability. Social anxiety was almost palpable as people watched the prospect of a vision of middle-class urban existence slipped from their grasp. To make the point, perhaps one statistic might suffice. According to the United Nations "World Population Prospects," the annual increase in life expectancy at birth as late as 1975 was not quite 1 percent per year. By 1990, it had fallen to half of that. And there it remained until 2000.

What made things more difficult still in the 1980s was debt repayment—the very issue that precipitated the crisis of 1982. Debt repayment (in this case, to money center banks mainly in the United States) presupposed that consumption would fall, of course. Yet consumption tends to be the largest share of expenditure for the poorest classes in society. Therefore, debt repayment was linked to growing inequality in the 1980s, and a falling share of wages in national income.[86] At the same time, the falling value of the peso—itself related to the mechanism of repayment in the reserve currency of dollars—spilled over into higher domestic inflation. By the mid-1980s, trend growth in GDP per capita was *negative* and inflation had reached 150 percent per year. From 1983 to1988, real wages fell an estimated 40 percent. As if this were not enough, a devastating magnitude 8.1 earthquake hit Mexico City in September 1985, killing 40,000 people and costing into the billions of dollars. This was truly, as President de la Madrid (1982–1988) put it, "an emergency" and emergency measures to stabilize the economy, most notably, an unorthodox incomes policy known as the *Pacto Económico de Solidaridad* (PES, 1987), explicitly to avoid "an excessive increase in prices that threatened to get out of control."[87]

While the PES was ultimately successful, the measures taken to implement it were politically controversial, divisive, and economically stressful: The private sector essentially pledged to limit price increases; organized labor was compelled to accept restricted wage increases; the public sector undertook an austerity program that was little short of a dismantling of much of productive and financial infrastructure of stabilizing development; foreign competition was allowed to impose far greater price discipline domestically than it had in the past; and measures were taken to reduce the burden of external debt payments that had reached as much as 5 to 6 percent of GDP annually. As a result, when the Presidential elections of 1988 were held—during considerable controversy as to their integrity—the PRI and Carlos Salinas (1988–1994) held on to power, but even its "official" share of the vote barely exceeded 50 percent. If anything, as José Woldenberg observed, whatever its considerable successes, and however obvious its manifest failures, the model of "stabilizing development" that could function in a smaller, less urbanized, and less heterogeneous society than Mexico was well on the way to becoming, had clearly reached its limits.[88]

Nevertheless, the 1990s were a kind of an epilogue to the Miracle. Under the auspices of a market-based debt reduction scheme, known as the Brady Plan, the ratio of the external debt to GDP was reduced from 59 percent in 1988 to 39 percent in 1990. The net outflow of resources from Mexico was cut from 6 percent of GDP to 2 percent, which implied that there would now be more funds for productive investment. The number of quasi-state entities fell from 1,155 in 1982 to about 425 by the end of 1990, with the proceeds of their liquidation used for debt reduction. The operating government deficit that reached 16 percent of GDP in 1987 fell under 4 percent in 1990. These changes were anticipated to bring macroeconomic stability to Mexico, and until 1994–1995, they did. Then, once again, a sharp devaluation at the end of the Salinas *sexenio* occurred, producing another short, sharp economic contraction. The causes and responsibility for this episode, known colloquially as "the error of December" or the "Tequila Crisis," have been widely discussed. There is wide agreement that the short-term debt was badly mishandled and that the exchange rate was inconsistent with monetary and fiscal policies. At the very least, these policies brought further discredit to the PRI.[89]

To complicate matters, internal tensions in the PRI—themselves nothing new, but typically settled behind closed doors—literally had blown the party apart. The PRI candidate for President, Luis Donaldo Colosio, was assassinated in broad daylight in 1994 (the murder was never solved) and replaced by Ernesto Zedillo (1994–2000), who did little to quell factiousness within the now-aging hegemonic party. Open rebellion in Southern Mexico, in Chiapas, in 1994, ostensibly directed against the neoliberal economic policies of President Carlos Salinas (its outbreak coincided with the enactment of NAFTA), fractured the party even more deeply, and publicly reducing the standing, power, and prestige of Zedillo, who was compelled to deal with rivals for leadership in the PRI, such as Manuel Camacho Solís, who ultimately broke with the PRI itself.[90] The open disintegration only turned worse with the murder of the Secretary General of the PRI, José Francisco Ruiz Massieu, on September 28, 1994, ostensibly at the behest of the former President's brother, Raúl Salinas, who served ten years in prison before being released in 2005. There is no point in trying to sort the truth of any of this, because, likely, the truth will never be known.[91] What can be said is that the party, in deep disarray, finally lost its stranglehold on power in the election of 2000, when the PAN candidate Vicente Fox was elected president, amid continuing controversy, although no one really disputed the outcome of the election. Since 1982, what the PRI had long delivered, at least to some, was a share in the benefits of modernization, the Miracle, and the Mexican Revolution. By 2000, that era, the Miracle, and the Institutional Revolution were clearly and decisively over.

Notes

1 "Delimitación de las zonas metropolitanas de México 2015," 57, accessed June 12, 2024, www.inegi.org.mx/contenidos/productos/prod_serv/contenidos/espanol/bvinegi/productos/nueva_estruc/702825006792.pdf.
2 David M. Gould, "Mexico's Crisis: Looking Back to Assess the Future," *Federal Reserve Bank of Dallas: Economic Review* (2nd Quarter, 1995): 3–4.
3 In Spanish, see Felipe Ávila and Pedro Salmerón, *Breve Historia de la Revolución Mexicana* (Mexico City: Planeta, 2017). In English, Alan Knight, *The Mexican Revolution: A Brief Introduction* (New York, NY: Oxford University Press, 2016). I have been much influenced by Héctor Aguilar Camín, *La frontera nómada: Sonora y la Revolución Mexicana* (Mexico City: Siglo XXI, 1976). Also invaluable is Aguilar Camín's *Después del Milagro* (Mexico City: Cal y Arena, 1988).
4 Manuel Odorica and José Luis Lezama, "Consecuencias demográficas de la Revolución Mexicana," in *El Poblamiento de México: Una Visión Histórico-Demográfica*, 4 vols (Mexico City: CONAPO, 1993), 4: 47.
5 Lourdes Márquez and América Molina del Villar, "El otoño de 1918: las repercusiones de gripa en la ciudad de Mexico," *Desacatos*, no. 32 (2010): Graph 3, accessed June 13, 2024, http://ref.scielo.org/b8y4rb. I am grateful to América Molina del Villar for her discussions of these issues.
6 Amilcar E. Challú and Aurora Gómez-Galvarriato, "Mexico's Real Wages in the Age of the Great Divergence, 1730–1930," *Revista de Historia Económica. Journal of Iberian and Latin American Economic History* 33 (2015): 110–22, Table A.
7 For cotton textiles, especially, see Aurora Gómez Galvarriato, *Industria y revolución: Cambio Económico Y Social En El Valle De Orizaba, México* (Mexico City: Fondo de Cultura Económica, 2017).
8 Gómez Galvarriato, *Industria y Revolución*, 262, Gráfica VII and 37, Cuadro 1.2.
9 Razo and Haber, "Mexican Cotton Textile Industry," 502.
10 Jonathan Brown, *Oil and Revolution in Mexico* (Berkeley, CA: University of California Press, 1992).
11 Charles C. Cumberland, *Mexican Revolution. The Constitutionalist Years* (Austin, TX: University of Texas Press, 1974), 391. Stephen Haber, Noel Maurer, and Armando Razo, "When the Law Does Not Matter: The Rise and Decline of the Mexican Oil Industry," *Journal of Economic History* 63 (2003): 1–32.
12 *Tariff Act of 1921*. United States, 67th Congress, Senate, Committee on Finance (Washington, DC: GPO), 4663.
13 The point is made in Blanca Rubio, "Análisis tendencial de la economía mundial y el campo mexicano, 2015–2035," in *El Futuro de México al 2035. Una Visión Prospectiva*, eds. Manuel Perló Cohen and Silvia Inclán Osegura (Mexico City: Universidad Nacional Autónoma de México, 2018), 619.
14 Nathan Whetten, *Rural Mexico* (Chicago, IL: University of Chicago Press, 1948), 68; Virgilio Partida-Bush, "Demographic Transition, Demographic Bonus and Ageing in Mexico," accessed June 13, 2024, www.un.org/en/development/desa/population/events/pdf/expert/9/partida.pdf.

15 Whetten, *Rural Mexico,* 90.
16 Frank Tannenbaum, *Mexico The Struggle for Peace and Bread* (New York, NY: Alfred A Knopf, 1950), 136.
17 Stanley J. Shadle, *Andrés Molina Enríquez: Mexican Land Reformer of the Revolutionary Era* (Tucson, AZ: University of Arizona Press, 1994).
18 For an extensive discussion and specific cases, see Manola Sepúlveda Garza, *Vaivenes de la Historia Ejidal. Dolores Hidalgo, CIN, Guanajuato, 1900–1970* (Mexico City: Instituto Nacional de Antropología e Historia, 2011), esp. 51–112.
19 Whetten, *Rural Mexico*, 146, 594; *El minifundismo: una realidad del siglo xxi* (Mexico City: CEDRESSA, 2014), 10.
20 Secretaría de Economía, Direccion General de Estadística, *Segundo Censo Ejidal de los Estados Unidos Mexicano 1940. Resumen General* (Mexico City: Talleres Gráficas de la Nación, 1949), 7. This figure could be misleading, but on the whole, it is in line with expectations: pasturage, forest, and fallow are another matter entirely.
21 The single best modern work from which virtually my entire discussion is drawn is Arturo Warman, *El campo mexicano en el siglo xx* (Mexico City: Fondo de Cultura Económica, 2001). Also see P. Lamartine Yates, *Mexico's Agricultural Dilemma* (Tucson, AZ: University of Arizona Press, 1981).
22 Molina Enríquez, *Los grandes problemas*, repr. ed. (1909; Mexico City: Ediciones Era, 1978), 152–53, 174–75.
23 Warman, *El campo mexicano*, 216.
24 Eyler N. Simpson, *The Ejido: Mexico's Way Out* (Chapel Hill, NC: University of North Carolina Press, 1938), 556, where Simpson himself alludes to the problem.
25 Kirsten Appendini, "Tracing the Maize-Tortilla Chain," *UN Chronicle*, June 27, 2013, accessed October 8, 2022, www.un.org/en/chronicle/article/tracing-maize-tortilla-chain. Equally revealing on the same issue is Cynthia Hewitt de Alcántara, *La modernización de la agricultura Mexicana, 1940–1970*, 7th ed. (Mexico City: Siglo XXI, 1999), 99–115. For an early attempt, see R.S. Weckstein, "Evaluating Mexican Land Reform," *Economic Development and Cultural Change,* no. 18 (1970): 391–409.
26 Sources for change in agricultural productivity in Mexico are US Department of Agriculture, Economic Research Service, *Sources of Change in Mexican Agricultural Production, 1940–1964* (Washington, DC, 1971); and US Department of Agriculture, Economic Research Service, *International Agricultural Productivity,* accessed June 14, 2024, www.ers.usda.gov/data-products/international-agricultural-productivity/, September 2023 update.

For guarantree prices, Hewitt de Alcántra, *Agricultura Mexicana,* 93. Kirsten A. de Appendini and Vania Almeida Salles, "Algunas consideraciones sobre los precios de garantía y la crisis de producción de los alimentos básicos," *Foro Internacional,* no. 19 (1979): 407–8n. Sergio Reyes Osorio, *Estructura Agraria y Desarrollo Agrícola en México* (Mexico City: Fondo de Cultura Económica, 1974), 101–4, 143. The size of the resource transfer is the subject of considerable debate, but it was large and growing ever larger.
27 IndexMundi, accessed June 14, 2024, www.indexmundi.com/agriculture/?country=mx&commodity=corn&graph=imports.
28 See Gómez Galvarriato, *Industria y Revolución*, 362–78 for a valuable discussion.
29 "Alarmed Mexico Spends Heavily to Build Farming," *New York Times*, November 6, 1981.
30 Pedro Aspe, *Economic Transformation the Mexican Way* (Cambridge, MA: MIT Press, 1993).
31 Gabriela Torres-Mazuera and Kristen Appendini, eds., *La regulación imposible: (i)legalidad e (i)legitimidad en los mercados de tierra en México al inicio del siglo XXI* (Mexico City: El Colegio de Mexico, 2020). Kindle ebook.
32 *New York Times,* February 18, 2007.
33 Steven Zahniser et al., "The Growing Corn Economies of Mexico and the United States," USDA, FDS-19F-01 (August 2019) for this and what follows, accessed June 17, 2024, www.ers.usda.gov/webdocs/outlooks/93633/fds-19f-01.pdf?v=5103.

34 The United States International Trade Commission. *Economy-Wide Modeling of the Economic Implications of an FTA with Mexico and a NAFTA with Canada and Mexico*, USITC Publication 2516 (Washington, DC: USITC, May 1992), with the conspicuous exception of Levy and van Wijnbergen, "An Intertemporal, Linked, Macroeconomic CGE Model . . ." which explicitly considered agriculture and migration but even then underestimated the impact.

35 Antonio Ortiz Mena, *El Desarrollo estabilizador: reflexiones sobre una época* (Mexico City: Fondo de Cultura Económica, 1998).

36 Richard Salvucci, *Textiles and Capitalism*: *An Economic History of the Obrajes, 1539–1840.* (Princeton, NJ: Princeton University Press, 1987), passim.

37 *Globalization and the Poor Periphery Before 1850* (Cambridge, MA: MIT Press, 2006), 16.

38 Richard J. Salvucci, *Politics, Markets and Mexico's "London Debt," 1823–1887* (Cambridge, UK: Cambridge University Press, 2009), 16.

39 Haber, "Obstacles to Industrialization," passim.

40 Anthony F.C. Wallace, *Rockdale: The Growth of an American Village in the Early Industrialization* (New York, NY: Knopf, 1978), 244–45.

41 Jordan Bryan, "The California School and the British Empire," accessed June 17, 2024, https://histempire.wordpress.com/2014/12/01/the-california-school-the-british-empire/.

42 Stephen Haber, *Industry and Underdevelopment. The Industrialization of Mexico, 1890–1940* (Stanford: Stanford University Press, 1989).

43 Gómez Galvarriato, *Industria y Revolución*, 82, 37, Cuadro 1.2 for a comprehensive summary of 1870 through 1930, and 59–66 for subsequent statistics.

44 Donald B. Keesing, "Structural Change Early in Development: Mexico's Changing Industrial and Occupational Structure From 1895 to 1950," *Journal of Economic History*, no. 29 (1969): 716–38, esp. 726.

45 Banamex, *Examen de la Situación Económica de México* (1925–1945) (Mexico City: Banamex, 1976). Translation mine. September–October 1932, 121–22.

46 Cf. Friedrich Katz, *The Secret War in Mexico. Europe, the United States, and the Mexican Revolution* (Chicago, IL: University of Chicago Press, 1981).

47 Michael K. Bess, *Routes of Compromise. Building Roads and Shaping the Nation in Mexico, 1917–1952* (Lincoln, NE: University of Nebraska Press, 2017), 155–56. Most other statistics in this section are drawn from NAFINSA, *La Economía Mexicana en Cifras, 1990*, 11th ed. (Mexico City: NAFINSA, 1990).

48 Rosemary Thorp, "The Latin American Economies, 1939-c. 1950," in *Cambridge History of Latin America*, 11 vols (Cambridge, UK: Cambridge University Press, 1984–1995), 6 (1): 127. There were always exceptions. The state of Veracruz, for example, was one. See Paul Gillingham, *Unrevolutionary Mexico. The Birth of a Strange Dictatorship* (New Haven, CT: Yale University Press, 2021), 51–52.

49 Banamex, *Examen de la Situación Económica de México*, esp. 262, 270, 284, 288.

50 Ingrid Bleynat, Amílcar E Challú, and Paul Segal, "Inequality, Living Standards and Growth: Two Centuries of Economic Development in Mexico," *Economic History Review*, no. 74 (2021): 584–610.

51 Jeff Bortz, *El salario en Mexico* (Mexico City: El Caballito, 1986), 34–35. As we will see, this may bias the estimate of the share of wages downward, perhaps considerably. One scholar found that real wages in 1970 were twice that of 1939. See Juan Moreno Pérez, "Mi relación con el profesor James W. Wilkie," in *Wilkie: historia, economía y elitelore*, 2nd ed., coord., Samuel Schmidt (Ciudad Juárez, CHI: El Colegio de Chihuahua, 2017), 92.

52 M. López-Alonso, "Growth with Inequality: Living Standards in Mexico, 1850–1950," *Journal of Latin American Studies*, no. 39 (2007): 81–105, esp. Fig. 1. Thanks to López-Alonso for a thorough discussion of these issues on several occasions.

53 Martha Mier y Terán, "Dinámica de la población en México: 1895–1990. El gran cambio demográfico," *Demos* 4 (1991): 1–2. Patricia M. Rowe, *Mexico: Country Demographic Profile* (Washington, DC: Bureau of the Census, 1979), 1.

54 Edgar W. Butler, James B. Pick, and W. James Hettrick, *Mexico and Mexico City in the World Economy* (New York, NY: Routledge, 2019), 261.
55 Butler, Pick, and Hettrick, *Mexico and Mexico City in the World Economy,* 189. The modern program originated in 1965 according to Lawrence Douglas and Taylor Hansen, "Los orígenes de la industria de maquiladora en México, *Comercio Exterior*, no. 53 (2003): 1045–56.
56 "Program of Manufacturing Industry, Maquila and Export Services (IMMEX)," accessed July 17, 2024, https://en.www.inegi.org.mx/programas/immex/.
57 "Pobreza en México," accessed June 18, 2024, www.coneval.org.mx/Medicion/Paginas/PobrezaInicio.aspx.
58 Jaime Ros, "Los retos de la política económica," *Economía UNAM*, no. 16 (2019): 16–22, accessed July 17, 2024, https://doi.org/10.22201/fe.24488143e.2019.46.419.
59 Moisés González Navarro, *La pobreza en México* (Mexico City: Colegio de México, 1985), 194.
60 Oscar Altimar, *La Dimensión de la Pobreza en América Latina* (Santiago de Chile: CEPAL, 1979), 73.
61 Manuel del Castillo Negrete, *La magnitud de la desigualdad en el ingreso y la riqueza en Mexico* (Mexico City: CEPAL, 2015), 63.
62 M. Browning, "Engel's Law," *The New Palgrave Dictionary of Economics*, 2008, accessed June 18, 2024, https://doi.org/10.1057/978-1-349-95121-5_681-2.
63 Naomi Lamoreaux and Ian Shapiro, eds., *The Bretton Woods Agreements* (New Haven, CT: Yale University Press, 2019).
64 Ortiz Mena, *El desarrollo estabilizador*, 331–32. Also see *Raúl Prebisch y los desafíos del Siglo XXI*: *La restricción de la balanza de pagos al crecimiento*, accessed June 18, 2024, https://biblioguias.cepal.org/PortalPrebisch.
65 González Navarro, *Pobreza*, passim.
66 Kenneth Edward Mitchell, *State-Society Relations in Mexico. Clientelism, Neoliberalism, State Reform, and the Case of Conasupo* (London: Routledge, 2001), 40–41.
67 Moramay López Alonso and Roberto Vélez-Grajales, "Mexico: A History of Stunted Growth," *Revista de Historia Económica*, no. 37 (2019): 271–96.
68 Juan Ramírez Hernández, Pedro Arroyo, and Adolfo Chávez, "Aspectos socioeconómicos de los alimentos y la alimentación en México," *Comercio Exterior* (August 1971): 676–90.
69 *Foreign Relations of the United States, 1969–1976*, vol. E—11, Part I, Documents on Mexico; Central America; and the Caribbean, 1973–1976, "Memorandum From Secretary of the Treasury Simon to President Ford," Document 101, August 24, 1976, accessed June 18, 2024, https://history.state.gov/historicaldocuments/frus1969-76ve11p1/d101.
70 An authoritative account of the exchange rate regime in Mexico is Banco de México, *Exchange Rate Regimes in Mexico Since 1954* (Mexico City: Banco de México, 2009).
71 For a good summary, see Jeffrey A. Frieden, *Global Capitalism. Its Fall and Rise in the Twentieth Century* (New York: Norton, 2006), 339–46.
72 John Maynard Keynes, *The Economic Consequences of the Peace* (New York, NY: Harcourt, Brace, 1920), 15.
73 Mario Cimoli and Gabriel Porcile, "Learning, Technological Capabilities, and Structural Dynamic," in *The Oxford Handbook of Latin American Economics*, eds. José Antonio Ocampo and Jaime Ros (New York: Oxford University Press, 2011), 546–67. Ricardo Ffrench Davis, "The Latin American Economies, 1950–1990," in *Cambridge History of Latin America* (Cambridge, UK: Cambridge University Press, 1985–2008), 6 (1): 182.
74 Héctor Aguilar Camín, *Después del Milagro* (Mexico City: Cal y Canto, 1988). Pedro Aspe, *Economic Transformation The Mexican Way,* passim.
75 Jeffrey Garten, *Three Days at Camp David. How a Secret Meeting in 1971 Transformed the Global Economy* (New York, NY: Harper, 2021). Frieden, *Global Capitalism*, 339–59. Lamoreaux and Shapiro, *Bretton Woods*, 217–33.

76 A recent survey, Douglas A. Irwin, "The Rise and Fall of Import Substitution," *World Development*, no. 139 (2021), accessed June 20, 2024, www.sciencedirect.com/science/article/abs/pii/S0305750X20304332?via%3Dihub.

77 Victor Bulmer-Thomas, *The Economic History of Latin America Since Independence*, 3rd ed. (New York, NY: Cambridge University Press, 2014), esp. 20–285. For a summary of the terms of trade argument, see Linda K. Salvucci and Richard J. Salvucci, "Cuba and the Latin American Terms of Trade: Old Theories, New Evidence," *Journal of Interdisciplinary History*, no. 31 (2000): 197–222.

78 The Ambassador in Mexico to the Secretary of State, Mexico, DF, February 2, 1945. United States, Department of State, Office of the Historian, *Foreign Relations of the United States, 1945*, vol. 9 (American Republics), accessed June 20, 2024, https://history.state.gov/historicaldocuments/frus1945v09/d944.

79 Jaime Ros, "Mexico's Trade and Industrialization Experience Since 1960: A Reconsideration of Past Policies and Assessment of Current Reforms," in *Trade Policy and Industrialization in Turbulent Times* (South Bend, IN: Kellogg Institute, University of Notre Dame, January 1993), 186.

80 Rowe, *Mexico: Country Demographic Profiles*, 6.

81 "The Monetary and Fiscal History of Mexico, 1960–2017," 1–3, accessed June 20, 2024, https://bfi.uchicago.edu/wp-content/uploads/The-Case-of-Mexico.pdf.

82 Clark Winton Reynolds, *The Mexican Economy: Twentieth-Century Structure and Growth* (New Haven, CT: Yale University Press, 1970), 298: "Mexico . . . represents an economy that has combined the advantages . . . of individual economic freedom together with political regulation in the public interest."

83 Memorandum of Secretary of State Rusk to President Johnson, Washington, December 11, 1968. United States, Department of State, Office of the Historian, *Foreign Relations of the United States, 1964–1968*, vol. XXXI (South and Central America; Mexico), accessed June 20, 2024, https://history.state.gov/historicaldocuments/frus1964-68v31/ch9.

84 Most data on petroleum are taken from Schlumberger Oil Services, *Cien años de la Industria Petrolera en México* (Mexico City: Schlumberger Oilfield Services, 2004), esp. 195–221. See also M.A. Adelman, *Genie Out of the Bottle. World Oil Since 1970* (Cambridge, MA: MIT Press, 1995).

85 *Treasury Reporting Rates of Exchange* (Washington, DC: Department of the Treasury, 1982). This figure is still in "old pesos." As of January 1, 1993, Mexico introduced a new monetary unit called "new pesos." One "new peso" in equivalent to one thousand (1,000) old pesos. For example, in new pesos, the 1960 peso-dollar exchange rate was 12.50, which would be 0.0125 in "new" pesos. Banco de México, *Exchange Rate Regimes Since 1954* (México City: Banco de México, 2009), 10, accessed July 16, 2024, www.banxico.org.mx/markets/d/%7B397668FC-BB0B-5F0C-D4A6-241EBE9F0812%7D.pdf and www.govinfo.gov/content/pkg/GOVPUB-T63_100-7ed1d5321219f14ba8158efeaf193ef3/pdf/GOVPUB-T63_100-7ed1d5321219f14ba8158efeaf193ef3.pdf.

86 Carlos Ibarra and Jaime Ros, "The Decline of the Labor Incomer Share in Mexico, 1990–2015," *World Development*, no. 122 (2019): 570–84, esp. 570. Also see Andrés Fernández and Felipe Meza, "Informal Employment and Business Cycles in Emerging Economies: The Case of Mexico," *Review of Economic Dynamics* 18, no. 2 (2015): 381–405.

87 Presidencia de la República, Unidad de la Crónica Presidencial, *Las Razones y Las Obras. Crónica del Sexenio, 1982–1988. Sexto Año* (Mexico City: Fondo de Cultura Económica, 1988), 187. Translation mine; For real wages, see page 204 OECD Economic Surveys. Mexico, *Overview*, January 2015, accessed November 15, 2022, www.OECD.org/economy/surveys/Mexico-Overview-2015.pdf. The earthquake statistics—very much contested—came from the Mexican Seismological Institute account of the 1985 earthquake which is no longer online.

The summary description of the PES is derived from Unidad de la Crónica Presidencial, *Crónica del Sexenio,* esp. 793–814.

88 José Woldenberg, Pedro Salazar, and Ricardo Becerra, *La mecánica del cambio político en México* (Mexico City: Ediciones Cal y Arena, 2000).
89 Matthew Shane and David Stallings, *The Mexican Economy in the 1990's: Markets are In; State Control is Out* (Washington, DC: USDA, Economic Research Service, 1991). Sidney Weintraub, *Financial Decision-Making in Mexico: To Bet a Nation* (Pittsburgh, PA: University of Pittsburgh Press, 2000). Nora Lustig, *The Mexican Peso Crisis: The Foreseeable and the Surprise* (Washington, DC: Brooking Institution, 1995), accessed July 16, 2024, www.brookings.edu/articles/the-mexican-peso-crisis-the-foreseeable-and-the-surprise/.
90 All documented presciently by Juan Molinar Horcasitas, "Hacia un Cambio en el Sistema de partidos," *Cuadernos Políticos,* no. 56 (1989): 64–84. George A. Collier, *Basta! Land and the Zapatista Rebellion in Chiapas* (Oakland, CA: Food First, 2005).
91 Alma Guillermoprieto, "The Riddle of Raúl," *The New Yorker*, June 2, 1997, 36–47.

Bibliography (Including Official Publications)

Adelman, M.A. *Genie Out of the Bottle. World Oil Since 1970.* Cambridge, MA: MIT Press, 1995.

Aguilar Camín, Héctor. *La frontera nómada: Sonora y la Revolución Mexicana*. Mexico City: Siglo XXI, 1976.

Aguilar Camín, Héctor. *Después del Milagro*. Mexico City: Cal y Canto, 1988.

Altimar, Oscar. *La Dimensión de la Pobreza en América Latina.* Santiago de Chile: CEPAL, 1979.

Aspe, Pedro. *Economic Transformation the Mexican Way*. Cambridge, MA: MIT Press, 1993.

Ávila, Felipe, and Pedro Salmerón. *Breve Historia de la Revolución Mexicana.* Mexico City: Planeta, 2017.

Banamex (Banco Nacional de México). *Examen de la Situación Económica en México, 1925–1945.* Mexico City: Banamex, 1976.

Banco de México. *Exchange Rate Regimes in Mexico Since 1954.* Mexico City: Banco de Mexico, 2009. www.banxico.org.mx/markets/d/%7B397668FC-BB0B-5F0C-D4A6-241EBE9F0812%7D.pdf.

Bess, Michael K. *Routes of Compromise. Building Roads and Shaping the Nation in Mexico, 1917–1952.* Lincoln, NE: University of Nebraska Press, 2017.

Bleynat, Ingrid, Amílcar E. Challú, and Paul Segal. "Inequality, Living Standards and Growth: Two Centuries of Economic Development in Mexico." *Economic History Review*, no. 74 (2021): 584–610.

Bortz, Jeff. *El salario en México*. Mexico City: El Caballito, 1986.

Brown, Jonathan. *Oil and Revolution in Mexico*. Berkeley, CA: University of California Press, 1992.

Bryan, Jordan. "The California School and the British Empire." https://histempire.wordpress.com/2014/12/01/the-california-school-the-british-empire/.

Bulmer-Thomas, Victor. *The Economic History of Latin America Since Independence*. 3rd ed. New York, NY: Cambridge University Press, 2014.

Butler, Edgar W., James B. Pick, and W. James Hettrick. *Mexico and Mexico City in the World Economy*. New York, NY: Routledge, 2019.

Challú, Amílcar, and Aurora Gómez-Galvarriato. "Mexico's Real Wages in the Age of the Great Divergence, 1730–1930." *Revista de Historia Económica. Journal of Iberian and Latin American Economic History*, no. 33 (2015): 83–122.

Cimoli, Mario, and Gabriel Porcile. "Learning, Technological Capabilities, and Structural Dynamic." In *The Oxford Handbook of Latin American Economics*, edited by José Antonio Ocampo and Jaime Ros, 546–67. New York, NY: Oxford University Press, 2011.

Collier, George A. *Basta! Land and the Zapatista Rebellion in Chiapas*. Oakland, CA: Food First, 2005.

Cumberland, Charles C. *Mexican Revolution. The Constitutionalist Years*. Austin, TX: University of Texas Press, 1974.

De Appendini, Kirsten A., and Vania Almeida Salles. "Algunas consideraciones sobre los precios de garantía y la crisis de producción de los alimentos básicos." *Foro Internacional,* no. 19 (1979): 402–23.
Del Castillo Negrete, Manuel. *La magnitud de la desigualdad en el ingreso y la riqueza en Mexico*. Mexico City: CEPAL, 2015.
Fernández, Andrés, and Felipe Meza. "Informal Employment and Business Cycles in Emerging Economies: The case of Mexico." *Review of Economic Dynamics*, 18, no. 2 (2015): 381–405. https://doi.org/10.1016/j.red.2014.07.001.
Ffrench Davis, Ricardo. "The Latin American Economies, 1950–1990." In *Cambridge History of Latin America*. 12 vols, edited by Leslie Bethell, 6 (1), 159–252. Cambridge, UK: Cambridge University Press, 1985–2008.
Frieden, Jeffrey A. *Global Capitalism. Its Fall and Rise in the Twentieth Century.* New York, NY: Norton, 2006.
Garten, Jeffrey. *Three Days at Camp David. How a Secret Meeting in 1971 Transformed the Global Economy*. New York, NY: Harper, 2021.
Gillingham, Paul. *Unrevolutionary Mexico. The Birth of a Strange Dictatorship.* New Haven, CT: Yale University Press, 2021.
Gómez Galvarriato, Aurora. *Industria y revolución: Cambio Económico Y Social En El Valle De Orizaba, México*. Mexico City: Fondo de Cultura Económica, 2017. Kindle ebook.
González Navarro, Moisés. *La pobreza en México.* Mexico City: Colegio de México, 1985.
Gould, David. "Mexico's Crisis: Looking Back to Assess the Future." *Federal Reserve Bank of Dallas: Economic Review* (2nd Quarter, 1995).
Guillermoprieto, Alma. "The Riddle of Raúl." *The New Yorker*, June 2, 1997.
Haber, Stephen. *Industry and Underdevelopment. The Industrialization of Mexico, 1890–1940.* Stanford, CA: Stanford University Press, 1989.
Haber, Stephen. "Assessing the Obstacles to Industrialisation: The Mexican Economy, 1830–1940." *Journal of Latin American Studies,* no. 24 (1992): 1–32.
Haber, Stephen Noel Maurer, and Armando Razo. "When the Law Does Not Matter: The Rise and Decline of the Mexican Oil Industry." *Journal of Economic History*, no. 63 (2003): 1–32.
Ibarra, Carlos, and Jaime Ros. "The Decline of the Labor Income Share in Mexico, 1990–2015." *World Development*, no. 122 (2019): 570–84. https://doi.org/10.1016/j.worlddev.2019.06.014.
Instituto Nacional de Estadística e Geografía. "Programa de la industria manufacturera, maquiladora y de servicios de exportación (IMMEX) – 2007 en adelante." www.inegi.org.mx/programas/immex/.
Katz, Friedrich. *The Secret War in Mexico. Europe, the United States, and the Mexican Revolution*. Chicago, IL: University of Chicago Press, 1981.
Keesing, Donald B. "Structural Change Early in Development: Mexico's Changing Industrial and Occupational Structure From 1895 to 1950." *Journal of Economic History*, no. 29 (1969): 716–38.
Keynes, John Maynard. *The Economic Consequences of the Peace*. New York, NY: Harcourt, Brace, 1920.
Knight, Alan. *The Mexican Revolution: A Brief Introduction*. New York, NY: Oxford University Press, 2016.
Lamoreaux, Naomi, and Ian Shapiro, eds. *The Bretton Woods Agreements*. New Haven, CT: Yale University Press, 2019.
Lewis, Colin. "CEPAL and ISI: Reconsidering the Debates, Policies and Outcomes." *Revista de Estudios Sociales*, no. 68 (2019): 8–26. https://doi.org/10.7440/res68.2019.02.
López Alonso, Moramay, and Roberto Vélez-Grajales. "Mexico: A History of Stunted Growth." *Revista de Historia Económica*, no. 37 (2019): 271–96.
Lustig, Nora. *The Mexican Peso Crisis: The Foreseeable and the Surprise*. Washington, DC: Brooking Institution, 1995. www.brookings.edu/articles/the-mexican-peso-crisis-the-foreseeable-and-the-surprise/.

Márquez, Lourdes, and América Molina del Villar. "El otoño de 1918: las repercusiones de gripa en la ciudad de Mexico." *Desacatos*, no. 32 (2010): Graph 3. www.scielo.org.mx/scielo.php?script=sci_arttext&pid=S1607-050X2010000100010. (online only)
Meza, Felipe. *The Monetary and Fiscal History of Mexico, 1960–2017*. Macro-Finance Research Paper. Chicago, IL: Becker-Friedman Institute, 2019.
Mier y Terán, Martha. "Dinámica de la población en México: 1895–1990. El gran cambio demográfico." *Demos*, no. 4 (1991): 1–2.
Mitchell, Kenneth Edward. *State-Society Relations in Mexico. Clientelism, Neoliberalism, State Reform, and the Case of Conasupo*. London, UK: Routledge, 2001.
Molina Enríquez, Andrés. *Los grandes problemas nacionales*. Repr. ed. Mexico City: Ediciones Era, 1978. First published 1909.
Molinar Horcasitas, Juan. "Hacia un Cambio en el Sistema de partidos." *Cuadernos Políticos*, no. 56 (1989): 64–84.
Moreno Pérez, Juan. "Mi relación con el profesor James W. Wilkie." In *Wilkie: historia, economía y elitelore*, edited by Samuel Schmidt. Ciudad Juarez, CHI: El Colegio de Chihuahua, 2017. www.colech.edu.mx/cont/wilkiejames.pdf.
Nacional Financiera, SA. *La Economía Mexicana en Cifras*. 11th ed. Mexico City: NAFINSA, 1990.
Odorica, Manuel, and José Luis Lezama. "Consecuencias demográficas de la Revolución Mexicana." In *El Poblamiento de Mexico: Una Visión Histórico-Demográfica*. 4 vols, 4, 32–53. Mexico City: Secretaría de Gobernación, Consejo Nacional de Población. CONAPO, 1993.
OECD. *Economic Surveys: Mexico*. https://doi.org/10.1787/19990723.
Ortiz Mena, Antonio. *El Desarrollo estabilizador: reflexiones sobre una época*. Mexico City: Fondo de Cultura Económica, 1998.
Presidencia de la República, Unidad de la Crónica Presidencial. *Las Razones y Las Obras. Crónica del Sexenio, 1982–1988*. Mexico City: Fondo de Cultura Económica, 1984–1988.
Ramírez Hernández, Juan, and Pedro Arroyo, and Adolfo Chávez. "Aspectos socioeconómicos de los alimentos y la alimentación en México." *Comercio Exterior* (August 1971): 676–90.
Reynolds, Clark Winton. *The Mexican Economy: Twentieth-century Structure and Growth*. New Haven, CT: Yale University Press, 1970.
Ros, Jaime. "Mexico's Trade and Industrialization Experience Since 1960: A Reconsideration of Past Policies and Assessment of Current Reforms." In *Trade Policy and Industrialization in Turbulent Times*, 186. South Bend, IN: Kellogg Institute, University of Notre Dame, 1993.
Rowe, Patricia M. *Mexico: Country Demographic Profiles*. Washington, DC: Bureau of the Census, 1979.
Rubio, Blanca. "Análisis tendencial de la economía mundial y el campo mexicano, 2015–2035." In *El Futuro de México al 2035. Una Visión Prospectiva*, edited by Manuel Perló Cohen and Silvia Inclán Osegura, 617–52. Mexico City: Universidad Nacional Autónoma de México, 2018.
Salvucci, Richard. *Textiles and Capitalism in Mexico: An Economic History of the Obrajes, 1539–1840*. Princeton, NJ: Princeton University Press, 1987.
Salvucci, Richard J. *Politics, Markets and Mexico's "London Debt," 1823–1887*. Cambridge, UK: Cambridge University Press, 2009.
Salvucci, Linda K., and Richard J. Salvucci. "Cuba and the Latin American Terms of Trade: Old Theories, New Evidence." *Journal of Interdisciplinary History*, no. 31 (2000): 197–222.
Schlumberger Oil Services. *Cien años de la Industria Petrolera en México*. Mexico City: Schlumberger Oilfield Services, 2004.
Sepúlveda Garza, Manola. *Vaivenes de la Historia Ejidal. Dolores Hidalgo, CIN, Guanajuato, 1900–1970*. Mexico City: Instituto Nacional de Antropología e Historia, 2011.
Shadle, Stanley J. *Andrés Molina Enríquez: Mexican Land Reformer of the Revolutionary Era*. Tucson, AZ: University of Arizona Press, 1994.

Shane, Matthew, and David Stallings. *The Mexican Economy in the 1990's: Markets are In; State Control is Out.* Washington, DC: United States Department of Agriculture, Economic Research Service, 1991. https://doi.org/10.22004/ag.econ.309588.
Simpson, Eyler N. *The Ejido: Mexico's Way Out.* Chapel Hill, NC: University of North Carolina Press, 1938.
Tannenbaum, Frank. *Mexico. The Struggle for Peace and Bread.* New York, NY: Albert A. Knopf, 1950.
Tariff Act of 1921. United States, 67th Congress, Senate, Committee on Finance. Washington, DC: GPO, 1921–1923.
Thorp, Rosemary. "The Latin American Economies, 1939–1950." In *Cambridge History of Latin America.* 12 vols, edited by Leslie Bethell, 6 (1), 159–252. Cambridge, UK: Cambridge University Press, 1985–2008.
Torres-Mazuera, Gabriela, and Kristen Appendini, eds. *La regulación imposible: (i)legalidad e (i)legitimidad en los mercados de tierra en México al inicio del siglo XXI.* Mexico City: El Colegio de Mexico, 2020. Kindle ebook.
United Nations, Economic Commission for Latin America (CEPAL). *La restricción de la balanza de pagos al crecimiento.* New York, NY: CEPAL, 2012. https://biblioguias.cepal.org/PortalPrebisch.
United States, Department of State, Office of the Historian. *Foreign Relations of the United States: Diplomatic Papers, 1945.* Vol. IX (The American Republics). https://history.state.gov/historicaldocuments/frus1945v09.
United States, Department of State, Office of the Historian. *Foreign Relations of the United States, 1964–1968.* Vol. XXXI (South and Central America; Mexico). https://history.state.gov/historicaldocuments/frus1964-68v31/ch9.
United States, Department of State, Office of the Historian. *Foreign Relations of the United States, 1969–1976.* Vol. E–11, Part 1, Documents on Mexico (Central America; and the Caribbean, 1973–1976). https://history.state.gov/historicaldocuments/frus1969-76ve11p1.
United States, Department of the Treasury. *Reporting Exchange Rates, 2001–2024.* https://api.fiscaldata.treasury.gov/services/api/fiscal_service/v1/accounting/od/rates_of_exchange.
United States, International Trade Commission. *Economy-Wide Modeling of the Economic Implications of an FTA with Mexico and a NAFTA with Canada and Mexico.* USITC Publication 2516, Washington, DC: USITC, 1992. www.usitc.gov/publications/332/pub2516.pdf.
Wallace, Anthony F.C. *Rockdale: The Growth of an American Village in the Early Industrialization.* New York, NY: Knopf, 1978.
Warman, Arturo. *El campo mexicano en el siglo xx.* Mexico City: Fondo de Cultura Económica, 2001.
Weckstein, R.S. "Evaluating Mexican Land Reform." *Economic Development and Cultural Change,* no. 18 (1970): 391–409.
Weintraub, Sidney. *Financial Decision-Making in Mexico: To Bet a Nation.* Pittsburgh, PA: University of Pittsburgh Press, 2000.
Whetten, Nathan. *Rural Mexico.* Chicago, IL: University of Chicago Press, 1948.
Williamson, Jeffrey G. *Globalization and the Poor Periphery Before 1950.* Cambridge, MA: MIT Press, 2009.
Woldenberg, José, Pedro Salazar, and Ricardo Becerra, *La mecánica del cambio político en México.* Mexico City: Ediciones Cal y Arena, 2000.
Zahniser, Steven, Nicolás Fernando López López, Mesbah Motamed, Zully Yazmin Silva Vargas, and Tom Capehart. "The Growing Corn Economies of Mexico and the United States." USDA, FDS-19F-01, August 2019. www.ers.usda.gov/webdocs/outlooks/93633/fds-19f-01.pdf?v=5103.
Proceso
New York Times

EPILOGUE

When Harvard Business School professor Raymond Vernon published *The Dilemma of Mexican Development* in 1963, he raised an interesting question. If Mexico were to continue to pursue the development strategy that was bringing it apparent success, could it do so indefinitely? There were, in essence, two problems. One was diminishing returns. Absent technological change, nothing could grow at the same rate forever. That much was plain common sense, not to say arithmetic. The other was the question of finance. Growth was a function of investment. Investment was a function of savings. Public savings start with taxes. There was then no real evidence—and much to the contrary (after Cambridge economist Nichols Kaldor recommended sweeping tax reform in 1960)—that the Mexican private sector was willing to bear the burden of growing taxes indefinitely.

There was, at that point, no mechanism for the international transfer of capital of the magnitude necessary for massive public sector investment. Indeed, under a regime of fixed nominal exchange rates, it probably was not even possible. So however much Mexican politicians and technocrats might find the Mexican way convenient, even self-serving, or desirable from a professional point of view, it could not continue forever. Nor would it end well.

Even if there was at least some private support in Mexico for Vernon's views, and perhaps public support outside, Vernon's reception in Mexican official circles was far from enthusiastic. One Mexican economist, Ifigenia de Navarete, publicly compared Vernon to the mythic figure of Quetzalcoatl, the fair-skinned deity who would bring down the Aztec Empire. This was emphatically not intended as a compliment, and Vernon, clearly wounded, beat a retreat and concentrated his later efforts on multinational enterprise.[1]

But we concluded with the epochal Presidential election of 2000, one in which the PAN candidate (later President) Vicente Fox, promised 7 percent per year growth,

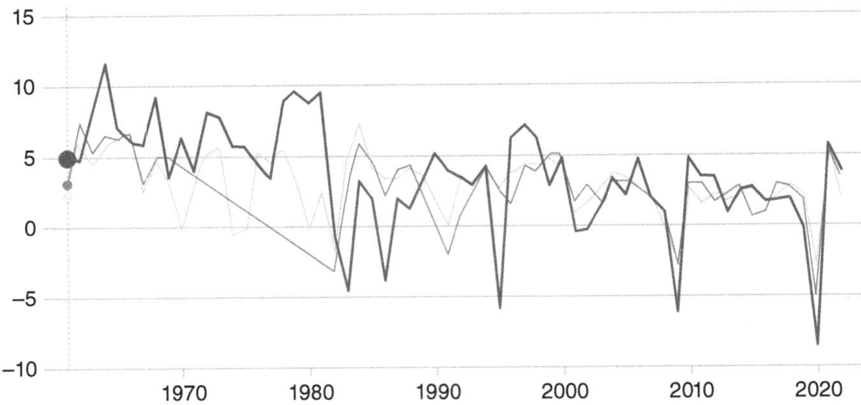

FIGURE EPILOGUE 1 Rate of Economic Growth in Mexico, 1960–2021 (the left axis represents the percentage and the heavy line denotes Mexico)

or, to put it differently, the Resurrection of the Miracle before his *sexenio* was over.[2] So Vernon, whatever his errors, was not completely wrong. He was somewhat premature, thus leaving himself open to the proverbial "stopped watch is correct twice a day" wrong. But in 1980, as it turned out, the Miracle was over once and for all. Indeed, if measured by the growth of GDP, subsequent rates rarely reached half of their pre-1980 level, when they reached it at all. See Figure Epilogue 1.

By 1990, the dimensions of the problem were becoming quite clear. Héctor Aguilar Camín, no "neoliberal," put things quite succinctly: "the urgent need in Mexico in the 1990s can be summarized in one word: *growth.* No growth, no production, or jobs; no production or jobs, no nothing."[3] But the longer the situation persisted, the more perplexing—and polarizing—the issue became. Since Vernon had essentially—and, pretty much, uniquely—predicted there would be a problem, one was tempted to fall back on his logic. It was—and is—a kind of arithmetic and economic *reductio.* Nothing is forever, nothing can grow forever, nothing lasts forever, all good things. . . . A cliché is not an explanation, much less a nostrum for reversing a problem. And the fact that virtually all the explanations given were, of necessity, *post hoc*, made them, if anything, less convincing. Over time, the usual suspects were rounded up, interrogated, and dismissed. Explanation became an exercise in frustration.[4]

There are only two lines of thought that seem very convincing and even these are more hypotheses than established conclusions. One, basically, attributable to the economist Jaime Ros, is that the Mexican economy has been demand-constrained. Since productivity growth is a function of demand itself, anything that acts as a brake on demand will reduce productivity growth in something of a vicious circle.[5]

Ros explores various dimensions of the problem, including incentives for the low productivity informal sector to grow. But he also alludes to a second hypothesis, which is the role of the Banco de Mexico, the central bank, in constraining growth. Ros argues (if only implicitly) that the central bank's single-minded focus on restraining inflation (unlike, say, the dual mandate of the Federal Reserve Bank of the United States on price stability and full employment, which is also the mandate of the Full Employment Act of 1946) was a severe drag on economic growth.[6]

Considering Mexico's experience with inflation in the 1980s, one might argue, such caution is understandable. But understandable or not, the constraint has real costs. An unwillingness to face them squarely helps nothing. In fact, any present or future *sexenio* that tries to stimulate growth by enlarging public spending or running public sector deficits will succeed mostly in raising interest rates and the real value of the peso, both of which will only aggravate the problem of slow growth. And that is simply the beginning, not to mention the effect of capital flows and the supply of money of foreign origin, which is indeed a problem that Andrés Manuel Lopez Obrador faces in the waning days of his *sexenio.* A house, divided, one recalls cannot stand.[7]

The other possibility is to place the narrative of Mexican "exceptionalism," especially the end of the Miracle, in a broader context. This context would emphasize the end of the Bretton Woods gold-exchange, fixed exchange rate system in 1971. It would discuss the removal of capital controls, a keystone of the Bretton Woods system. The example of the so-called Tequila Crisis of 1994–1995 would also be invoked, so that a delayed response to the changes that began in 1971 in the world economic regime, including the OPEC oil shocks of 1973 and 1979, all of which had confounding effects on the Mexican economy, would assume pride of place. It is useful to recall there were other "miracles" in places like Japan, Italy, and even Greece. None of them survived the 1970s. In some ways, Mexico, too, was an artefact of the postwar Golden Age of Capitalism. When Presidents Echeverría and López Portillo pursued unsustainable monetary and fiscal expansion—"unsustainable" in light of what was sustainable under Bretton Woods but inconsistent with the goal of pursuing social justice without fundamental economic reform—the edifice of postwar economic policy collapsed, and so did the "miracle" along with it. The political system and control of the country, focused traditionally on the President in Mexico City, the source of state largesse, went with it. And large parts of the country slowly pulled away from the control of the central government or Federation. It felt, in some way, like the nineteenth-century redux. There are indeed lessons from the past.[8]

Notes

1 The entire story is well retold in Soledad Loaeza and Graciela Márquez, coord., *Raymond Vernon en 1963. Los dilemmas de entonces y de ahora del desarollo mexicano* (Mexico City: El Colegio de México, 2023).

2 Interview with Vicente Fox, "Commanding Heights," *PBS*, April 4, 2001, accessed June 24, 2024.

3 Héctor Aguilar Camín, *Después del milagro*, 4th ed. (Mexico City: Cal y Canto, 1990), 285. Translation mine.

4 Jesus Cañas, Sewon Hur, and Braden Strackman, "Mexico's Productivity Woes Limit Nearshoring, Growth Potential," *Federal Reserve Bank of Dallas, Southwest Economy*, April 16, 2024, accessed June 25, 2024.
5 Jaime Ros Bosch, *Algunas tesis equivocadas sobre el estancamiento económico de México* (Mexico City: El Colegio de México, 2013), esp. Chapter 1.
6 "The main objective of the Banco de Mexico is to maintain a low and stable inflation," accessed June 25, 2015.
7 Jorge A. Chávez Presa, "Mexico's 2024 Public Debt Surge: Defying Prudence. A Cause for Concern?," Wilson Center, November 20, 2023, accessed June 25, 2024, www.wilsoncenter.org/article/mexicos-2024-public-debt-surge-defying-prudence-cause-concern.
8 Stephen A. Marglin and Juliet B. Schor, eds., *The Golden Age of Capitalism. Reinterpreting the Postwar Experience* (Oxford, UK: Clarendon Press, 1992); and especially Andrew Glyn, Alan Hughes, Alain Lipietz, and Ajit Singh, "The Rise and Fall of the Golden Age," 64.

Bibliography

Aguilar Camín, Héctor. *Después del milagro*. 4th ed. Mexico City: Cal y Canto, 1990.

Banco de Mexico. www.banxico.org.mx/indexen.html.

Cañas, Jesús, Sewon Hur, and Braden Strackman. "Mexico's Productivity Woes Limit Nearshoring, Growth Potential," *Federal Reserve Bank of Dallas, Southwest Economy*, April 16, 2024.

Chávez Presa, Jorge A. *Mexico's 2024 Public Debt Surge: Defying Prudence. A Cause for Concern?* Washington, DC: Wilson Center, November 20, 2023. www.wilsoncenter.org/article/mexicos-2024-public-debt-surge-defying-prudence-cause-concern.

Loaeza, Soledad, and Graciela Márquez, coords. *Raymond Vernon en 1963. Los dilemmas de entonces y de ahora del desarollo mexicano*. Mexico City: El Colegio de México, 2023.

Marglin, Stephen A., and Juliet B. Schor, eds. *The Golden Age of Capitalism. Reinterpreting the Postwar Experience.* Oxford, UK: Clarendon Press, 1992.

Public Broadcasting System. Interview with Vicente Fox. "Commanding Heights," April 4, 2001.

Ros Bosch, Jaime. *Algunas tesis equivocadas sobre el estancamiento económico de México*. Mexico City: El Colegio de México, 2013.

DATA APPENDIX

Anyone doing historical work for Mexico faces the problem of data and sources, and particularly primary sources, the accessibility of which is often problematic. Many would say, correctly, that the situation today is immeasurably better than it was half a century ago. Systematic efforts to locate, preserve, classify, calendar, and even digitize archival materials have opened a new world to scholars. Yet serious problems remain, and some of them are the consequence of the very effort to organize materials since the 1970s.

Economic historians face a particular problem. It is no longer sufficient, according to the standards of the field in Anglophone or developed countries to simply present anecdotal data. Ever since the so-called cliometric revolution, historians were expected to use rigorous hypothesis testing on homogeneous collections of serial data employing standard economic theory. In principle, that sounds reasonable. And yet one reflects that in Mexico, and in many other places besides, the bureaucratic mechanism needed to create, collect, and catalog such data did not, by force of circumstances, exist before the twentieth century, if then. So one either writes off most of the country's history as literally unknowable or makes do with what is at hand. The results (and methods employed) are not always orthodox, but that is just the reality of things. Telling economic historians "whereof one cannot speak one must be silent" is not very helpful. Perhaps better to light one candle than to curse the darkness. But always admit you are lighting *one* candle. Trying to oversell the results of any econometric exercise will only fool those willing to be fooled, or those who simply know no better.

It is not so much a matter of whether our numbers are "correct" as they are what they seem. I prefer to think of probability distributions or confidence intervals—in simple English, a range, if only implicitly, if not a point estimate, for a given number. We know that much of what we say is tentative, so why not admit it? And why not search for other nonquantitative evidence that supports or contests our claims? History is dialog and dialectic anyway. Anyone looking seeking objective truth is advised to look elsewhere.

That said, we count and measure whenever we can. We use all the resources we have at our disposal, and that sometimes requires either imagination or a willing suspension of disbelief, or both. Sometimes, one assumes the existence of a can opener, as an old joke in economics goes. Sometimes, one must assume the existence of the can itself. Complete markets in Mexico at any time are few and far between.

Similarly, the impact of climate change on history is a subject that is wildly, and justifiably, in vogue. I take this concern into account as much as possible by drawing on two kinds of evidence. One is provided by dendrochronology, or the study of tree rings as evidence of periods of wetness or dryness. There are now well-established protocols and a variety of data sites that are accessible even to a nonspecialist (e.g., http://drought.memphis.edu/). I use the evidence to bring controlled speculation about the impact of rainfall, or its absence, on an agrarian society in which such considerations were crucial. I use standard indices (such as the PDSI), all of which are explained in detail on the database and its associated publications and in the text. I present the data in simple graphic form, always asking if it confirms or rejects what we *think* we know. I employ other evidence, such as tithe collections, or vital statistics, to establish correspondence or its absence. Dendrochronology is a tool, not a magic wand. But there are serious caveats.

For one thing, the geographic reference I employ is a point in the Mexican Bajío, Amealco, precisely because it is a broad proxy for climatic effects on cereal agriculture in Central Mexico. Note, I do not say "Mexico," because, as the reader will soon find, the idea of an integrated colonial or early national "economy" is an anachronism. We have long gotten past the point of doing Mexican regional history and trying to make some limited generalizations from it. Economic history is no different. A classic study of Mexico was once entitled "Many Mexicos." In economic history, one inevitably must ask, about which Mexico are we speaking? Someone may object that the observation remains true today as well. And indeed it should. If we cannot speak of "Mexico" overall, then we will not. "Amealco" is not "Mexico." Shift the geographic focus 100 kilometers in any direction and you are likely to get rather different results from climate reconstruction. A little humility is a good thing. A lot is even better.

I also construct a continuous index of ecological, environmental, and agricultural stress for the colonial period. I utilize the rather remarkable collection of anecdotal data assembled by Virginia García Acosta and her colleagues in *Desastres agrícolas en México (958–1822)*. There is also a volume for the nineteenth century, but I decided against using the results: its coverage seemed less thorough. Moreover, the advent of railroads and industrialization after 1870 seemed to make climate as an explanatory economic factor somewhat less compelling. But in any event, here is a brief attempt to explain how I constructed, the so-called IEEAS, or index of environmental, epidemiological, and agricultural stress.

The raw material for the IEEAS is provided by an archival survey done by Virginia García Acosta, Juan Manuel Pérez Zevallos, and Ameríca Molina del Villar. The survey has been described as the first joint result of an initiative begun in 1992 whose goal was to obtain, arrange, and systematize information on agricultural disasters coming basically from primary sources. It accumulates, catalogs, dates, annotates, and documents all (then) known references to agricultural disasters. A particular focus was evidence of drought, but the researchers included citations documenting dearth, harvest failure, epidemic disease, excess rainfall, hailstorms, frosts, flooding, and windstorms. Nearly 40 archives and libraries were examined, not to mention printed primary sources. Central and West Central Mexico are most heavily documented, but peripheral areas are included as well. The result is the availability of the single most comprehensive guide to early agricultural failure and its causes and consequences. The key problem is to reduce the literary evidence to something numerical because basic measurement—which is all we attempt—requires it. And thus, the qualitative descriptions were reduced to a simple coding scheme.

The scheme is arbitrary, as it must be, but I applied it consistently, or as consistently as I could. I experimented with different techniques and levels of formality but concluded that simpler was not only practical but probably more flexible, given the wide range of meteorological phenomena were included. The aim was inclusion more than precision since the archival sources themselves are frequently imprecise. The results are a very general picture, mostly valuable for large trends and in the long run, although sometimes the index' s results must hinge on a single year or so.

Using each described episode (and I used *each*, and not a sample), I coded each episode in the following way, and then computed an annual sum as a measure of stress. In theory, a given year could score anywhere from 0 (no stress) to 30 (maximum stress). Since long-term results tend to be more meaningful, I computed simple moving averages of appropriate duration, usually ten years. The averages must be consistently computed to be comparable, obviously. Rarely do single year observations tell us much, and then these tend to be years of exceptional stress (or tranquility) of which there are few. Even notorious episodes, such as 1785–1786, the year of hunger, reflect the peculiarities of archives and data collection, so in no sense should be considered "objective." It is rather, as one economic historian once used the phrase, "controlled conjecture." How difficult, comparatively speaking, were environmental, epidemiological, and agricultural conditions over time: better, worse, or much better, or much worse? And if so, what were the larger political, economic, and social consequences, if any? Thinking about climate and its connection to the fiscal results of the Spanish Inquisition in the seventeenth century is certainly different. Yet historians, such as Geoffrey Parker, have suggested that it is possible.

Coding Values Applied
To *Desastres Agricolas*, and then Summed
Annually

Local (L) drought or excess rain	1
Regional (R) drought or excess rain	2
Multiregional (M) drought or excess rain	3

L hunger	4
R hunger	5
M hunger	6
L pestilence	7
R pestilence	8
M pestilence	9
L Epidemic	10
R Epidemic	11
M Epidemic	12

The calculated results are displayed graphically in Figures 1.2, 1.5, and 1.10 in the Chapter 1. One could in theory combine all three graphs in a kind of summary for New Spain, but I could see no advantage in doing so, especially if the effects of climate change are long term, but the triggers and memories of the events with which it is associated are short. My goal was modest: not a grand theory, but at least some sort of potentially measurable indicator of how tight things really were. It takes a great deal of work to get there; the reader will decide if the results are worthwhile. The inspiration for the exercise was Jack Goldstone's computation of what he called a psi-function in *Revolution and Rebellion in the Early Modern World* (Berkeley: University of California Press, 1993). My goal was more modest than Goldstone's: not a theory of what environmental, demographic, and other conditions produce (rebellions or revolutions) in the face of an inflexible state structure, but just a sense if, in Mexico, there was much of a connection at all. Evidently so at some times; evidently not at others.

Finally, there is a caveat about sources and bibliography, particularly in the digital age. Unfortunately, "persistent" links come and go, although I have repeatedly tried to verify the accuracy of the ones I provide. In Mexican archives, changing classification schemes have sometimes resulted in alternative ways of naming record groups so that what was cited in, say 1990, may no longer be so named (or even exist per se). To make matters worse, whole digital archives sometimes appear and disappear—in this case, SEDENA, of the archives of the Secretary of Defense. Not only that but also the search engine for this collection produced unreliable results. Even online one was forced to hunt for the correct bundle of documents containing the material located by keyword. These difficulties are no secret to working historians in Mexico. Nor are they particularly unique to Mexico. But finding digitized documents can frequently be a challenge, especially for a novice. Even for those with many years of experience, the task can frequently be frustrating. All a researcher can do is to do their best and present the results as transparently as possible.

INDEX

Abad y Queipo, Manuel (Bishop-Elect) 28, 46, 61, 64
Adame, Ramón 59–60, 81n66
agrarian reform *see* Mexico, agrarian reform
Aguilar Camín, Héctor 118n3, 121n74, 129n3
Ajuria, Gregorio de 65–66
Alamán, Lucas 49
altepetl 13, 33n17
Amealco 9
Andrien, Kenneth J. 37n68, 37n72, 85n115
Angostura 57, 58, 61
Antuñano, Estevan de 49
Arnaut, Javier 7
Arroyo, Leticia 18, 35

Bajío 10, 22, 25–26, 28.43, 46–48, 51–56, 132
Bakewell, Peter 22, 36n52
Balbontín, Manuel 58, 80n55
Banco de Avío 49
Banco de México 129, 130n6
Bandidos of Río Frio 82n78; *see also* Payno, Man
Bazant, Jan 56, 79n46, 81n66, 83n93, 83n95–83n97
Berkeley School 8, 30
Black Death 7
Borah, Woodrow 3, 8, 17–18, 35n39
Boserup, Esther 26
Bourbons 27–29; *see also* Mexico, Bourbon Reforms
Brading, David 3, 25, 26, 36n59–36n62
Brenner, Robert 3, 5n2, 11, 16, 33n12
Bretton Woods 4, 111–112, 129
Buena Vista *see* Angostura

California 63, 93
calpolli 14
Camacho, Sebastián 78n31
Canales, Antonio 6
Cárdenas, Lázaro 97
Carlota (Charlotte) 69
Carrasco, Pedro 13, 34n20
Casasus, Joaquín 85n115
Celaya 31, 37n80, 70
CEPAL (Economic Commission for Latin America) 108–109
Chalco 13, 27, 34n24
Challú, Amílcar 65, 76n1, 77n19
Chaunu, Pierre 2
Chen, Angus 33n7
Chevalier, Francois 17, 34n28
Chihuahua 60, 81n72
chinampas 14, 15, 30, 34n29
Chowning, Margaret 56, 79
CIDOSA 103
CIVSA 103
climate *see* Mexico, climate
Coatsworth, John 28, 65
Cocoliztli see salmonella
Colosio, Luis Donaldo 117

Comonfort, Ignacio 65–66
CONASUPO 109–110
congregación 13, 17, 33n17
Conquest *see* Mexico, Conquest
Cook, Sherburne 8
Cortés, Hernán 11, 12
Crosby, Alfred 6, 32
Cuba 27, 32, 79

David, Paul 54–55, 65
dendrochronology 7; *see also* Palmer Drought Survey Index (PDSI)
depression 16–20, 24, 31, 35n39
De Vries, Jan 26, 36n63
Díaz del Castillo, Bernal 21
Díaz Ordaz, Gustavo 97
Diáz, Porfirio 76, 92
Dilemma of Mexican Development 127
Domar, Evsey 11, 33n12
Durango 60, 81n72

Echeverría, Luis 97, 128
Ejército del Norte 57, 59, 60
ejido see Mexico, agrarian reform
encomienda 8, 30
Escamilla, Iván 37n68
Escandón, Manuel 50, 83n68
Essay on the Nature and Significance of Economic Science see Robbins, Lionel

factor endowments *see* Mexico, factor endowments
Findlay, Ronald 33n6
Florescano, Enrique 29, 36n65, 85n119
flota system see Mexico, Bourbon Reforms
Fowler, Will 83n103

Galindo 83n102
Galveston 79n37
García de Acosta, Virginia 7, 12, 32n4
García Martínez, Bernardo 35n37
Garner, Richard 15, 24, 37n79
Gayón Córdova, María 83n97
GDP *see* Mexico, output estimates
General Crisis 16, 20, 24
Gibson, Charles 3, 11, 15, 17, 33n10
Goldsmith, Raymond 79n40
Goldstone, Jack 134
Gómez Galvarriato, Aurora 5, 65, 74, 76n1, 77n19, 79n43, 94, 118, 120n43; and "slavery" of the metate 55
Grice-Hutchinson, Marjorie 36n54
Guanajuato 22–23, 24, 49, 56, 60
Guardino, Peter 61, 80n48, 81n74
Guedea, Virginia 77n8
Guerrero (region) 17, 19, 66, 98, 110

Haber, Stephan 5, 85n115, 102, 120n42
hacienda 15, 17, 46, 62, 81n66, 96
Henige, David 32n2
Hernández y Dávalos, Juan E 77n8
Hidalgo (state) 49, 110
Hidalgo, Miguel (historical figure)
Hirth, Kenneth 21, 33n8
Historia del Capitalismo en México see Semo, Enrique
Hobsbawm, Eric 5
Horn, Rebecca 12, 34n21
Humboldt, Alexander von 28, 54, 64

import substitution industrialization (ISI) *see* Mexico: import substitution
index of environmental, epidemiological and agricultural stress (IEEAS) 4, 9–11, 16, 18, 20, 29–30, 47–48; calculated 132–134
Insurgency *see* Mexico, Insurgency
Israel, Jonathan 34n32

Jalisco 53, 56, 98
Juárez, Benito 69
Judt, Tony 3, 5n2
Junta Central 62

Keen, Benjamin 33n9
Keesing, Donald 103, 120n44
Keynes, John Maynard 121n72
Klein, Herbert S 43
Kuntz, Ficker, Sandra 36n57, 72, 85n116

Lamíkiz, Xabier 37n69
León 25
Lerdo de Tejada, Sebastián 54
Ley Lerdo 66–67, 70
Lezama, José Luis 92–93, 118n4
Lizardi, Manuel Julián 50, 66, 70
Lockhart, James 13, 21, 34n19
López Alonso, Moramay 74–76, 85n120, 106, 110
López Obrador, Andrés Manuel 101, 109, 128
López Portillo, José 99, 128
Los Grandes Problemas Nacionales 13, 33n15, 96

Madero, Francisco 76, 92
Mairot, Mark Joseph 78n35
Maldonado, Celia 71, 84n113
Mangino, Rafael 78n23

market, labor *see* Mexico, factor endowments
Márquez Morfín, Lourdes 32n2, 93, 118n5
Marx, Karl 2
Maya 14
McCaa, Robert 32n2, 71, 84n113
McLeod, Murdo 36n55
Medina Rubio, Arístides 34n29
Mejía, Demetrio 51
Melville, Eleanor 6, 32n1
Mendieta, Jerónimo de 8
Mendoza, Antonio de 22, 34n30
Mesilla (Treaty) 66, 83n95
Mexico, agrarian reform 5, 92, 95–101; Bourbon Reforms 24, 26, 27–29; climate 9–10, 16, 29, 47–48, 67, 132–134; Conquest 6–7, 11, 16; exchange rate 49, 74, 100, 102, 111–112, 116, 117, 129; factor endowments (land and labor) 1, 7–12, 14, 16–17, 21, 26, 30–32, 34n28, 43, 57, 73–74, 92, 93, 94–95, 107, 110; finances 22, 28, 46–47, 56–63, 65–67, 70, 80n60, 81n64, 82n82, 110, 111, 117; import substitution industrialization (ISI) 5, 49, 101–110, 112–114, 115–116; Insurgency 4, 43–47, 69, 70, 92; mining 22–23, 25, 44–48, 49; "Miracle" 4–5, 91, 92, 108, 109, 110, 117; oil 94–95, 105, 112, 115–116, 129; output and cost estimates 46, 47, 48, 50, 54–56, 61–63, 65–66, 68, 70, 71, 82n82, 91, 111, 128; population change 8–9, 15–16, 19, 24–25, 50–54, 56, 71, 82n83, 91, 92, 95, 96, 99, 104–106; Porfiriato,70–76; property rights 12–15, 66–68; railroads 72–73, 84n114; Revolution 92, 93, 99, 101, 118n11; tariffs 49–50, 58, 59, 80n60, 99; textiles 27, 56, 64, 74, 93–95, 99, 101–103; wage-rent ratio 12, 14, 17–19, 22, 24, 25, 26, 29, 31, 43–45, 48, 63, 64–65, 70, 73, 75–76
Michoacán 24, 27, 52, 56, 60, 66, 98
Miller, Simon 72, 76n2
Mixteca Alta 19, 25
Molina del Villar, América 7, 32n4, 93, 118n5
Molina Enríquez, Andrés 13, 33n15, 37n83, 98, 119n17
Monclova 57
money 20–24, 36n48, 76n4
Monterrey 57, 61, 80n54
Morelos, José María 53
Morin, Claude 17, 25, 35n41, 36n57
Morineau, Michel 36n49
Moya de Contreras, Pedro 24

NAFTA (North American Free Trade Agreement) 100–101
Nahuas After the Conquest see Lockhart, James
New Laws 8, 11
New Orleans 61, 81n76
New Spain *see* Mexico
North, Douglass 13, 33n14
Noticias Históricas de la Nueva España see Suárez de Peralta, Juan
Noverint Universi 13
Nuevo León 61
Nuevo Mexico 60, 81n72

O'Rourke, Kevin 33n6
Oaxaca 19, 25, 56, 98, 101, 110
obrajes 9, 12, 22, 26, 27, 31, 36n64, 45, 50
Odorica, Manuel 92–93, 118n4
Olivares Sandoval, Omar 33n16
Olivares, Conde-Duque de 20, 35n43
Orizaba 67, 94
Ortiz Escamilla, Juan 47
Ortiz Mena, Antonio 120n35

Palmer Drought Survey Index (PDSI) 9–10, 19–20, 29, 47–48, 132
Palo Alto 57
PAN (Partido de Acción Nacional) 118
Pandemic of 1918 92
Paredes, Mariano 81n67
Parker, Geoffrey 16, 34n31
Patch, Robert 14
Patch, Robert 14, 33n7, 34n22
Payno, Manuel 62, 82n78, 83n94, 83n95, 84n108
Pearce, Adrian 37n70
Peñafiel, Antonio 70, 71
Pérez Herrero, Pedro 35n48
PES (Pacto Económico de Solidaridad) 116, 121n87
peso *see* Mexico, exchange rate
petroleum *see* Mexico, oil
population *see* Mexico, population change
Portilla, Anselmo de 78n34
Postconquest Coyoacán see Horn, Rebecca
Prebisch, Raúl 5
Prebisch-Singer thesis 112
PRI (Partido Revolucionario Institucional) 98, 117
property rights *see* Mexico, property rights
Puebla 12, 15, 18, 19, 26, 27, 28, 34n29, 35n37, 57, 66, 80n54, 102, 103, 110

Querétaro 19, 22–23, 25, 35n41, 43–48, 50, 51–57, 60–69, 71, 75, 76n4, 79n39, 82n85, 102–103
Quirós, José María 36n48, 54

Rabell, Cecilia 36n58
Raso, José Antonio del 50–53, 71, 77n13, 78n28; biographical data 50–51
Rea, Joaquín 57, 80n53
Real del Monte 49, 76n1
repartimiento (labor draft) 17–18, 30
Resaca de la Palma 57
Reséndez, Andrés 33n13, 81n70
Revolution and Rebellion in the Early Modern World 134
Revolution *see* Mexico, Revolution
Reynolds, Clark 113, 115
Robbins, Lionel 1–2, 5n1
Rojas Rabiela, Teresa 14, 79n43, 85
Ros, Jaime 113, 121n58, 122n79, 129, 130
Rosenzweig, Francisco 28
Rubio, Cayetano 50, 55, 66, 102

Salas, Mariano 58
Salinas de Gortari, Carlos 100, 117
salmonella 8, 9
Saltillo 57, 60
Salvucci, L.K. 37n72, 84n105
Salvucci, R. J. 37n73, 77n19, 78n24, 84n114, 120n38
SAM (Mexican Food System) 100
San Juan de Ulúa 47
San Luis Potosí 22, 25, 48, 56–57, 59
Santa Anna, Antonio López de 50, 57, 59, 62, 65–66
Santa Inés Zacatelco 35n41
Say's Law 22
Scheidel, Walter 76, 85n124
School of Salamanca 24
Scott, Winfield 57
Semo, Enrique 3, 5n2
Sempat Assadourian, Carlos 33n13, 35n42, 36n53
Simpson, Eyler 98, 119n24
Sluiter, Engel 24
Smith, Adam 26, 32, 73, 96, 101
Sonoran Dynasty 92
Stein, Barbara, H. 37n70
Stein, Stanley J. 3, 37n70
Storey, Rebecca 32n2
Suárez Arguello, Clara Elena 82n79

Tacubaya 68
Tamaulipas 60, 68
Tampico 57, 68, 80n51
Tannenbaum, Frank 96, 119n16
tariffs *see* Mexico, tariffs
Taylor, Zachary 57, 58
TePaske, John 24
Tepeaca 12
Tetzcoco 32n3
Texas 53, 60, 76n4, 79n37, 93
textiles *see* Mexico, textiles
Thomson, Guy 37n74
tithe 18, 25, 46, 51, 53, 132
Tlatelolco 21
Tlaxcala 12, 18, 110
Toluca 18, 33n16, 35n41
Torget, Andrew J. 79n37
Torre Villar, Ernesto de la 33n17, 36n56
Torres, Medina 80n59
Treaty of Guadalupe Hidalgo 63
Tucker, Spencer 80n53
Tutino, John 82n83

Urquiola Permisán, José Ignacio 12
Urrea, José 57, 60, 80n51
USMCA (United States-Mexico-Canada-Agreement) *see* NAFTA

Valladolid 32
Vázquez, Josefina 81n65
Veracruz (port) 27, 34n27, 47, 73, 102
Veracruz (region) 15, 19, 67, 98, 103
Vernon, Raymond 127–129
von Wobeser, Gisela 17

wage-rent ratio *see* Mexico, wage rent ratio
war, with the United States 4, 44, 56–63; French Intervention 4, 65; Reforma 4, 65, 67–69; spending 57, 65–66
Warman, Arturo 98, 119n21
Weiland, D.J. 37n65
Williamson, Jeffrey 3, 28, 37n67, 74, 85n122
Wool, John 60, 81
Wyllie, Robert Crichton 77n21

Ycaza, Antonio 62
Yucatán 15, 33n7, 110

Zacatecas 22, 35n42, 36n52, 60, 81n68
Zacutla 17
Zaragoza, Ignacio 67
Zavala, Silvio 2, 33n10, 35n35
Zedillo, Ernesto 117
Zorita, (Zurita) Alonso de 8, 9

FSC
www.fsc.org
MIX
Papier | Fördert
gute Waldnutzung
FSC® C083411

Kolibri 360 GmbH
Ferdinand-Jühlke-Straße 7
99095 Erfurt, Deutschland
produktsicherheit@kolibri360.de